COBRAS IN THE PLAYGROUND, RABBITS IN THE MOON

Cobras in the Playground, Rabbits in the Moon

✦

Letters and Reflections of a Reluctant Expatriate

Mary Ned Fotis

iUniverse, Inc.
New York Lincoln Shanghai

Cobras in the Playground, Rabbits in the Moon
Letters and Reflections of a Reluctant Expatriate

iUniverse books may be ordered through booksellers or by contacting:

iUniverse
2021 Pine Lake Road, Suite 100
Lincoln, NE 68512
www.iuniverse.com
1-800-Authors (1-800-288-4677)

ISBN-13: 978-0-595-40156-7 (pbk)
ISBN-13: 978-0-595-84536-1 (ebk)
ISBN-10: 0-595-40156-2 (pbk)
ISBN-10: 0-595-84536-3 (ebk)

Printed in the United States of America

To Frank, Jared and Leah
for sharing these adventures and misadventures
far away and long ago

Contents

Acknowledgments

Illustrations from the Egypt portion of this book, with the exception of Margo Veillon's "Nile Women," are from paintings by Halina Wlodarczyk, a most exceptional woman and artist, whom we had the great pleasure and privilege of knowing in Cairo. These paintings—in full color—are from our private collection. Images in the Thailand portion of the book are less illustrious, composed as they are of portions of an old menu from Bangkok's Oriental Hotel cafe, a painting on silk from India, and photographs of memorable characters and amusing encounters in Burma, Nepal and other travels.

No book about life in Cairo would be complete without special mention of Karen Stubbs, driver of *Karen's Khan Krawler*, co-celebrant and co-creator of Knight of Knights, and expatriate par excellence, ferrying her magic box of spices and culinary artistry from continent to continent, leaving a trail of memories behind her.

I'd like to offer a special note of thanks to Jeff Erickson for his lucid and pithy explanations when I needed tech support in transforming the graphics.

And to Jeanne Kightlinger Smith, who would not allow me to abandon the graphics, no matter how hard I tried. For that, and for everything else, I thank her.

Preface

"Well, I've seen the pyramids—and never again as long as I live will I ever set foot in this country again!" I announced as we boarded the plane and left the desert sands behind.

Two years later, we moved to Cairo.

No wonder I was a reluctant expatriate. My first experience with Egypt had been a combination business trip/honeymoon for which I was ill-prepared. Clad in jeans and tee-shirts, whisked from the airport from our overnight flight from South Africa, we were—to our amazement—escorted to the presidential suite of a new luxury hotel overlooking the Nile. Due to a shortage of hotel rooms and series of miscommunications, and unable to switch hotels until the next day, we spent our first night in these "luxurious" surroundings, quickly learning that all that glitters is not gold. Perched on a French provincial settee, surrounded by marble tables, bizarre crystal lamps, incredibly ornate furniture and watered silk wallpaper, I gazed out of one of our many bay windows overlooking the Nile to the splendor of Cairo's domed and minaret-dotted skyline. We had—for the two of us—three bathrooms (the "green room," the "brown room" and the "blue room"); it took us a while to learn which one had a functioning shower, which one to use for a toilet that flushed, and which one's faucet didn't drip—no wonder there were three of them, as we needed all three. In addition, we had three balconies with chairs and tables (where were our friends so we could throw a party?) and three separate living rooms, or perhaps I should say salons, with (dusty) crystal chandeliers, (cracked) marble tables and (uncomfortable) brocade and silk-upholstered furniture. Oh, where to sit? Where to sit? We soon emerged from our awestruck state as we explored our surroundings and realized that we were indeed in Egypt, and therefore: Not one of the three built-in radios worked; there were glasses, but no water to drink; there were oriental carpets, but we had to hopscotch over the cigarette ashes; none of the three bathtubs had been cleaned, which was odd considering that water spurted from the showerhead sporadically and without provocation, and the suite's elegantly molded and gilded doors were covered with black fingerprints. Nonetheless, we were humbled, clad as we were, to be "presidential" for a night.

The next day we removed ourselves to Cairo's legendary Shepherd Hotel, first built in 1814, famed as an historic hotel which hosted emperors, kings and queens. We soon discovered to our dismay that the original structure had burned down during the rebellion against King Farouk in 1952, and that the present Soviet-style structure bore the name only, not even the same location. We were more down to earth in our spartan surroundings with early American motel furnishings with a little fringe added for the oriental touch. The Persian carpets' brilliant hues were obscured by strata of overlying dirt (which dynasty?), further blurred by the funereal pall cast by what appeared to be torchieres straight from a funeral parlor. We did enjoy our several balconies overlooking Cairo's noisy and chaotic street scene, so much better viewed from above. Eventually we plunged in, accosted by frenetic guides awaiting their prey, much as it must have been for centuries, or should I say millennia? After several hours of touring, we escaped the busy street scene with what we thought would be a relaxing sailboat ride on the Nile, cut short when the boat's real owner rowed up, yelling and screaming, forced us onto another boat, threatened to extort double-payment and called the police when we refused. Meanwhile, the boatman who literally "took us for a ride" and whom we had paid generously, fled the scene, leaving us to deal with the boat's owner and the police, surrounded by a crowd of curious bystanders—most of Cairo, it seemed to us, except for "the guy in a long brown robe" who was surely by now well on his way to Luxor.

We won't even get into the food and how I left the contents of my stomach at the Great Pyramid of Khufu (Cheops).

So you can now perhaps understand my horror at Frank's pronouncement, two years after this original initiation to Egypt: "Well, it looks like we'll be moving to Cairo for two years."

We were finally getting settled in our New England suburb, I had at last made some friends in the neighborhood, and our son was just a year old. Life was good. How could we possibly be uprooted to go back THERE—and with a baby!?! Well, thank God we did. Those two years in Cairo stretched to three and then four, and more. When we did eventually depart, it was with great sorrow on my part, as I grew to love that crazy and exasperating place. The only consolation was that we were leaving for another adventure, an assignment in Thailand, which couldn't have been more different—where yells were replaced by whispers, brusqueness by refinement, sand by water, and camels and donkeys by elephants and water buffalo.

I was a reluctant expatriate no more.

Greek Interlude

July 1980

This is it—my traveling letter #1, and I'm not to be held responsible for its contents or organization. A series of rambling impressions from my disordered as yet mind is the best we can hope for. I'm really doing this for *me* as I have no one to phone, and the only one I speak English to is Jared, but it tends to be limited to "No! No! You'll break it! Don't throw it off the balcony. See the big bus." So I need a friend for my petty complaints as well as to share amusements of cultures that don't quite mesh.

I had forgotten the meaning of the word "hot"—the true meaning—till I got to Athens. I'm sitting up, sweating, at midnight. Jared gets three baths a day and is still a sticky goo. We go to bed and wake up sweating.... *Po! Po! Po!*

Tomorrow marks one week that Jared and I have been with Frank's mom in her apartment in Athens while Frank is already hard at work in Egypt. The first few days she had me worried that Jared was starving, and she still wants to shove in the food—more than the little body can hold—as a show of love. Tonight we had a fruitless discussion on why I give him water instead of milk when he goes to bed. She pointed out all the relatives who drank milk from the bottle at every bed and naptime and whose teeth haven't fallen out—yet.

Jared's newest word is "TAKI"—for souvlaki (shish-kebab), which we buy at a corner stand at night. He took his first bus ride today...very exciting due to all the bumps...and says "buth" (bus) in his sleep, which, by the way, begins sometime just before 11 P.M., due partly to change of time zones and partly to the Greek custom of keeping kids up late—really late! He eats "oh-go" (yoghurt) and sweet overripe Greek watermelon. We eat good Greek food at "noon" (3-4 P.M.), meticulously prepared by Frank's mom, who is really a workhorse. She washes out clothes by hand every few hours, it seems, or mends, or crochets, or whatever. "A woman's hands must never be idle," I overheard her telling her granddaughter, as she shoved a piece of embroidery into the girl's hands. After cleaning, preparing lunch, serving lunch and then cleaning up after lunch, it's time to get out

1

the ole embroidery or doily and pass a few hours stitching or crocheting. Me—I just want to sit, but I feel guilty…and end up chasing Jared anyway.

It is now 12:30 A.M., not so very late for any self-respecting Greek, and here I sit in bed, sweating. I had wanted to visit Dora and family, but it appears that everyone is out of Athens on vacation or at the family village to escape the heat. In the summer, families generally stay in their ancestral villages, and the men go up for weekends. That accounts for the lack of chaos in the streets when we came in from the airport. I now completely understand why anyone who can escapes from Athens at this time of year.

I begin to appreciate American stores already. We looked unsuccessfully for a port-a-crib today cuz it takes so long to get Jared to sleep on the mattress on the floor, and when he wakes, he goes roaming. At 5 A.M. this morning, he took my hand and dragged me to the kitchen. *He* went back to sleep, not I. He loves the balcony. He yells "HI!" to whoever passes beneath, throws things off ("dat" included) and yells "BIKE!" every time a motorcycle races by. He yells "BU-EE!" (boy) to every male who crosses his path.

Thus we pass our days here, waiting to go to Egypt.

Marhabaa, Masr! Welcome to Egypt!

Marhabaa, Masr!

September 1980

Marhabaa, Masr! Welcome to Egypt!

Long-lost friends—

Excuse my long delay in corresponding, but any earlier letters would have been a bit gloomy. However, *now* we are at last looking forward to moving into our apartment in a few days, and I can actually *do* something productive, i.e., endless errands. We've been five weeks in a hotel room—at the historic Mena House just next to the great pyramids, with pool, restaurants, and elegant trappings (such as marble stairs with a thin handrail and very few side supports to keep a wriggly toddler from tumbling through and plummeting four flights down to the marble floor below). A luxury hotel with a two-year-old is **no** luxury, I'll tell you. We know every hiding place in most of the restaurants, and now we settle for room service and French fries most of the time—it's easier. We've had our bouts with "mummy tummy," as I've rechristened "Montezuma's Revenge," also known as the "Bangla-dash." The first two weeks I had a new ailment every day. By the time we'd finally obtain the proper medicines, I'd come down with something else! There are compensations, such as awakening at 5 A.M. and seeing tiny flyspecks dot the top of the great pyramid—today's mountaineers. I was mad to climb it myself till I had to walk up six flights to Frank's office one day and nearly expired.

Cairo is dirty, noisy, dirty, crowded, dirty, hot, dirty, exotic—and exciting in a weird way. Donkey carts, camels, water buffalo, women in black, men in long robes and turbans are an everyday sight. The women are graceful and dignified, especially the poor, who balance every kind of load from suitcase to propane gas tank and gigantic earthen water jars on their heads. This morning I saw a young woman cross a crowded intersection with a huge wooden crate balanced on her head, a red plastic shopping bag balanced on top of that, and a baby clutched in her arms. And I could barely manage with a stroller and a big bag of groceries.... The people are friendly and kind (even though they yell a lot like all their Mediterranean counterparts), and what used to seem like a beady-eyed sly calculating look is actually from years of squinting to lessen the intensity of the sun and pro-fusion of dust from desert winds. I've enjoyed poking around Cairo's seamier sec-tions in my errands, such as the street of the marble tombstone-makers and the street of the ironmongers where, in my quest to create a dining table of Egyptian marble on an iron base, I sketched my idea for a table base, handed it to the iron-mongers and hoped for the best. We'll see.

I haven't visited museums or tourist spots at all yet. (Can you imagine Jared in the museum, thumping on the mummy cases to see the hair fall out?) We've given up on the swimming pool. From there Jared runs to (1) the crowded park-ing lot, (2) the restaurant kitchen, (3) the roof of the outdoor discotheque. He does enjoy helping the maids dust and vacuum, though one day he stuck a feather duster in a bucket of soapy water. But we'll have plenty of time, we hope, to explore in depth later. We did drive one day to an oasis, Fayoum, an incredibly lush and green series of villages in the middle of the totally dead, totally barren desert. Really amazing contrast. We bought some local baskets with the help of our very kind driver. We've been to the *souk*—bazaar—once to buy a large hand-hammered and blackened copper bean pot, and ended up with three pots, one carved wooden mirror, and two antique Egyptian chairs (and no money for a while). Our apartment should be rather exotic with these elegant additions in contrast to the $3.00 large earthen water jar I bought as well. These jars are seen on every corner in Egypt with a tin can attached for passersby to drink from.

The Corniche, the romantically-named road from Cairo to our village of Ma'adi, runs alongside the timeless Nile, which is amazingly wide and whose waters seem to traverse not only land but time zones, separating the more "mod-ern" environs of Ma'adi and outlying Cairo from the rural villages and farms on the other side, which look like illustrations from old Sunday school Bibles. The majestic river is plied with large-sailed boats called *feluccas,* whose design, so I'm told, has remained unchanged since ancient times. Long thin river islands of bamboo wave in the desert winds. In the canals, people wash their clothes, water buffalo lie nearly submerged, and village children frolic. Life is hard for most. Poverty is overwhelming. If you slow the car, boys pop out of nowhere to wipe windows, direct you, or offer any other service for some *baksheesh*—tips/hand-outs. On the other hand, you're as likely to be approached by an old man selling a fragrant necklace of jasmine or tuberoses, which I find impossible to resist. (By the way, roses are so inexpensive here! For the least occasion, I'll buy two or three dollars' worth of roses—two to three dozen!! We'll have flowers in our house con-tinually for two years!) You tip everyone for everything—and nothing—here. Since many people don't work, it's how they exist. The average traffic policeman makes $40 a month; our driver, one of those fortunate enough to work for the *farangs*—foreigners (from a word meaning "French")—makes $135 for a six-day week, plus $30-$45 in tips. Our friends' driver is a brain surgeon! He's doing his residency and makes much more money by driving us foreigners than operating on patients. By the way, we had a maid—for one day. It's a long story, for another letter, but we'll gradually learn the local ways.

Our landlords are warm, friendly, helpful people. Coupled with our architecturally bizarre building, with lowered ceilings, triangular rooms and sunken bathtubs, in the old quiet section of Cairo's distant suburb of Ma'adi, amid cacti and flowering trees, we're anticipating a wonderful stay here. Of course, I haven't had to cope with cooking and cleaning Western-style in a Middle Eastern country, but just having fresh roses on the table will inspire me, I'm sure. Our landlady, who prefers to be called "Madame Hajja," denoting her having completed the *hajj,* or pilgrimage to Mecca, wears black robes from head to toe, with a beige knitted veil...we don't even notice anymore. She's wonderfully kind and helpful and calls me "Madame Mary." Jared is, most unfortunately, "Jerry" to most (how can I spell it in Arabic so they will understand?), and I mutter my way through such Egyptian names as Basiera, Naziah, Fraycheka, Nasmi and Rasmi, along with the usual masculine assortment of Achmeds, Mahmouds and Mohammeds.

Jared's language is flowering like the flora here. An occasional Arabic *"quiis"* (nice) intermingles with the Greek "asssst" (for "asto"—leave me alone!) and of course his running commentary of surrounding events ("bus go," "horse eat," etc.). We find ourselves talking the same way. He hasn't been on a camel yet but has added "bamel" to horse and goat, doggie and kitty in his verbal menagerie. Occasionally he tries to telephone his relatives in Greece and his friends back home. Last night he picked up the phone and said, "Amboogoo, beese" (hamburger, please), expecting room service to appear. He has a two-year-old friend, Simon, whose British "hallo" he now imitates, and now we look forward to being in our own home with toys and room to run as at Simon's.

Egyptians love children—and are even more attentive to them than Greeks are, if such a thing is possible. Can you imagine the effect on the hotel staff of an exuberant little blond fellow? He has free rides on the dirty towels and sheets in the laundry cart, and kisses from every direction. On the other hand, many of his clothes—and some of ours—are disappearing day by day, as well. I was forewarned by a departing expatriate, but disregarded her rather bitter words of warning. "Children's clothes are always the first to go," she said. Apparently she was right.

We're gradually adapting, i.e., switching from exorbitant little six-ounce bottles of apple juice to guava and mango juices. Soon we'll probably be eating *"fool"*—fava beans—like the rest of the country. It must be the national dish! There's a ban on meat this month, and people are scrambling for the chance to buy pingpong-ball-sized eggs.

We can't complain about Egyptian inefficiency and lack of system too much. I unpacked our air shipment this morning and found my towels and tablecloths wrapped around the bottle of Clorox, which of course was squashed and had eaten through most of my linens and other surrounding objects. Books were tossed in—open!—and are bent, ripped and mangled; lampshades were destroyed, etc. I rather dread receiving our sea shipment with all the furniture, dishes, glasses, clothes and toys. Even Jared's crib was broken in spots. But my initial upset cannot overcome the sudden euphoria of the prospect of finally moving in, even without any furniture. No more twenty plus mile drives through the hot and crowded streets of Cairo twice a day, sometimes foodless and waterless.

Frank works constantly, weekends included (broken promises!), rising at 5 A.M. to write his reports (no other choice in a hotel room with Jared), and now he's traveling again—back to Boston in early October for a few weeks. (Actually it's fortunate, as none of our sheets or curtains fit….)

We're so much farther south here that sunset is at 5:30-6 P.M. But it shouldn't be so terribly early in winter—I hope. Without daylight savings time, it's light here before 5 A.M., so we always wake up quite early…and our hotel room window looks directly at the Great Pyramid!

At Home in Cairo

December 1980

Christmas Greetings from 34 Oraby Street #1, Ma'adi, Cairo! At last we are reasonably settled into our new home, thankfully removed from hotel life, and nostalgically recalling good friends abroad. The only visible sign of the Christmas season, and not intentionally so, is the abundance of flowering poinsettias by the roadsides, sometimes reaching to three storeys high! They are actually trees here, and quite common ones at that—nondescript during most of the year, but truly magnificent now. There are also brilliant yellow-flowering trees, and something which should be called the "cookie-crumb tree," for the ground underneath seems littered with crumbs—until you look closely and find nearly microscopic blossoms of perfect symmetry and beauty—winter snowflakes of the tropical climes? At last "the cold" is setting in—which means cold nights and mornings…and very damp, chilly houses inside…but still sunny, warm mid-days. I still haven't learned how to dress accordingly—either I'm freezing or smothering, depending on time of day…and also being in or out of the sun. When taking a walk yesterday, we found ourselves constantly donning and discarding our coats, then realized the incredible temperature differential between sun and shade. In spite of occasional murky days—all pollution—the sun is victor here in Egypt, and it's wonderful! (Don't ask us in the summer….) Never a rainy day, but still mud puddles!!!! No rain, so everything is flooded twice a week, *really* flooded, practically submerged with Nile water, thus accounting for the tropical lushness. And only a mile away….barren Saharan sands as far as the eye can see.

Though the exotic has become commonplace, we are still amazed and amused by it. Yesterday our friends had the local snake charmer in to catch two very large snakes in their garden. I still think the snake charmer planted them there, because the week before he "caught" two snakes on a neighbor's roof! A "butcher" rides up on his bicycle with a plastic garbage can of meat in tow. It's beef or buffalo, depending on what he thinks you want. We don't know if we're eating *boeuf* bourguignon or *buff* bourguignon. The street sweepers go by in their long robes and turbans with primitive bramble-brush brooms. In such a dusty climate, the result of their labors soon disappears. And now, the knife-grinder just walked by carrying his heavy grindstone. Someday I'll take a series of photos—"Views from Our Window," beginning with the old women in black from veil to toe nearly obscured by the huge bundles of brambles of their heads. Now there are four men in robes and turbans delivering a refrigerator to the apartment above us. A few days ago, a herd of sheep and goats scampered by, depleting our newly sprouted patch of grass bordering the road. Our windows are practically part of the road. We are observed as much—and probably more intently—as we observe the scene outside. Jared in his highchair especially draws quite a reaction.

We are very happy to be in our little community of Ma'adi, south of Cairo just off the Nile. Its tropical lushness and old-world splendor of villas and gardens blend well with the village atmosphere of the foreign community here. Our six-floor apartment building will have two American, two British, one German and one Egyptian family, one per floor. We selected the ground floor apartment during construction, wisely avoiding a hot and tiresome daily climb with car seat, stroller and tricycle in tow. My favorite neighbor is the German woman, but all we can do is nod, smile and say, "*Ja, ja, das ist schön.*" (That's nice.) I find myself spouting off little British-isms unthinkingly. And Jared yells "Come here!" in Arabic to everyone who passes the window. I still don't know where he learned it, but at last I understand what he's saying. Sometimes he yells the same thing in Greek. He speaks in sentences completely now, and we love listening…well, most of the time: "I can't dood it…. I falldown (one word)…. Daddy my boy…. My Daddy Frankie…. I dives car (his obsession)…. I eep (sleep) bed…" Poor boy—he broke his arm (both bones) during a fall, and while the doctor was putting on his knuckle-to-shoulder cast, he looked up with tears in his eyes and said, "I all-done." He wished he were! But he has adapted incredibly well and seems not to be bothered at all by it. (I, on the other hand, after giving him a bath in a sunken bathtub and holding a plastic bag over the cast, am ready for a week's rest!) He has now recovered from his mild concussion suffered during another fall (when Frank was in the U.S., of course). The Egyptian doctor advised against taking him to a hospital. "It's safer to observe him every hour and make sure he doesn't throw up or fall asleep." As soon as the doctor left, Jared threw up and fell asleep, leaving me—phoneless, carless and husbandless—to cope. Hence, we do occasionally long for Boston's medical services. The *exotisme* of the scene palls when you take your crying child into a filthy hospital with uncertain staff. (Some assistants who can't read or write are swathed in doctor's white while the doctor, if any, might be the only one in argyle socks and old sweater.)

We enjoy life without phone or TV, though it's a bit inconvenient. Therefore, "dropping in" (which I have always enjoyed as either dropper or droppee) is more acceptable here. In fact, there's little alternative. I was just thinking a few months ago how well I had adapted to our new life here, when I looked down and discovered lice in Jared's hair. We have since recovered from our two-week ordeal of scalp-burning ointments, boiling clothes, etc., and cutting his beautiful hair *a la* U.S. Marines, and are now equipped with adequate U.S. medicine in case of a recurrence, but I've learned not to gloat over my adjustment—or something else will strike....

Cooking "from scratch" might be challenging and enjoyable for some, but not me! We have had some interesting and exotic dinner-party cuisine, however, which I'll long remember. I never would have believed I would serve baby buffalo ("buff stroganoff," as a friend put it), sweet potato soup, fresh mangoes and dates, and frozen fermented rice, as a standard meal for guests. Now that everyone has been served that, I'm searching for a new menu. This weekend I tried "buffalo-weinerschnitzel scaloppini"—that's about as close a description as I can get to what appeared on the plate! I think for Christmas I'll ask for a cook! Oh, for a McDonald's!

Frank, I think, is working even harder here than at home. At least we're in the same country now. We're celebrating because he has just taken his first two-day weekend since we arrived in Egypt. I'm hoping for more! Last week we celebrated our fourth wedding anniversary. The first was spent at Jeanne and Frank's wedding reception, the second with Daddy and Dorothy and Grandpa at the Wayside Inn with six-week old Jared asleep in his "shoe" under the table, the third climbing around in Grandpa's attic in Missouri organizing his move to assisted living, and now the fourth in a felucca (those tall old graceful sailboats) on the Nile! As Grandpa would say, "Who woulda thunk it?" We wonder what the fifth will bring....

We think of our good friends so often, even more so now at Christmas, and we wish some of you could join us in our first "tropical Christmas."

Every day we wait for the strawberry man to appear, bearing luscious
red berries under the leafy lid of his basket

From "Rest and Recreation" to "Rip-Off and Ruin"

January 1981

Back at last in our beloved Ma'adi, Cairo, gazing out on the giant eucalyptus trees, imported from Australia at the turn of the century for shade, filtering morning sunlight onto the streets, I can at last begin—with regret—to relive the details of our first R&R ("Rest and Recreation") in Greece, or rather "Rip-Off and Ruin," as we have renamed it.

In addition to using two of Frank's precious vacation weeks, we spent nearly $3,000 on a series of calamities, which are painful—but surely humorous—to recount:

ARRIVAL—Halfway over the Mediterranean we entered swirling gray clouds which remained with us until our departure two weeks later when the sun again reappeared halfway over the Med. We landed in an Athens covered with SNOW! As if in a Swiss ski resort, we looked around to surrounding hills and mountains, Hymettos, Parnassos, and Parnitha, all starkly white. Lacking front yards to display their ingenuity, Greeks made snowmen and voluptuous snow-women on the hoods of their cars, supported by sticks and strings, donning scarves, hats, mittens, and with a variety of facial features. What a treat to see three or four cars in a row, all sporting their Hellenic snow-people. Aside from the snowmen, the rest of the weather's aftereffects were grim. "SIBERIA!" proclaimed newspaper headlines four inches tall. After the snow vanished several days later, we were treated to two weeks of rain, unheard of in Greece. Where was the famous Greek light, of winter as well as summer? Well, I think it was vacationing in Egypt. So we huddled around Yiayia's oil stove....

In addition to family difficulties which cast a pall over everything, even overshadowing Frank's younger brother's (rainy) wedding, we were all three sick with various maladies, and I fell into the hands of a highly-recommended "society doctor" whose 18th century treatment, inflationary prices and nightly four-hour ordeals of waiting and undergoing assorted "therapy" for my herniated spinal

13

disk destroyed our first week of vacation. Our initial appointment was for 9:30 P.M. Asking if we could come earlier, because of Jared, we were told, "Certainly. Come at 9 P.M.!" We did—waited till after 11 P.M. to get in, waited for X-rays, this and that, and got home at 2 A.M. Thereafter, four hours of every evening were spent in waiting, in traction, in despair and in disgust, ending with a grand finale of a five-minute appearance by the doctor for a painful "Zorba the Greek" bell-cup suction treatment on my bare back and three injections into my back nightly! Odd that every patient, no matter what the problem, had the same treatment.

After one week of this "treatment," at incredible expense but in desperation (for what could we do in Cairo? We had been waiting for Greece! Oh, to be near Mass General now!), we found another orthopedic surgeon who was shocked at the painkillers and excessive medication given by the first doctor (of whom I had requested NO painkillers). For example, I was taking medicine for rheumatism, which I didn't have. I was getting daily injections of cortisone (too strong!), and xylocaine (the painkiller I'd had during Jared's birth!!!), and a muscle relaxant which I could have had in pill form. I was also taking three a day of a painkiller that the second doctor gave only a maximum of two a day—and that only for cancer. Well, once we discovered I was being given massive doses of painkillers under the guise of other medicines, we immediately dropped the society doctor and his opulent office full of Persian carpets, oil paintings, statuary and crystal (I figured we bought him several new crystal vases with every night of "The Cure," which, by the way, was supposed to be for a minimum of twenty days.... I would have had to remain in Greece with Jared after Frank left. And after that, a series of three operations on both feet, each of which required nearly a month in the hospital and forty-five days without foot touching floor! Can you imagine! Four and a half months in bed and with a two-year-old!) This society doctor also would not give us our X-rays, necessitating a late-night visit to a hospital to take more, during which our borrowed car broke down and had to be abandoned, etc., etc.

And the final blow: Dr. High Society had to be paid in advance in cash, as was the custom, and gave us NO RECEIPTS to submit to our insurance...because then he'd have to pay Greek taxes on his income. We threatened, we cajoled, we reasoned. Finally, we gave the final payment to Frank's younger brother with strictest instructions not to fork over a single drachma until receipt was in hand. Unfortunately, he succumbed to the doctor's aura, surrounded by the magnificence of the office, and agreed to give over our money with the doctor's promise to mail a receipt as soon as he received his office stationery, which he was temporarily out of. Well, you know what happened—or rather, what didn't happen. In other words, in every way, a disastrous encounter! Anyway, to end this tale quickly, the second doctor referred me to a physical therapist where I learned exercises every day during the second week and which I now continue here in Cairo.

We had taken cabs everywhere but in the daily downpour found I was spending more time standing in the rain than sitting out of it. One day I got in three separate cabs (twenty minutes apart) only to find they didn't know our location and so I had to get out and find others in a more deserted place. So Frank borrowed his brother's car to pick me up one day from my physical therapy (another downpour) and we finally did something together—went to a store. While inside, police ticketed our car (none of the others we had parked among received a ticket) and removed the license plates, so our one evening together we spent at the police station paying fines and unsuccessfully trying to convince them not to ground the car for ten days. This was the only car of the family which could operate on the upcoming weekend due to even-odd plate restrictions. And on and on.

We did eat well (and we did have one evening of pleasure with Jared's godparents before we left). In compensation for illness, weather, emotional turmoil in family, we stuffed ourselves with spaghetti, stuffed cabbages, loads of fresh fruit—and the other compensation is that we did not get divorced. So it could have been worse. But we are not looking forward to our next R&R with great anticipation and glee.

MA'ADI

Back to Cairo with joy and wonder. What a switch from our other arrivals here! Evening arrival at the empty, clean (my standards have changed) airport, with little hassle, little traffic (only one near-accident on the Corniche) and back to our cavernous—by comparison—apartment with SUNSHINE the next day, a new maid who doesn't leave deathtrap dustpans and brooms all over, and HOME. I've stayed in since, though shivering in the interior winter chill, enjoying the outdoor street life pass by (turbaned knife-grinder, two men with 20-25 foot ladder on bicycle who pass daily, women balancing groceries on head, donkey carts). Someone brought us some of Cairo's beautiful roses, plentiful and inexpensive, so we use them for the slightest occasion. So I'm so relieved to be back and even more fond of our exotic surroundings and our new home.

And to make our return even more joyful, we re-celebrated Christmas, not a major holiday in Greece, where gifts are opened at New Year's, which is the festive occasion, rather than Christmas Day itself which is a rather somber religious occasion. Naturally, we left just after the somber Christmas and before the festive New Year celebration. While in Greece, I had prepared a Christmas dinner for the family. Frank's mother took the precaution of preparing a separate meat and potatoes meal for anyone who wouldn't eat my Christmas turkey dinner, made with a pathetic little turkey which paled in comparison with any Perdue chicken. She had earlier told me that I couldn't use celery for the stuffing, as it was used only in soups. When I persuaded her to let me use my grandparents' recipe for stuffing, instead of the traditional Greek hamburger and chestnut stuffing, she procured the limpest little celery, gave me the wispy leaf-tops and threw the stalks into the trash. She was most amazed to see me retrieve the useless stalks, chop them and use them in the turkey stuffing. Later, she scratched her head in bewilderment and said, "Well, it was not so bad. It was OK." That, however, was my final attempt at introducing new foods in Greece.

Many cards and some packages had arrived at Frank's office in our absence, so Jared opened presents ("More, please") and we spent a wonderful evening reading letters and cards. What a joyous return to Ma'adi. Our R&R made us appreciate our Cairo home even more! We actually have the best of both worlds—an exotic home with new friends, wonderful climate, and much of interest, but with the underlying stability and sense of closeness with our good friends back home. So when things aren't quite right here, we remember whom we've left and to whom we will eventually return.

Jared is flourishing. He's shed his cast and is wiggly as usual and suddenly quite proficient on his Christmas tricycle, which we have already disassembled and reassembled. (Over a hundred parts and no assembly instructions! I was quite proud to have completed the task with only four pieces left over.) He is in a great period of language development and astonishes us daily with his mixture of English, Greek, and Arabic. Actually, I think he does not understand much of his new vocabulary but mimics with abandon. At 3 A.M. last night he yelled out, "I don't like my bed! I want Big Bed!" When I ask if he is Mommy's baby, he says, "NO. I Daddy's boy. Daddy's big boy." When asked where he lives, he replies, "In my house. Ma'adi, Cairo, Egypt."

"I want to go outside."

"Where?"

"England." (His little girlfriend was there for Christmas, so it made a big impression. His other girlfriend was in Australia, but it's too hard to pronounce.) His name is David Fotis (David is as close as he can get to pronouncing Jared at the moment). His daddy is "Big Daddy Frankie Fotis" and his mommy is "Manin Fotis." He knows the last names of all his friends and their sexes and animals. I'm amazed at the correctness of his grammar. Size is expressed along family lines. For example: Big Daddy truck, Mommy truck, Little Baby truck.

A group of girls in gray skirts and pants walks by. Each school has its own uniform, so troops of blue, gray, brown, even powder blue may pass. We are half a block from an elementary school, so the neighborhood is full of "khaki kids." Egypt is proud of its literacy rate and high educational level compared to much of Africa and the Middle East. Cairo abounds in doctors, but since one earns the title after only two to three years past high school education, it's a bit difficult to choose with confidence.

Hopefully, future letters will cover some of Cairo's ancient archeological and medieval Byzantine sites. There is so much to see and up till now we have mainly just been settling in.

We may return to the States this summer for "home leave" which hopefully will be a great improvement over our first R&R. Until then, we hope to hear from some of you and wish health and contentment to you. We are now prepared to receive overseas visitors, and hope you'll come and share the pyramids with us!

Frank's new assignment—fixing the phone system in Egypt—looks like it'll take some magic to accomplish!

Un-Maid, But Not Undone

October 1981

I'll take time out from chasing the mouse in the kitchen (and studying for my Arabic class in one hour, which I defer and avoid if possible, since it's typically unorganized as are all things here) to attend to a more pleasant task—writing to you. Greetings from afar…. I finally have a quiet house for half an hour—Jared's in school, no one is here, especially all the repairmen who *promised* to come. Actually, they come, look at the heater, etc., and say, "It's not working," and then leave, perhaps never to return….

Back in Cairo again! After our month of seeing family and friends after such a long absence, we are now settling back into our semi-tropical surroundings and beginning to establish this year's routine. Hopefully, we can experience Egypt more fully now that the household is settled, Jared is happy in his little school, and I have time for a course on visiting monuments of Islamic Cairo as well as joint chairmanship of a committee to seek out and purchase Egyptian arts and crafts for the local women's organization. We are looking forward to a year of good health and fulfillment for all, *Insha'allah* ("God willing"—attached to nearly every statement).

We returned to our home amid turmoil and confusion (how else could it be in the Middle East?) with our landlords seeing lawyers about evicting us because they still objected to our maid—a very pleasant and pretty girl whom Jared likes and who performed many services for us—whose short skirts and friendly manner were anathema to our fanatical black-gowned (enshrouded, I should say) landlady. Let me back up and give some history of how we have been unmade by our maids. Upon arrival, our so-lovely and helpful landlady "gave" us a maid and suggested a salary. The homely young girl, Gamila (whose name means "beautiful" and not "camel" as it sounds), was rather sweet, but very shy—illiterate and fearful of displeasing. We had never had a maid before, so I worked along with her and enjoyed her company. She always seemed so very tired, however. We paid her well and treated her with friendliness and respect. Finally, one day, with Jared's elderly Egyptian babysitter to translate, she broke down and explained her condition. She was basically a slave of our revered religious landlady. She had been taken from her country village as a child and trained to clean and cook for the landlady's family. She slept on their kitchen floor. So while she was OUR maid, she was also working fulltime for the landlady upstairs, who even took all the money we paid the poor girl! Gamila wanted to return to her far-away family in the country—and we gave her more money to help her get there. Unfortunately, the landlady, Madame "Hajja" of the pilgrimage, found out—and that was the beginning of the end for us in our lovely apartment. We stayed for the duration of the lease, but not without troubles, broken equipment, and threatened lawsuits for various matters. We had to find another maid, and happily settled upon the lovely Soraya—just the opposite of poor Gamila—pretty, quick, and sociable.

Back to the present—we finally very regretfully let our maid Soraya go and did without household help for the first month. (Life without a maid? It doesn't sound so bad till you think of no babysitting, of all the vegetables to be bleached, water boiled, floors washed daily, and the constant battle against the desert dust. I hired a man one day just to wash the floors—it took him two full days to do what our maid had done in an hour or so.) Now we have a new maid with a pretty name, Aziza. Jared still hasn't adjusted to her, perhaps because she's quite overwhelming in size and rather frightful in appearance, unlike petite Soraya, as well as not speaking much English. Whenever I called Soraya, she would respond, "Oui, Madame?" With Aziza, it's a deep throaty blast, "W-H-A-A-T???", reverberating through the house, rattling glasses and dishes. No wonder Jared won't let her near him!

Aziza is well-known in the foreign community for her skill in leg-waxing, so I thought I'd give it a go. It was so surprisingly painful when she ripped off the hard dried wax cemented to my legs that I felt a certain kinship with medieval martyrs being flayed. That's the last time for me. Aziza still gives "treatments" to her former employer, additionally including arms and—OUCH!!—underarms, too! I gave a dinner party last week, left the dirty work (bleaching and chopping fruit, veggies and salad, picking bugs out of the rice) for the incomparable Aziza—who never showed up!! So I spent much of the evening cloistered in the kitchen, fortunately before the arrival of our resident mouse.

Our building is still "under construction"—actually nothing's being done but all the old rubble is still on the unpaved "sidewalks" and the cement walls with pipes and wires haven't been plastered. Now that the landlords are living in the building (with the landlady hanging out her window observing *everything*), all their efforts and money go into their own apartment rather than the public parts of the building. I'm so used to treading on rubble that I would probably appear to be goose-stepping if I walked across a smooth surface. But *ma'alesh* (never mind, oh well)....

Thus far we have escaped the ringworm fungus, which some of our friends have contracted. I still take samples from Jared to the lab for parasites and worse, as he still complains of his tummy—for over six months now. My hepatitis must be gone by now—I feel much better. Still no liquor till late March, but really it's no loss at all. I don't even miss it. Egyptian wine is so full of sulfates—sulfites?—that one pays the next day in pounding headaches for even a slight imbibing...and imported wines cost more than Scotch. And with a 43% rabies rate in cats, even, we can't adopt the lovely cat abandoned by people next door. I still slip it food, though.

The Fotis achievement award this fall goes to Frank who has lost fourteen pounds since our return and is aiming for another 15-20. Soon his tapered shirts will really taper! His nose is beginning to wriggle as he consumes kilos of carrots and tomatoes, allowable between-meal snacks. We're all clucking, as we practically live on boiled chicken (frozen American AID chicken—complete with the handshake and American flag logo, sold both in stores and privately. I wonder if the poor Egyptians for whom the chicken was originally destined ever get any?)

Frank is still working many weekends and holidays. Jared and I took advantage of one of those days by traveling with friends to a famous but little visited pyramid and then entering via a ladder up a vertical wall to an opening, then descending eighty meters down a forty-foot ramp (Jared backed out by then) into the solid bedrock where wooden pillars and rafters were planted for the pulleys for the sarcophagus. Actual 5,000-year old wood (of course the guard gave us some chips in spite of our protests).... When we "surfaced," we had acquired mustaches of "pharaonic dust" from the murky depths of the tomb. Aside from the omnipresent guard, only wild desert dogs were within miles.

Our little community of Ma'adi still retains its exotic elements described in previous letters. They, however, are commonplace to us now, and what is truly shocking and amazing is the incredible progress of Westernization among the little shops in just the last year—electronic cash registers, painted storefronts, canned soup, and—gasp!—tiny jars of—truly!—Sanka!!! (We of course had returned from our summer R&R in the U.S. with practically a suitcase full.) Now if only someone would import Cheerios for Jared! I'm afraid our lifestyle won't seem nearly so adventuresome and primitive to those who visit us this year. We now have a telephone (can receive, but not make long distance calls; our number: Cairo 630-362), and we even have TWO people we can call now. We have our

TV, though it seems to broadcast mostly the Koran now, and Frank buys the daily Egyptian Gazette and scrambles to get an imported *TIME* Magazine every week. So we're actually quite, quite, quite civilized, you see.

The weather during this long, languid fall is beautiful as usual—cool mornings, hot afternoons (90s still!) with refreshing breezes and mild warm evenings. Some trees are in a second flowering—one with brilliant yellow clumps of flowers, an occasional purple jacaranda and many trees with bright-green new leaves at the end of dusty summer-worn branches.

We were getting slightly concerned with the religious turmoil here, as we live next door to Cairo's newest and one of the largest Coptic (Christian) churches. During the Sunday evening services, cars drive around, honking continuously for several hours to disrupt the services. Armed guards are now stationed in front of the church (sometimes coming to us for water—we're so convenient to everyone, being on the first floor). The nation mourns Sadat during this forty-day official mourning till November 15. We were all of course shocked and confused, relying on scratchy old BBC for any news. I'm sure you all at home knew of his assassination before we did. Fortunately, the city remained quite calm, eerily so, though everyone was uneasy. And life now continues normally. Mubarak seems to be a stable, well-trained leader, and Sadat paved the way for a smooth transition of power. We just hope and pray that Mubarak remains safe and in control. We get little news here, but all is calm and well around us and we're all fine, so we hope no one will worry about us. The one minor, but real, inconvenience is that Jared and I can no longer walk to his little school with ease. His school is just past an army barracks, and now the streets are blockaded with sandbags and helmeted soldiers with machine guns, so where we once walked twice daily saying an Arabic good morning ("*Sabaa el kheer*") to our friends the soldiers, we must now detour three more blocks through the busiest street with careening cars, raucous honking, and sidewalks of alternating manure and rubble, forcing us into the street with the mad rush-hour traffic. So large loom life's minor inconveniences. Anyway, we mourn Sadat, we revere his memory, and we hope his Egypt will continue as he wished. At least he died in moments of glory for himself.

Later: Our lives are calm, though atop a current of rumor. We think all will be OK, but unfortunately Ma'adi, rather than the quiet village we imagined, seems to be a sort of center for terrorist meetings and weapons caches (a load of weapons was uncovered, hidden in the elementary school *next door* to us!) There have been several shoot-outs and minor bomb incidents (at my grocery store!), so we're lying low. I think, hope, it won't get worse. Foreigners seem to attract the Khomeini-style anti-Western pro-Islamic groups. Thus, no Halloween this year, and our bazaar, which we've been working on all fall, will probably be cancelled, or transformed into house parties. Oh, well. Better to be safe. (I just hope I can get all my prized copper pots and trays out safely—with us, of course—when the time comes.)

Here I am again, days later, struggling with the problem of ridding my kitchen of its unwelcome visitor—a mouse! No car to go to the store for a trap…probably the Egyptian mousetrap would backfire anyway. Of course, we can't rely on the mother cat who lives in the basement to keep the mouse population down. She seems interested only in sneaking in our door whenever she can to pee on Jared's rug.

Ever go to a cemetery to buy glassware? I found a little primitive oven and glassblower in the City of the Dead and we've been going there to order (for the upcoming bazaar) liqueur and wine glasses of aqua blue—made from melted down bottles…very interesting to see it blown into shape.

We think of our moments together this last summer and look forward to sharing some of our Egypt with some of you. It is a truly beautiful country in many different ways, from the fertile lushness and brilliant greens of the Delta and Nile Valley to the rich yet somber desert hues concealing bursts of color in hidden tombs and Bedouin garb. In the next letter, I'll relate some of the beauties of early Islamic and medieval Cairo remains as well as the typical string of confusions and minor misfortunes which pursue us all in the Middle East.

Zeinab prepares beans

Cairo Christmas

December 1981

It must be near Christmastime here—the poinsettias are roof-high with bright red blossoms. Yet still the leaves haven't fallen…they will, as real winter hits us in January and February. Grass is green, green, and street men continually trim the towering eucalyptus trees, so many street corners are piled high with branches, brambles, and bundles of leaves. Occasional donkey carts stop as black-robed and veiled women rummage through the piles for a bit of firewood, whether giant palm fronds or tiny twigs.

We looked for a "Christmas tree" yesterday. Last year we chose a rather large cactus-type tree, fuller than most of the tall spindly cypress trees and rather exotic for our first Middle-Eastern Christmas, we thought. However, after rigging nearly every branch with twine to support ornaments, and getting coated with the sticky white substance oozing from within, we decided this year to try one of the spindly cypresses, tall and gangly but at least smelling of Christmas, and now covered with two hundred and fifty malfunctioning lights. And for the first time since our departure, we will have Christmas music this year! There are no copyright laws in Egypt, so American/British records are taped and sold without penalty. I just bought a cassette of assorted Christmas music (Johnny Mathis' carols interrupted by a boys choir, etc.), so we don't feel quite as isolated as last year. Our only snow is in the kitchen—on our new New England calendar. And that's enough for me.

Jared's major concern now is the fate of the three wise men. We saw a live nativity pageant at the local expatriate church—complete with camels, goats and other animals. Now every time we pass the church, Jared wants to find the three wise men on their camels. (I explained that they'll be back next year, but that explanation was insufficient.) I'm afraid Jared's skiing skills are put on hold for a few years, but his daring exploits on camel will suffice in the meantime.

Jared is back in his "Teacher Judy school" and has learned the colors—his favorite is blue, so he wants everything blue—his clothes, his food, etc. He's a big tall fellow, as energetic as ever, and still a charmer. His best friend, in addition to

Simon, David and Samir, is his "Curious George" monkey, who accompanies him to school, to bed, and everywhere else. "Georgie Porgie" is now a solid family member. The pre-school, held in the home of his teacher, another ex-pat, lasts three hours four days a week—what a lifesaver for both of us. Tomorrow I have a course on discipline a la Rudolf Dreikurs, who was popular in the U.S. two years ago. For our personal goal in the course, I put "7 P.M. bedtime." Everyone else had more grand aspirations, such as "family harmony."

By the way, we did have Halloween after all—or didn't actually, as was the case. For security, American families hired a wagon to transport costumed kids and parents to a list of "safe houses" in Ma'adi for trick-or-treating. So excited to celebrate Halloween, which we had earlier thought would be canceled due to unrest surrounding Sadat's assassination, we assembled baskets of treats for the wagonload of kids. We waited…and waited…and waited. At last, greatly disappointed, surrounded by loads of undistributed candy, we went to bed. The next day we asked why the Halloweeners had passed us by. They hadn't! When twenty costumed children and adults approached our doorway, they were intercepted by the building *bawab*, or doorkeeper—a cross between guard, custodian and concierge seen lounging around the doorway of most apartment and office buildings. The robed and turbaned *bawab*, who lived with his family in the basement, intercepted the threatening crew—who must have appeared to him like alien invaders—shooing them away before they could get close to our doorbell. He then spent the night, he informed us through gestures the next day, sleeping on our doorstep to protect us from further attack. He indicated that substantial *baksheesh* was expected for his heroic efforts to guard our safety. (Perhaps we did not reward him adequately, as the next thing we knew…his children gave Jared a small but potent gift—lice.)

We're still enjoying Egypt's sunny days, though we'd be warmer in Greece sitting by the stove or even in New England with its central heating. The houses in Egypt are extremely damp in winter, so we open windows during the day to dry out the atmosphere, even by letting cold air in. As our time remaining grows shorter, I'm aware of so much of Cairo and Egyptian history and life that we haven't explored or experienced. The possibility of a June return appalls and panics me—though it would be great to be with friends again, I've just settled and adapted and started to explore. Why quit after all the hassles and just as the fun begins? (But not for poor Frank—it's all work, work, work, work.) Much as I enjoy life in Lexington, I wish we could extend our stay here. Where else would the cleaners' delivery man carry your clothes over his head with one hand and steer his bike with the other? And gardeners adorn doorways with greenery and poinsettias for Christmas (naturally, for baksheesh—but so what?)? Or park all day by the Hilton and give the "street man" 10-15 cents for "guarding the car"?

My most enjoyable activity of the year has just ended—seeking out local artisans and craftsmen and purchasing their wares for sale at a Christmas charity bazaar, which was a great success. Seeking out and procuring goods for the fair enabled me to explore hidden corners of Cairo—from the medieval street of the tentmakers to a small courtyard where primitive mud kilns melted glass to be hand blown...among the water buffalo, goats, sheep, and numerous cats...and even a trip to a desert oasis for baskets. In a creative leap, I designed and had sewn a large supply of kitchen aprons from some beautiful heavy cotton fabric I had discovered with wonderful ancient Egyptian motifs. All went well until I washed my own apron and ended up with an Egyptian Jackson Pollack blend of colors and designs intermingling in chaotic (well, that's typical for here) fashion. Next time we'll have to figure out a way to set the dyes prior to sewing....Well, actually, there will probably not BE a next time for those aprons—will come up with another brilliant idea for next year!

We miss you all very much, and hope that 1982 brings you peace of spirit, joy of heart, and us!

Just Another Day

January 1982

To our armchair travelers—

This first travel letter of '82 was slow in production. Most travel letters occur during a sudden spurt of euphoria, which has become a rarer commodity these days. However, a few events of yesterday and today have pushed me as close to it as I'll probably get now—so a long-overdue letter is ready. Strangely enough, the local scissors and knife sharpener provoked this mood. I was staying home on my weekend Saturday to wash six loads of clothes, piled up since the washing machine broke a week before. The GE man actually did come and actually did fix it, after a fashion, with a total bill of five dollars for labor, parts, and house call! (Believe me, getting anything fixed here is rare.) So I happily washed and ironed twenty-one shirts, all the kitchen curtains, etc. Fortunately, our maid was here to hang them out in shifts. Anyway, the grinder-man walked by, clinking his metal wheel as advertisement. I rushed out with three dulled knives, and Jared and I watched from our kitchen window as the purple-turbaned knife-sharpener pedaled the grindstone round with his foot, looking proud of his craft and smiling at us as he worked. The cozy neighborhood feeling of visiting grinders, apple vendors, Buta-gas tankers, butchers and bread-men enveloped us. The knife-sharpener man never knew what a mood of happiness he had instilled.

Today I suddenly stopped and smiled as I jotted a list of things to be accomplished. Among the more mundane not-worth-mentioning chores were several which I'll never again put on my shopping and errand lists after return to the U.S.:

- Rent car to visit medieval caravansary-inn for displays of local arts and crafts

- Return broken Bedouin oasis pendant to medieval bazaar for repair

- Get info on visiting handmade rug factory in the Delta

- Take friend to alleyway rug repair shop (where one old fellow in crocheted prayer-cap sits shoeless and cross-legged all day repairing Persian carpets)

- Take another woman to street of the tentmakers to buy appliquéd tent squares

- Return to native village to complain about missing tassels from a camel saddle blanket previously purchased

- Invite Greek artist and her German archeologist husband to dinner.

I could spend years here exploring—there's so much unseen, especially in other parts of Egypt—the oases, the Delta, Alexandria (spent only three hours there in one and a half years), the Nile Valley. Well, I'll content myself with a few medieval monuments.

The other day, we actually rejected a street vendor's offer of roses for a dollar a dozen! We said two dozen for one dollar; he said three dozen for two dollars; we said, "Too expensive!" and drove off—then sat there stunned. How our values have changed! (Of course, the roses would have wilted within hours….)

There are many family-style activities for Egyptians. We went to an outdoor "family night club" in the afternoon—a sort of dinner and floor show combination with dancing horse, singers, and—if you can believe it—a transvestite dwarf belly dancer (that one was a bit much!), and a woebegone Salvation Army-looking brass band trudging through the audience. We ordered shish kebab whose distinctive flavor (special secret ingredient) may have been imparted from the charcoal "chips" used in the barbecue pit, according to Frank who explored the outdoor kitchen. Many customers had hookahs—water pipes—delivered to their tables to enjoy the "HIGH-lights" of the show.

Imagine dining al fresco in mid-January! But it has been unusually warm this winter. Today was the first real chiller—windy, dusty, damp. My ski parka was a lifesaver, especially *inside* the house. Actually, it was just a fall-spring day in Boston. I'll be glad to use some of the beautiful sweaters Jared received for Christmas at last.

Frank is not enjoying Egypt as much as I—he never sees it! Just the traffic and his office. Of course, he's working again tonight and the five-day workweek (which never really was) will officially become six-day, it seems. Sigh…. He did get a chance to visit the local Imbaba camel market, however, where white-garbed Sudanese bring their camels on a forty-day journey from Sudan. They walk by night, rest by day. What a wild and wooly place! Frank said the pitch-black white-turbaned Sudanese characters at the camel market make Cairo's exotic residents seem like Boston suburbanites. Camels were hobbled (with one leg tied, completely bent at the knee) to slow down escape attempts and came in a variety of shades from pure white to dark brown. Next door was the water buffalo market, where local stalls sold grilled entrails and other delicacies (with a clothing stall set up in the corner displaying orange and purple bras. The women may dress in black, but beware what lurks underneath.) Nearby was a cane-making stall, and we couldn't resist buying a cane after watching them heat and curve the handle of the knotted wood.

Healthwise, we wish we had nothing to report. Aside from my accidental discovery that the tetracycline I've been taking for five months should be prohibited to anyone with hepatitis, as it destroys the liver (at least I have a reason for feeling poorly lately and can now look forward to improvement since I stopped the medicine), the major tragedy is Jared's front teeth…WAS Jared's front teeth, that is, after a severe fall on the pavement at his school. One of them (and they were so white, straight and beautiful) lies lost somewhere in the grass in the garden of his nursery school, root and all, while the other progressively grays due to the death of the nerve. We've had several dentist visits (one of them leading to the purchase of two Persian carpets, oddly enough) and a great trauma. Our prayers have so far been answered, as the body has not yet rejected the other front tooth, which is out of place and very insecure. Poor little Jared nightly asks God to help his teeth, among his recitations of friends here and abroad to be thankful for. He looks like a precocious three-year-old who'd fit right in among all those 6-and 7-year-olds missing their front teeth. He will know "All I Want for Christmas Is My Two Front Teeth" very well by the time his other teeth eventually come in.

Jared's a very sociable little fellow (sorry, a "big strong boy") who enjoys his Ma'adi friends and remembers all his Bostonian cronies from the summer. He places people well, knows whose parents are whose (especially his "Frankie Daddy Fotis"), and is very concerned about any illness or misfortune to befall anyone. His longest and saddest moment of the day (and mine, too) is his bedtime. He has a great grasp of foreign countries, as so many of his friends live and travel abroad. He is finally learning that a pyramid shape is called a triangle. Previously all shapes were categorized into squares, circles, or pyramids. His daily life is full of a variety of vehicles and animal life. Last week as we walked to his school, we were delayed by watching a garbage truck (from Richmond, Virginia!) with eight to ten long-robed and hooded garbage men and then turned the final corner, only to intercept a herd of goats, sheep, two donkeys, two sheepdogs and three puppies shepherded by a ten-year-old girl in bright scarf and long patterned dress. We are now back on our "little street" (*al-hamdulellah*!) and greet the soldiers as we walk past.

Interestingly enough, many foreign service and business wives, when I say how much I enjoy Cairo and all its hidden little corners, reply that it's really nothing next to Indonesia, and proceed to extract from their bags primitive jewelry and then tell tales of island visits, native crafts and scenic splendor. (All we have here is the setting sun behind the pyramids behind the towering silhouetted palms behind the wide and swift-coursing Nile....) I'm so thankful for this chance to share in and experience the exotic side of life, even if I have to tramp through heaps of garbage—which I literally do—to realize it. Last year I wrote letters to pull you closer to me, to strengthen the tenuous ties, to shorten the distance. This year, this is my home, I love its corners, its nooks and crannies, its possibilities. I write to offer a taste to you and hope your appetite for more will bring some of you here so I can show you unbelievable places and say, "See what I stumbled on? See what's here waiting for you?"

Bordering the Khan el Khalili, Cairo's medieval bazaar, into whose
narrow labyrinthine paths Jared disappeared, following a cat

Rabies and Rides

March 1982

Spring is here! There's a morning chill in the air, and houses are still cold and clammy, but I put on my sandals yesterday, so it must be spring! Midday has been quite warm—but you'd never guess from staying in the house. Also, the unmistakable aroma of gar-b*ah*ge is in the air, so it must be warmer. Spring winds are beginning, and there's always a whirlwind of dust and leaves around one's ankles. Soon the full-scale *khamseen*, or sandstorm, period begins when Saharan sands permeate every crack and crevice and settle on every inch of household surfaces. One has the strange sensation of breathing soil. Tongues and nostrils are coated in a layer of fine yellowy powder—rather like superfine flour. Even the air inside the house appears slightly tan. Oh, but that's to come. For now, we'll enjoy the last few remnants of winter and get a few more days' wear of corduroy and wool.

The latest in our ongoing series of health tragic-comedies has been a double-hitter: rabies shots for Jared, along with a possible abscessed tooth and future root-canal on his one remaining upper front tooth. We kept a local cat in one bathroom for a day and a half to observe him on the ninth and tenth days after he "bit" Jared, according to Jared when questioned about two small puncture wounds on his arm. Jared also said that another yellow cat bit him, so we had to run around for two weeks in search of rabies serum, until the U.S. Embassy in a formal document stated that it was "in the best interests of the United States of America" to sell us rabies serum from their private stock.

Meanwhile, I had dragged the poor cat, a stray, clear out to Heliopolis where the U.S. Naval Medical Station is located, to be tested for rabies—in a brain autopsy. The cat escaped its various boxes three times, and finally the maid, the driver and I stuffed him into a tiny basket which we roped excessively. Halfway out there (Jared was at home in bed with a high fever from the abscess or a mystery illness), it occurred to me that the cat fit the description of the cat of the old Austrian lady several blocks away. I couldn't have them euthanize the cat till I'd made sure it wasn't her cat! I found out later that it was not—and the doctor and

I decided to observe the poor kitty in our bathroom for another day. Such relief! I felt I hadn't the right to take the poor cat there, though it was a stray and this was the proscribed procedure in potential rabies cases. I gave him a fine last supper of steak, deviled eggs and milk. *Al-hamdulellah!* (Thanks to God!)…the cat seems fine and is my constant companion now. I'll try to take him to a vet this evening for rabies shots. Jared will feel better if he's not the only one! Jared has five shots to go. Thank goodness we were allowed to buy the special vaccine; otherwise Jared would have to go through twenty-one injections in the stomach. Now to top it all off, I must say that this cat must be Watson's African cousin—he's a beautiful fluffy (though matted) golden tomcat with white front and is very affectionate (we'll see if he still is after his rabies shot today!). Sixty per cent of cats here are rabid (and a higher percentage of dogs), so this is a very serious concern in our neighborhood. The population explosion of people here is matched or superseded by that of the animal world.

Only in Egypt…

…would your phone bill for $5 arrive one month after the phone has been disconnected due to nonpayment of the bill. This happened to us as well as to our friends, so must be routine procedure.

…would liquid milk be unavailable for two months. (Probably someone did not pay someone off….)

…could you buy a stalk of celery nearly three feet long (and then tell the maid to put it in the refrigerator, and find it frozen and withered in the freezer the next day).

…would we be invited to the Austrian Embassy to bid adieu to the Ambassador of Ecuador (whom we've never met) because we met the Austrian commercial attaché at a party to say goodbye to the Greek embassy press officer (whom we'd never met) going to Romania because I admired the Bedouin jewelry collection of a Greek artist married to a German archeologist, both of whom speak Greek, German, English, French, Arabic, Italian and one other language I forget, and invited them to dinner to meet a Polish artist and our British-Indian friends. Whew! I am the only person at the whole affair who speaks only one language. I came away with great resolve to pursue language studies, but alas…

…would I receive for a birthday present a tiny carved sunflower religious amulet, knowing it had been carved for someone over 3,000 years ago! The sunflower is the sacred flower of the pharaoh Akhenaten, the first person in recorded history to proclaim that there is only one god. When succeeded by his son, the child Tutankhamen ("King Tut"), Akhenaten's new capital at Amarna was abandoned and his "heretic" monotheistic religion reverted to the standard polytheistic religious practice, thus ensuring the high priests continued employment and power. So my little sunflower will remind me of a time long ago and far away when an enlightened ruler tried to change the course of history—a man before his time.

Come with me! Here I go on my one errand of the day—off to the "glass factory" to pick up a friend's order. I love to go there, even though I must wade through garbage and awful offal inside the open courtyard in the middle of the medieval City of the Dead, now occupied by squatters due to the shortage of shelter. This old necropolis is laid out geometrically with house-like tombs where each family could rest when they came to visit their departed dead relatives on feast days. Now the various tomb-houses are filled with poor families, shops, etc., and even have electricity. Our glass-blowers' courtyard is next to the inspiring mausoleum of Quait-Bey, considered the gem of architecture of the Mameluk ("slave") period of medieval Egypt, which was ruled by kidnapped East Asian slaves who were then trained in military and political mastery. It is just a stone's throw from the brilliance of design and décor of this mausoleum from the fifteenth century with its ornately carved minaret and dome, gilded ceilings, inlaid marble and stained glass—to the crudeness of the glassblowers' tiny courtyard, complete with dogs, cats, donkey, goats, and two huge water buffalo!

Here we go—down the Corniche along the Nile with green fields and palm trees on the distant shore, smokestacks vying with minarets, and now the pyramids of Giza and desert sands beyond. I never tire of this Ma'adi-Cairo commute. It's a clear day, for a change—I can even see some of the tiny wives' pyramids alongside the major three monumental ones. And—remnants of winter still—fluffy white clouds. Soon the clouds will disappear for eight or nine months. Felucca masts punctuate the river shoreline—those ancient boats live on in today's felucca, little changed in design through the millennia, with hand-sewn sails and towering masts. …And now that gray Cairo appears under the clouds far ahead, we turn away from the Nile onto Salah-Sa'alem, street of the ovens, through billowing black smoke of hundreds of tiny ovens burning old tires for heat to slake the limestone rock for whitewash, paint and whatever else comes of it. An other-worldly spectacle, with sky here black as night, and yet life goes on (but for how long?) with brightly-dressed toddlers clinging to black-garbed women with huge metal tins on their heads.

…And now in the distance, a series of medieval signaling towers, twenty-five round ones and five three-storey square ones with arches. What is their history? …And now (sorry—bumpy road!) past "Garbage City" where a non-Muslim group of people lives amid the garbage heaps, rummaging through the mounds of fetid garbage, picking out old plastic for the shoemakers, bits of cloth for the rug-weavers, and food for the pigs they raise. If not for these very poorest of workers, the Egyptian economy would tumble even further, for these ultimate recyclers provide invaluable services that automation could not duplicate.

...Now Fustat, remains of the first Islamic city in Cairo, 7th century, where pottery shards still abound. ...Now along the medieval aqueduct of Saladin, huge arched wall with some squatters claiming arches and cardboarding them for privacy. ...Now the Mokattam Hills, huge beige limestone cliffs towering up from the city, where early monasteries used to be. ...Now on the left, the Citadel, medieval fortress of Saladin, built from stone stripped from the pyramids, with rounded towers, and huge thick crenellated walls with slots for arrows—the landmark of Cairo. ...Now minarets and mosques of the medieval city when Cairo was the highlight of the existing world. ...And now at last the City of the Dead, square, immense, domed and minareted, aging and ageless, full of present-day life amid the dead of the past.

"Double, double, toil and trouble

Rubble, rubble everywhere..."

Here we are...now wasn't that more interesting than driving to the Burlington Mall?

Uh oh...road's closed. ...Here we go again, giving someone a lift for directions. He wears a woman's metal and rhinestone ring on his little finger. ...Well, business is transacted and we're headed back to Ma'adi along the same route—wasn't that fun? Just in time to get Jared from school.

Jared: Mary.

Me: Mary who?

Jared: You know, MARY!

Me: A new Mary in your school?

Jared: No.

Me: Well, who is Mary?

Jared: You know, God's wife.

Of course!

Days later...and now the other side of the coin. Life in a tropical climate has its downside, such as a month-long sore throat, three-day diarrhea and stomach cramps, four-day zinger of a headache, plus chills and fever, all converging on the helpless one at the same time. So for the first time in Egypt, I called our general practitioner, an enterprising young man who makes house calls (for $12!). He proceeded to take my temperature with his thermometer, unwashed after whoever was last, examine my throat with a metal "throat horn?" (looked just like a shoehorn) in a similar state of sanitation, and then the ears, etc. Probably a few more germs couldn't do me much more damage; however, I feel sorry for who-ever gets *my* germs next. I was gathering my courage to refuse an injection from a used syringe; however, it was unnecessary. Result: the usual—a virus, and an infection, and stomach something. Better get penicillin and this and that and…. They really over-prescribe here, which is why I haven't been to a doctor yet.

A friend called this morning to inquire of my health. Aziza, our weightlifter maid, answered. My friend thought it was a man and asked, "Where's Mary Ned?"

"NO GOOD!" came the booming reply. True to character. As much unlike our last feminine, petite, courteous maid as could be. Aziza lifts our marble table-top, a feat previously performed only by two men together. (By the way, our heavy glass coffee table top broke yesterday "all by itself," according to a three-year-old witness.)

And so goodbye until the next traveling letter, an account of the glories of the Nile in Upper Egypt as we—at last after a year and a half—cruise from Aswan to Luxor, fly to Abu Simbel, and visit the Valley of the Kings. Au revoir…or *Ma'a salaama* (with peace), as we say here.

Additional notes to Frank's cousin:
May 17, 1982

Hope you can decipher this epistle, as much of it was written while traversing one of Cairo's bumpy roads! Alas, if I'd waited to remember the scene, I wouldn't. So a few bumps and some more local color direct to you from here—where yester-day it was 43° C (106+° F). Whew!

We hope to go to Alexandria this weekend to get Frank away from the office, where he seems to be chained this month. He's had ONE day off in a month, leaves at 7:30 A.M., returns at midnight!

Jared's growing as usual and is constantly inquisitive. Yesterday's first ques-tion: "How come monkeys don't take showers?!" His wonderful "Teacher Judy" school of this year is closing—so I'm madly hunting for one for next year (on *both* sides of the Atlantic) and without any success so far. Anything is second-rate compared to what he had this year. Sigh…. He will complete his rabies shots soon. Now he's quite aware of injections and their requirements. "Do you have to have a shot to go to England?" he asks. "No." Very well. He will go to England…but NOT to Kenya or anywhere else until he verifies that shots are not required.

We don't know (literally) if we are coming or going. We were supposed to find out in March. All the project funds expire at the end of May and some (including Jared's first and best friend Simon) have already departed—after only one week's notice! That's the way these projects run. Simon (originally known as "Mimon" to Jared's "Gedded") has been Jared's very good friend since our six-week period of transition at the Mena House by the pyramids in what seems an eternity ago—could it really have been less than two years? It's a hard lesson to lose those early friends…sigh. Now that the initial two years are nearly over, we don't know who will stay or go, so everyone's in a kind of limbo. The "Why Didn't I Visit a Desert Oasis? Syndrome"—fear of suddenly having to leave without having seen enough—pervades. Registering children in schools on both sides of the Atlantic—just in case. Some people have been notified two days before their departure that they would be staying. Others have been told to return to the U.S., and come back after three or four months, having moved everything back and given up their apartment. Ah, organization!

So we may or may not be back in Lexington this year. If the project is extended and we do stay next year, it won't be here in our wonderful apartment. I'll be crushed to leave it—except for the landlords, who are up to their old tricks—collecting double rent on some apartments, trying to take over furniture of departing tenants without paying, the usual. What will they pull with us? Right now they've opened a carpentry shop beneath us, so the happy buzz of power saws and friendly thud of hammers adds a bit of background to our daily life.

Nevertheless, I love this place. It's more like a house, really—only no garden (yard) and five layers of people on top of us. I love its odd-shaped rooms, its ups and downs, its sculpted ceilings. New architecture here is quite dramatic—you know, the Mediterranean soul with a touch of Africa added. Probably not too stable, as buildings keep falling down (hope ours doesn't, but with our bedroom wall cracking from their chipping away at the foundation support to add a walkway, we'll probably be safer somewhere else), but thankfully lacking the American cost-consciousness which leads to square rooms and lack of projecting exteriors. Residential buildings here, at least some of them, have waves, domes, curls, concave and convex surfaces. The new office buildings tend to be western boxes. Wish you could observe. I love the old Islamic (especially Mameluke/slave-ruler) designs—so graceful and lovely. How could such ruthless and cruel people have been so refined in their art? A recurring question….

Women carry water from the Nile in Upper Egypt
("Nile Women" by Margo Veillon)

Later addition:

Somehow the letter of the cruise down the Nile into the past never got written! Perhaps it was due to the fever and chills which followed me from temple to temple and tomb to tomb…my very own Curse of the Pharoahs. More likely, it was due to my instant obsession with the Boggle game of re-arranged word tiles, which our travel companions brought to me, and which left me with eyes glued to the tiles, creating as many words as I could within a minute or two, punctuated with a few quick glances at the timeless scenes floating by along the banks of the Nile. What folly!

Some hazy memories persist:

• The endless brown of dried-mud huts forming rustic villages along the banks of the Nile, brightened by orange, fuchsia, crimson and vermillion dresses and wraps of little girls

• Black-robed women who remain erect in spite of the burden of heavy terra cotta water jars atilt on their heads, cushioned by a coil of bright fabric forming a nest for the large heavy curved jars

• Water buffalo circling endlessly around primitive water-wheel pumps which haven't changed much from the time of Archimedes

• Ravaged temple walls whose cartouches and hieroglyphic names and images had long ago been defaced and gouged out by early Christians whose sensibilities were offended by ancient polytheistic culture

• Hundreds of mummified crocodiles, yes CROCODILES, piled up in a side temple at Kom Ombo

• The ethereal semi-submerged Temple of Philae, eerily receding beneath the waters with the creation of the Aswan Dam and subsequent flooding of the area, resulting in the very large Lake Nassar and the end of seasonal flooding of the Nile. Now there's water all the time, but the land no longer has time to rest and recover, the silt is dammed up, reducing the fertility of the land downstream towards the Nile Delta, and Nile water parasites no longer have an off-season during which their numbers are reduced, resulting in even more blindness and disease (and why we were warned NEVER to walk barefoot in our garden, as it was regularly flooded twice a week with Nile water).

• Colossal 60-foot tall cliff-side bas-relief statues of (what? him again?) Ramses II at Abu Simbel in Egypt's deep south near the Sudanese border. One could see where each statue had been cut into pieces, moved to higher ground and then reassembled, rather like a giant Lego pharaoh clinging to the cliffs.

- The long cool tomb chambers in the Valley of the Kings, adorned with still-brilliant paintings on walls and starry ceilings. Most frequently portrayed was the goddess Nut, goddess of the sky and of the dead. Tomb ceilings were covered with constellations, which—to an ancient Egyptian at least—were the embodiment of Nut.

- Climbing into smaller artisans' tombs and angling and lining up a series of handheld mirrors to direct the sunlight inside the darkness and onto delicate and detailed carved and painted scenes of hunting, cooking, merriment, nature and wildlife…just another day in the life of an ancient artisan

- Towering Nubian feluccas at Elephantine Island—or was it Kitchener's?—with their billowing white sails and gleaming interiors. The neatnik Nubians, with brightly knitted skullcaps and glowing ebony faces, polish every inch of their craft, unlike their neighbors to the north, and they make sure no wayward footstep leaves a spot of dust in their glorious feluccas.

- The many "antiquity-brokers" with deep pockets from which they extract priceless one-of-a-kind antiquities, available for a price to the gullible tourist, only to retrieve an identical item from deep within their billowing robes for their next victim

- The horse-drawn calèches in which we explored Thebes and Luxor, taking us back to another time when tourists arrived with many heavy sea-trunks full of fancy ball gowns and proper evening attire for their splendid nights at the Winter Palace. (We, on the other hand, stayed at a more modest establishment which was thrilled to have four *farangs* among its clientele, as it raised their status significantly. When we went to the desk asking for a bottle opener to slake our thirst at the end of a very long and very dusty day, the manager eagerly followed us back to our room, took our bottles and—voila!—pried open each one on the edge of a piece of furniture.)

- The monumentally huge Temple of Luxor, with its massive painted and carved columns stretching into the heavens, it seemed, just like in the scene from *Murder on the Orient Express*. In a few days *Aida* would be performed right where we stood, complete with camels, elephants, Luciano Pavarotti and an exclusive audience flown in from around the world. How's that for an authentic stage set?

Diplomatic Days—and Nights

May 1982

Happy May Day to all!

Our traveling letters are rather sporadic, for we wait to write till there's something to write about, even though the daily routine here is interesting by contrast to life in the States.

Last night was very interesting indeed. We were the only Americans at a party which included the ambassador of India, the ambassador of Austria, acting ambassador of Greece, assistant ambassador of Brazil, military attaché of Hungary, economic attaché of Austria, naval attaché of Britain, and some kind of attaché of Israel, an Italian couple and...us! The hosts? A Greek-Egyptian *dentist* and his beautiful young German wife. We began the evening in great style by introducing ourselves to the waiter, whom we assumed, by his formal attire and great dignity, was some kind of ambassador from black Africa. "Uh...uh...I am the waiter," he stuttered with some embarrassment, as I slowly retracted by hand and turned purple. There was much kissing of hands and bowing. My first ambassadorial conversation last year was with the American ambassador about his wife's pleurisy. My second was last night with the Indian ambassador. Sample of his comments: "And what brand of olive oil do you use? Where do you get your charcoal briquettes? When I was ambassador to Tanzania we were given two rabbits, and had two hundred by the time we left...." His wife, beautifully "wrapped" in a pink silk sari, shared his aristocratic British accent, as she discussed the German school in Bombay and a flowering tree in her garden. The Hungarian attaché produced a devastating colorless fruit liqueur which nearly felled us—the Hungarian national drink. The Brazilians mumbled "*boa noite*" to all and slipped out. The Israeli wife spoke perfect English and asked to switch to French, as her English was "so bad." Her Hebrew and Arabic she shelved for the evening. Our dentist host greeted everyone in appropriate tongues, switching smoothly from one language to another. Most spoke five or six languages—and there I was, fumbling with a Greek participle, craning an ear to decipher some French, and nodding agreeably to *je ne sais pas quoi*. The young German hostess (who has four children from twelve years to nine months, and speaks German, English, French, Arabic, and Greek) had created a masterpiece of German and Greek food—five meats, salmon, chicken, grape leaves, etc., which were wonderful—but only a precursor to her pastry table of mango (frozen from last summer) tarts and other delectable desserts.

Now HOW can we reciprocate? (I told them I'd invite them over for American hotdogs!) These same people had us to a picnic by the pyramids during "*Sham El Nessim*" ("Sniff the Breezes"), the big spring folk festival day in Egypt. They grilled steaks, built a tent for the day, and hammered desert stones to uncover geodes and agates hidden inside. (The dry parched desert sands give up other treasures as well with a little digging and prodding, including actual *seashells*, believe it or not, reminders of a wetter time zillions of years ago when the Sahara was a vast salt lake.) This elegant picnic was, of course, another multi-lingual occasion. So at last we are emerging from our social cocoon of ADL'ers, and thankfully so, because the men discuss business all evening (might as well have stayed at the office) while we women see who's sick now, etc. Actually, diplomatic life is similarly excruciatingly dull, as these social amenities must be performed again and again nightly, but for an outsider to glimpse the superficial glamour of it all is quite fun! (We're thinking of printing dinner invitations in French, too!)

Across the Nile, Mohammed the gardener eats with one hand and
whisks flies with the other, as the women who prepared the food look
on, waiting their turn to eat whatever remains after guests, men and
children have eaten their fill

Protocol is protocol, wherever one is—from rarefied formal embassy galas full of ambassadors and foreign dignitaries in full regalia—to a meal on the ground in a Nile village. I accompanied our Polish friend and artist Halina Wlodarczyk, who was the honored guest of her daughter's gardener Mohammed at his home in a typical village on the other side of the Nile. This special occasion was quite an honor for the gardener—as well as for us. Halina, whom we all called "Baba," Polish for "Grandmother," took a special interest in the young man and had drawn his portrait. Baba was most egalitarian, unlike many expatriates who tend to become rather lordly when placed in a foreign assignment with household help. When the big day arrived, Mohammed accompanied us to a local boat which continually criss-crossed the Nile ferrying many maids, cooks and gardeners to their jobs at *farang* households in Ma'adi. This was our first time in such local transport, and we—the only passengers without long robes or turbans—enjoyed our ride across the wide, wide river. Climbing up the muddy bank of the Nile, we walked to a grouping of houses, small ramshackle affairs of just one or two rooms, nestled in a grove of towering palms. We were directed to sit, on the ground, around a low round wooden table with the men of the family. Soon women and girls in long bright flowered dresses began bringing tin bowls of various foods, and one of meat, signifying the special honor accorded to Baba. As we reached into the bowl with our fingers, we each extracted a piece of meat from an orange-colored sauce, and proceeded to gnaw at it, trying to make conversation in our very inadequate and halting Arabic. Baba's animation and delight more than compensated for any lapses in language. The girls and women disappeared after bringing the food. When we had had our fill, the women returned and lifted the entire table and moved it over to another location where other members of the family, children and elderly, then sat down to dine from the same bowls. As we were finally saying our goodbyes, the poor women who had cooked the whole meal at last sat down to eat from the meager remains, the third and final shift in this traditional village dinner. Protocol had been followed to the tee.

I've had a wonderful weekend preparing and assisting Baba with her art exhibit. Just sitting in the room surrounded by the variety of painting styles and techniques is so satisfying. Halina, a most entertaining, talented and lively woman in her late sixties(?), had in her youth studied in Paris with Leger. When her architect husband died a decade or so ago, she joined the Peace Corps and served in Niger—quite a woman! I restrained myself—bought only one painting this time—but have enjoyed being closely involved in the matting, arrangement and presentation of each painting. All but eight of her forty-one on exhibit were sold within the opening hours, a great success, but I'm sad to see them go. At least, I know where some of my favorite paintings will reside: Kansas City, Cincinnati, Washington DC, London—and our fourteen in Boston! You will see them when we return. We have another artist friend here—Eleni Grossman, a Greek married to a German archeologist—who is exhibited in the National Gallery of Greece, and our (I should say *my*) hope is to have her paint a family grouping of us with a Greek island motif (Frank vetoed an Egyptian theme—though it would have been wonderful, as Eleni's ethereal desert and Bedouin scenes are fantastic). So it has been wonderful to observe the creation of painting from conception to sketch to paper and canvas, and to accompany Baba to downtown Cairo in her frequent and frustrating search for supplies—finally to find suitable imported paper in good condition, only to have the clerk mar it at the last minute with his dirty fingerprints while wrapping…and not have a clue as to the reason for our consternation at the damage. He could not for the life of him understand how big black thumbprints might have a deleterious effect on a lovely, limpid watercolor!

El Qahira, Mother of the World—Halina stopped to make this quick
sketch as we wandered around Cairo in search of art supplies

Frank is still completely immersed in work—at the office all weekend, etc. In desperation, I have reserved a weekend hotel special in Alexandria, hoping that the three of us will go, and no one can find us.

Jared is really growing. He vacillates between his charm and obstreperousness, both of which are quite overwhelming!

May whatever—much later....

Well, here it is, early May, and spring is nearly over. Most of the brilliant blossoms have passed their prime (without waiting for me to photograph them), and summer laziness has set in, although at the moment we're having an unusual cold snap (meaning it's not witheringly hot, but mild and pleasant).

Blue and lavender jacaranda blossoms tower over our lovely Orabi Street, creating an ethereal purple canopy to walk or drive under. The brilliant bougainvillea is faded now, and we must wait till next spring to catch our breath again at its incredible boldness of color—red, magenta, cerise, orange or pink. The American school campus is laden with springtime richness of pansies, cabbage plants, petunias (I shouldn't mention the roses, as they have bloomed throughout the winter), some lovely tiny blue plants, and huge pink and red geraniums—all this at ground level. Look up and you see blossoming *bauhinia* "orchid trees" with their mauve and white orchid-like blossoms. Later will come the flame trees with their vivid orange-red or yellow blossoms. Our grateful thanks to the British woman who, decades ago, arranged the planting of various streets in Ma'adi with rows of flowering tropical trees, one kind of tree per street, leaving us the gift so many years later of walking in springtime along the yellow "golden shower" tree street, the pink camel-leaf tree street, the flaming red Royal Poinciana *flamboyant* (whose Egyptian name is *gebennemiyya*—literally "hell-fire") street, and our own lovely lavender jacaranda street. And that's not all—there is the waxy beauty of the fragrant frangipani, the "Beard fo the Pasha" with white feathery flowers, the alluring but poisonous oleander, the modest blooms of seductively fragrant jasmine, and so many other floral delights!

Come and share all this with us. (Come also and share the broken telephones, the "aromatic plumbing," to put it politely…etc.) And now here comes some form of street peddler in long white robe and turban chanting his sales song…which of course I can't understand. Looks like a huge bag of potatoes or onions or—

(rest of letter is missing)

Alexandria
aka
The Glory of Greece Is Long Gone

May 1982

Our building has become a feline sanctuary for an assortment of local residents, primarily narrowed—through our good efforts, limited distribution of rations and occasional shoe leather—to two long-term occupants, "Yellow Kitty," the Watson of the East, and "Mrs. Puffin," a very pregnant and rather touchy calico, also known as Richard by the boys upstairs. So the pages of this traveling letter will be headed by a variety of feline poses, to reflect our current affairs. Actually, the most common position is not presented—our hesitantly opening the door with foot wedged between door and frame and then hopping out before the cats hop in. Of course, we cannot touch them—never mind the fleas…it's the possibility of rabies—and shooing two very determined kitties out without helpful hands feels rather like soccer must feel at the first attempts. Mrs. Puffin prefers to curl up in flower pots, absorbing any cool from the mud and shaded by the leaves of the plant. They both leave us assorted bones and bits of feathers on our doormat, which they favor, so we've moved it into the house. "Yellow Kitty" would glow like Watson if only he didn't seek the undersides of cars for winter warmth, summer shade, and scratching posts, adding an unnatural gray to his golden fleece.

This month's (spring's, year's) big adventure was our recent weekend getaway in Alexandria, familiarly known as "Alex" by nearly everyone. I can't get myself to abbreviate such a lovely long name so evocative of past grandeur. Alexandria! City by the sea! Mediterranean waves rolling down from Greece—so it seems. Cool! Winds! Clouds! Though small, only four to five million compared to Cairo's nearly fifteen million, the thin strip of city stretching east-west along the coast seems immense, as it's so long and narrow.

We went up on the train (Hungarian!) FIRST CLASS for three dollars one way, ensconced in once-plush seats which slid off their platforms if you didn't hug the backs. The slatted wooden shutters on the windows we raised—only we!—to observe the rich Delta countryside slide by for three and a half hours…water buffalos, donkeys, camels and the usual profusion of fowl. Stiff-backed figures bent in the fields, gathering what they could. Flapping Egyptian scarecrows, bits of white cloth on wire. Tiny fields of varying produce, with a shade tree or shack somewhere on each. Egrets. Tiny mud villages with newly piled thatched roofs. How many roofs a year? A strong wind could easily dislodge the rocks holding down bundles of straw. "It's like riding through the pages of *National Geographic*," we thought.

The eeriest sight was the shadow of our coach with all the soldiers' legs protruding from the top. The entire train was loaded with soldiers catching a free ride home for the weekend, sitting on the rooftops of each car. With every stop, we'd see some leap down beside us from above and hear the stomping of army boots over our heads.

At last the visually pleasing primitive mud villages, beautiful in their simplicity and design, gave way to "progress"—squat concrete squares with tin roofs, and then the innumerable high-rises, outlined in trash, until the actual urban sprawl overtook us. Actually, one could notice a change in the feel of the landscape as we neared Alexandria—a richness in the canal vegetation, towering fragmites and luxuriant growth. Life doesn't seem as hard here, even for the plants.

So to "Alex," where we saved the tourist sites for another day, but coincidentally happened into an American community barbecue (tiny foreign contingent here) by meeting an acquaintance at a Greek taverna, and even spotted our ex-driver on the street. Everyone who can comes to "Alex" for the weekend—or whole summer, preferably.

After a considerable wild goose chase with a very tired three-year-old boy (guess who?), we finally tracked down what should have been, and probably once was, one of the highlights of all Africa—the Orthodox Patriarchy of Alexandria, home of the fellow who heads the Orthodox Church for all of Africa, and one of the five divisions of all Orthodoxy worldwide. (Hope I have that right!) Well…like returning to an empty alma mater…the fabulously ornate church and grounds were silent, empty, gardens now sprouting corn and tomatoes amid remnants of once glorious formal rose gardens. Adjoining buildings which used to house church offices and students now were rented to local tenants, Muslim I assume, to whom the faded Greek inscriptions on their doors conveyed no purpose or meaning. After continued knocking on the immense doors, we gave up, but spotted an old caretaker just as we were leaving the grounds, and so were admitted to the grand church. This elaborate structure, incidentally, is not even the original, just another church now become the patriarchy with the collapse of the original. Alexandria was another Greece before Nassar and the massive exodus. How sad for those very few Greeks remaining to have seen great days and to live in the aftermath.

Alexandria is known for its seafood, and gorge we did—mmm!—including the long-awaited day when we drove to the famed village of Abu Kir, known throughout Egypt for its fresh and well-prepared seafood. We scouted about till we found "the Greek place," Zephirion, a huge indoor and outdoor restaurant right on the sea, all painted white and blue, with gargantuan platters of shrimp, lobster, barbouni, monstrous-long fish, urchins, sole.....mmmm! We'd waited a year and a half for this. Just as we were looking through the fish tanks trying to place our order, the *Decline and Fall of the Fotis Empire* began:

1. Jared developed a profuse nosebleed, drenching Frank's pearly white shirt and shorts with brilliant red.

2. Customers gasped, stared, glared, and some kindly ones gave us tissues.

3. The manager chased me through the entire restaurant trying to stuff a cone of wet tissues up Jared's nose, as I politely and then rudely refused in my halting Greek while Jared cowered in fear of him.

4. He caught us, performed the deed, and…

5. Jared promptly became hysterical at having the portly stranger force a foreign object up his wee little nose.

6. We returned to the table where Jared finally calmed down. Frank said, "YOU take him," and Jared dissolved into hysterics again.

7. Frank's frustration turned to fury, and by the time Jared fell asleep from exhaustion with his head on my purse on the table, I was no longer speaking to Frank, and he wasn't looking at me.

8. The shrimp and barbouni were stone cold, our driver and wife sat across from us eating the fish we had ordered, and when asked how she enjoyed the fare, the driver's wife shook her head and said, "It's better in Mansoura (her village)."

A day worth waiting for. I proceeded to drink a liter of beer.

(Actually, we never have much luck with the lethal combination of seafood and drivers. A day trip to Port Said on the Suez Canal had our previous driver, the lovely Mr. Samir, show us to the best place to order mounds and mounds of grilled shrimp, which are served on paper. Mr. Samir returned from the tiny take-out place absolutely laden with kilos of gigantic rosy shrimp hot off the grill. (And more expensive than what we could order at a fancy restaurant!) We sat in the car expecting to savor the first bite, trading ambience for flavor. FIRE!! Our mouths were on fire! Our tongues were singed, it seemed, as the powerful hot chili peppers imbedded in each shrimp began their fiery torment. "What is this?!" screamed Frank, eyes bulging and tongue searching for relief. "Oh, one must always eat shrimp with the spices," advised Mr. Samir, tucking into his portion with glee. "Well, never mind," mumbled Frank with disappointment. "You take them all. We don't like shrimp, anyway." And that was the end of that. I think we must have eaten a lot of bread that night upon our return from Port Said.)

We took the long way back from Abu Kir, through the Nile Delta village of El Rashid. ("Eau de Rashid" will long be remembered for its variety of noxious odors in such close confines—Po! Po! Po!). El Rashid is otherwise known as Rosetta, site of the discovery by Napoleon's army of the famous Rosetta Stone, carved in hieroglyphics, demotic, and Greek, which led to the deciphering of ancient hieroglyphics. Rosetta is the western branch of the Nile through the Delta, as Damietta is the eastern branch. So an interesting spot for a tour…though we never discovered the interesting old brickwork, disintegrated or plastered over, and though I never even got to stop for a pebble (MY "Rosetta stone"), we did enjoy the commuters' rush of horse-drawn "carts," actually just flat platforms full of farm bodies returning home, all dangling feet from the high wooden slatted platforms—we must have passed at least fifty of them—some with elderly respectable-looking turbaned gents, others all of women and chil-dren—the Lexpress of Rosetta—past marshy areas with tiny red and green striped canoe/rowboats all above the water on stilts!?!

Our most interesting venture was the four-hour drive to El Alamein (and then right back again—whew!), site of World War II battles where British forces repelled Rommel, denying Germans access to Cairo and the Suez Canal. Mile after mile after mile along the coast of brilliant otherworldly aquamarine waters and glistening white sand, only vehicles and shepherds herding woolly sheep and goats over the seemingly barren sand—on and on and on until the graveyards. The British lost 11,000 men in a few days here…and their individual tombstones revealed soldiers from South Africa, India, New Zealand, Scotland, Canada, Australia—all dying here in this alien desert, now all at peace amid the bougainvillea and graceful symmetry of arch and dome in this most beautiful, most touching and peaceful of cemeteries at El Alamein. Many tombstones were nameless: "Soldier of—Division, Australia…known only to God." One stone of a twenty-two-year old—and most were around that age at their deaths—read: "To the world, he was a soldier. To me, he was the world." And there they lie, nearly forty years later, many visited by far-away relatives who record whom they have come to visit in the visitors' books. How very, very sad.

And thus ends our weekend away, after a morning stroll through the grounds of King Farouk's Alexandria "retreat"—palace and gardens from which he sailed away, abdicating in 1952. Incredible wealth and luxury amidst his people's poverty…but then, were they really HIS people? Muhammed Ali, his grandfather, was Albanian…yet another in the thousands of years of foreign rule here.

Well! Here we are again in Ma'adi! In our lovely apartment…which the landlords are trying to rent right out from under us for twice the rent—$2,500 a month—and where we now sleep on the living room floor since the bedroom wall cracked clear through from one wall to the other after they knocked out the basement support walls under it. It's good to be back.

Sadly, we see newly-made friends departing. Our plans are still unsettled. We were supposed to know in March, then May, and now July. Jared, who's growing "like a weed," (things grow faster here), would like to visit America if he doesn't have to get a shot first.

Egyptian playground? Jared and friend slide down a pyramid

Mummies and Mud

November 1982

With mummy wrappings protruding from our pockets and shirts, we sifted through the crumbling mud bricks first molded perhaps 4,000-5,000 years ago. The original straw remains in these ancient building blocks, many now a fine powder forming wonderful landslides for Jared and his friend on the lower half of this Hawara pyramid near the fringes of the Fayoum oasis several hours south of Cairo. The upper level remains very nearly perfect, and we observed how each mud brick, perhaps sixteen inches long, rested on those beneath. The immutability of stone is omnipresent here in Egypt, but we were surprised at the longevity of this unfired mud brick.

We wandered through the extensive burial ground and ancient labyrinth at the base of the pyramid, where pieces of hand-woven linen peeked through the powdery soil, some still covering bones. One teenaged boy in our party uncovered TWO mummies! The rest of us stumbled among multifarious bones and cloth mummy wrappings. (An embassy employee wife later told me of uncovering an entire mummy head in her garden shed, perhaps left by a previous tenant. In fact, so many mummies have been unearthed from the Egyptian soil that "mummy" became a generic commodity in England in the 1800s.)

In the beginning, I carefully sneaked a tiny one-inch square piece of the ancient cloth into my pocket. One hour later, this "pharaonic fabric" had become so common that I was rejecting anything under eight inches long. And then my interest turned to pottery shards—chunks of ancient amphora, water or storage jars buried with the dead to provide ample sustenance for their eternal journey. We gradually discarded our November jackets, sweaters and hats, and stood—quite hot!—in short sleeves, basking under the same sun and lovely cloudy skies that canopied those early workers who—brick by brick—built this pyramid. I looked to my right—and saw my son in a tiny burial pit, digging away with a leg bone. With that, we departed for Fayoum, desert oasis a hundred and twenty kilometers south of Cairo, known for its straw baskets, as well as the world-famous 2,000-year old Fayoum Portraits, individual representative funerary masks painted during the Roman period on small boards to be placed over mummies' faces. To see the Fayoum Portraits, however, one must travel to museums in the U.S., England, France, Germany, Russia and Greece, as well as Cairo.

As usual, I was in search of typical Egyptian arts and crafts for the Christmas bazaar to be held in one week—enough to call for a two-car convoy on a beautiful Friday. After wild and frantic bargaining, we appeared to accomplish our goal for the bazaar, but a friend still wanted a very large square basket, and none remained. Thus we loaded one basket-lady, a pretty freckled young woman with a one-month-old infant, into one of the cars and set off for her home five miles away where she assured us were hundreds more baskets—and there were!

We stopped at a typical hut village by the water pump, which seemed to be the "town hall" as well. Girls in orange, fuchsia and purple dresses with earthenware pots and copper pans on their heads carried water for their households. Old women (old? perhaps thirty and up) in black sat chewing and spitting sugar cane. As we wound through the maze of alleyways past lovely old wooden doors and iron grillwork—on mud houses with dirt floors—we threaded our way in and out of groups of children, and then the entire passage was blocked by a camel, bearing four times its volume in sugarcane. We ducked into a doorway with ducks and hens—and finally reached the basket-lady's house, where we all bought more than we needed at more than we should have paid. The beauty of some of the people, the friendliness of nearly all, the poverty yet resilience of the human spirit amid the beauty of the palm trees, decorative brickwork, and colorful garb contrasted with the squalor—runny noses, fly-infested eyes, deformities. We were all appreciative for our brief glimpse into village life and somehow more quiet and thoughtful—and thankful—as we drove away.

A tisket, a tasket—to the oasis for a basket

Today we're thankful as well for an especially full and unusually interesting week. Hardly had I packed away our meager hoard of mummy wrappings, mostly reduced to "pharaonic dust" by now, than we prepared for our second pyramid picnic with our German-Greek diplomatic friends. Jared and I went with Italian friends, as Frank was still working. We were only an hour late—pretty good considering our two flat tires (in front of a gas station—but the attendants stood around nonchalantly while our Italian friend changed the tires himself) and a dog with carsickness! We arrived just in time to be introduced to the ambassador from Cameroon ("Where's Cameroon?" I whispered) before his early departure. I had nearly ignored the ambassador, recalling our gaffe in introducing ourselves to the waiter at a previous gathering, but then saw him with his glamorous wife escorted into a white Mercedes and driven off. How sleek he was—all ebon black dressed all in white—really TOO nice for a picnic! Frank arrived and we enjoyed a windy afternoon by the pyramids, Frank distributing German beer and Polish vodka, and I helping fry Tunisian crepes and trying unsuccessfully to sort the Italians from the Mexicans. Our host, the genial Greek-Egyptian dentist, of course addressed everyone in his or her native tongue—English, German, French, Greek, Italian, Spanish, Portuguese—and bargained with the camel and horse men in Arabic. Jared took a half-hour ride through the desert on horseback, with an older girl, as I watched him disappear behind the dunes.

These exotic experiences, which are certainly not daily occurrences for us, give us even more to be thankful for this year. I appreciate Ma'adi's towering trees and prolific flowers (ten-foot-high poinsettias are just beginning to turn red now), Egypt's sunny and temperate clime, our health (*Al-hamdulellah!* Thanks be to God!), and the thought of our friends here and those we'll be returning to. *Al-hamdulellah!*

Frank has a new interest—aerobics. He walks briskly around the American school track every morning, beginning in the pitch blackness of 5 A.M., logging three to seven miles daily. He's looking and feeling much healthier and trimmer.

Jared is quite a big fellow now that he has become four. He's decided he will be seven next. He'll skip over five and six, because seven-year-olds can do so much more. He's created a new style of coiffure—we call it the zigzag cut. He found the scissors one day and rearranged his hair. Part of his bangs are now ¼ inch long! He has quite a vocabulary, enjoys his school, and is as active as ever. He's a beautiful, sensitive, inventive fellow—and we're so thankful for him.

Scribbled postscript:

Written before we all got sick and Jared entered a "new stage," which, in the spirit of Christmas, is better left undescribed.

Preparing local *balady* bread in an earthen oven. Poor Egyptians, ironically enough, eat the healthiest foods: whole wheat and bran pita bread (much cheaper than rice or pasta), roasted sweet potatoes and lots of greens.

Leah in Lotus Land

[There seems to be an entire year of letters missing here. Surely the morning sickness wasn't *that* bad!]

November 1983

Home at last! Cairo welcomed Leah and her mom with balmy weather and a profusion of flowers. At last our family was reunited. Four months away for me and Leah's first visit to the Land of the Pharaohs! Villa Isis, our two-storey "little house near the desert" on a triangle of land bordered by three streets is wonderful, small but cozy, and we enjoy its intimacy and slightly crumbling quaintness even more than our previous architectural showplace apartment. Our family has increased by two—Leah and a little gray mouse who scurries in front of the fireplace when we sit down for a rest. I've searched high and low for a little mousetrap, but can find only large metal cages, large enough for a small cat and surely intended for Egypt's prolific rat population. When I protest and explain that it's just a little gray mouse, I get the standard reply: "Madame, here in Egypt, the mice are BIG!"

We settled in our lovely Villa Isis prior to my return for Leah's birth. We painted, carpeted, shuffled furniture, and prepared a welcoming home for the Fotis-to-be. Of course, this is still Egypt and even though we thought we had prepared for every contingency, we hadn't considered what cunning methods the local electric office or its agents would resort to. When Frank returned to the States on a business trip, I learned that we had been watched, and as soon as the man was gone, the vulnerable wife and child were fair game. (Most maids, cooks and gardeners are expected to report to the local police—the Ma'adi grapevine is quite extensive!) Someone was lying in wait to capitalize on a very pregnant *farang* alone in a house with a small boy. And that was the so-called "electric man" who appeared out of nowhere with a wrench and assorted other tools to turn off our electricity for nonpayment. Naturally, he didn't speak English—just gestured. I knew we had paid the bill, and quite a large one as we really needed the air-conditioning for the upstairs bedrooms. I had no car, no help, no neighbors—and the landlord had gone to Ethiopia! I pointed to my condition, and the "electric-man" retreated from the power box outside the house and gestured that he would return tomorrow—for the money. Frank's office sent out a local employee to resolve the issue; he read the bill, which was of course totally in Arabic, and told us we owed several hundred pounds, the equivalent of hundreds of dollars. I thought that perhaps the previous tenants had not paid their bill, but they had returned to Italy (oh, those Italians!), and so Frank's office advanced the money, which was paid at the electric office, not to the little man with the wrench, and I kept my lights and air-conditioner and the receipt. When the landlord returned from Ethiopia we gave him the receipt, expecting reimbursement, and his response was, "This is not for my house! It's a totally different address." And it was. And that's how you get bills paid in Cairo.

I returned to Cairo to the eminent loss of my three very good friends—such is life on a foreign assignment. Two years is the length of the standard overseas assignment—not enough! The first year is spent learning and adjusting, the second improves upon the first—and then just when you're about adjusted, functioning, and have a circle of friends....it's time to wrap it all up and return home where you go through culture shock all over again—in reverse. The third year is definitely the best. You're well adjusted, know where to find what you need, within reason, and still have friends. That's the year they hit you to preside over the various clubs and charitable organizations whose membership changes so dramatically with each year. You're an old hand by now. And then in the fourth year begins the slow sad decline—you're perfectly acclimated, but your friends start leaving one by one, or in my case three at once. Old hands gradually withdraw into a small social circle of long-timers or friends married to locals. It's a little sad to keep making new friends, only to have them leave in a year or two....

The blow of my friends' departure was softened slightly as Frank had bought for me my departing friend's second-hand white Mercedes so I could have some mobility in Ma'adi—at last! The Mercedes fell apart in less than a week—such is life in Cairo. It joins the washing machine, toilet, sink, water heater, gate and water pump all awaiting proper repair. Ah well, I was so euphoric the first week that I didn't mind returning to the "what new thing is broken now?" routine.

Life is easier now—we've broken in and purchased all those things we thought we could do without for the past three years—second car, video, color TV...a great help for Jared, Frank and his mom during my absence. (Even an electric steam iron, which we had eschewed the first few years since they cannot be grounded and are therefore very dangerous to use. However, watching the *muqwagi* [ironer] at work in his stall filling his mouth with water to spit on our clothes before pressing them with his charcoal-heated irons persuaded me to risk electrocution with an electric iron at home.) Frank's mom is a wonderful help with the baby. She has the Greek grandma's magic touch—a combination of humoring, rocking, and persistence to lull a crying baby.

Leah is lovely! Her rosebud lips, pale skin and dark hair are only the framework of her beauty. Her calm and trusting eyes and devastatingly pure and innocent smile are its core. We are really enjoying her early infancy, knowing how fleeting it will be. In the continuing saga of my brilliant plan (suggested by another expatriate mom who gets her disposable diapers without paying duty by shipping them through her husband's company) to ship a carton of diapers from Arthur D. Little by surface freight in time to meet us here—I admit defeat. The ADL shipping department shipped them by AIR since they were not wrapped in plastic to protect them from sea spray. So far the bill, prepaid by the company and deducted from Frank's pay, has reached $350 for the $30 carton of disposable diapers—and is climbing daily. First, the exorbitant air freight charges (I had told the company to send them by sea or not at all)—and then to top it all off, customs charges of $160. After much complaining, explaining and haggling, we got them to reduce the customs charges to $80, but could do nothing about the prepaid freight charges. I'll not ship anything else to Egypt for fear that Arthur D. Little will send it on the Apollo space shuttle for a multi-million dollar charge from NASA. Let's see, that's 192 diapers @ $1.75 each. I think I'll change her diaper every other day.

The big boy of the family is very enamored of his sister, also, and shows it in a most athletic way, which we are trying painfully to soften…. Jared is really growing, a tall blonde five-year-old now. He attends (at last, after two years on the waiting list!) "The Little Academy" in Ma'adi, taught by an esteemed matronly Egyptian woman and consisting of an international group of twelve four-and five-year-olds from the U.S., England, India, Egypt, etc.

We're so happy to be reunited with Frank. His six-day work week keeps him away too much, but we're thankful there is *no traveling* and we have most evenings together in our little villa.

As Christmas nears, the towering poinsettias are beginning to turn crimson. True "winter" will follow from January to March. Now is the lovely time—warm sunny days, pleasant evenings, slightly chilly nights and mornings—sleepable for a change. How we appreciate the climate and amenities here—in spite of the endless hassles.

This Thanksgiving and Christmas we're even more thankful—for our lovely Leah, Jared, our health, our friends.

Women of Cairo

Villa Isis

February 1984

Hello at last! Our long silence is broken! We've had a busy year of settling in to our "new" home, recovering from surgery and readjusting to our enlarged family size—four! We are very happily tucked into our Villa Isis, 4 Port Said Road in Ma'adi, enclosed in its own triangle of land bordered by three streets. Our tiny gated garden (definitely not a "yard," which means "vacant lot" here, as in Britain) is an attraction to local birds and cats seeking refuge from nearby traffic and desert dogs roaming the streets. The tiny terrace we have screened in will soon be a popular spot as spring approaches. We've adjusted to two bedrooms and a 25-step climb, due to the twelve-foot ceilings, to the upper regions to keep us in shape. We painted the green and brown walls beige and installed carpeting over the green and red checkered linoleum floors in the living room. The dining room buffet now resides in the hallway around the corner and has become the diaper-changing station. We've baby-proofed things as near as we could, considering what's available here.

Villa Isis is a charming little house with quite an appropriate name, as Isis is the ancient Egyptian goddess of motherhood, royalty (not quite sure how that fits in, except that some friends do refer to "Princess Leia," the Star Wars nobility having rubbed off on our infant daughter through the homonym), and family commitment. Isis was the mother of Horus, the mythological superhero who became the first ruler of a peaceful united Egypt (hear that, Jared?). Isis was one of the few Egyptian gods the Greeks took a fancy to—that must mean Frank! With the Christians she happily became identified as the Virgin Mary—well, at least they got the name right. Isis settled down to enjoy royal life, attending garden parties and state functions in her role as King's Mother, rather what I do now in a more limited fashion. Her exotic headgear features cow horns and sun disc—something I'll have to keep in mind for future events.

Although I miss our spacious and architecturally striking apartment a few blocks away on Orabi Street, it is a great relief not being pestered by an irritable landlord who thinks *he* should be paid when ladies come to tea! (After all, it is his property and he should share in the spoils....) Our current landlord is usually in Ethiopia and when he is around, he's not really *around*. We took over the apartment from Tiziana and Roberto, Italian friends we met at some of our diplomatic soirees. We are very happy here—and our happiness is magnified by our Leah, who is now in her "office"—the walker—moving backwards, her only direction, around the room until she hits a wall and needs rescuing. Our long-haired beauty is truly a joy! She awakens in her little mosquito-net covered "box" by our bed and happily sings and talks till Frank picks her up, rewarded by devastating smiles. She guffaws when tickled, smiles when addressed, complains when ignored, and waves and offers a throaty "Hi!" to people who stop on the street to comment on her beauty (no, it's not just parental pride). Her pale skin, long curly dark hair, blue eyes and tiny rosebud mouth are just the outer covering for her affectionate and friendly nature. We are just overwhelmed by this wonderful person who has come to join us! She is six months old now.

Leah and I spent her first two months of life in the States, as I needed emergency surgery. The four of us shuttled here and there, visiting my grandfather in Kansas City, stopping briefly at the airport in Chicago to introduce Leah to her future godparents, seeking medical advice in Philadelphia, and then we returned to Boston where we stayed in our friends' basement until I could go to Philadelphia for surgery. During these complicated days, I was trying to decide whether to have surgery or to return to Egypt without ("TOO RISKY!" warned the doctor), while simultaneously packing, shipping and storing my grandfather's household possessions in preparation for his transfer into the nursing home section of his retirement facility due to his blindness. We awoke one morning and, between steaming pans of water to cope with Jared's croup and shuffling boxes and crates, we heard the radio announce it was September 30—Jared's fifth birthday!! I couldn't believe we had overlooked such a momentous occasion. In desperation, I phoned McDonald's, reserved seating, somehow ordered a cake from somewhere, and called another family to come for Jared's "party." Well, the Law of Inverse Expectations prevailed, as Jared announced it was absolutely the BEST birthday party he had ever had. First of all, it was in America, that magical homeland so far away; secondly, it was at McDonald's—need more be said?; thirdly, he received the best gift of all: a little wooden car, hastily wrapped in newspaper by the family of twelve-year-old Nicholas, an older man much admired by Jared. "See?!! It's just like Nicholas' car! It even has the bangs and dents in the same places!!"

Jared and Frank returned to Cairo, where Yiayia flew in to assist, and Leah and I headed for Philadelphia, where she stayed with our *koumbari*, best man and his wife, while I went under the knife. But nothing is ever easy—and my night in the hospital before surgery was quite unnerving, as a dying woman in great agony was brought in during the night to the next bed, pleading for painkillers; she was refused any medication for well over an hour until a doctor could arrive to authorize it. The poor woman mercifully died fifteen minutes later. I will never forget her last hour of life—suffering, with her family watching, due to regulations and red tape. Couldn't someone have taken pity and given her some relief? From the other side of the curtain, I listened to the beautiful words of the Catholic Last Rites, to her husband's final words to her, her children's lamentations—and then to the nurses discussing how best to move the body and the funeral home attendants' maneuverings and badinage. Eavesdropping on anguish, eloquence, and comic relief.... Then it was my turn for the chopping block. My month-long recovery was hastened by our friend Betty's wonderful Greek cooking and by being reunited with lovely Leah. I had somehow survived the post-operative day and night and half the next day by lying absolutely rigid in my bed, as each breath and any movement was so painful, until I finally complained that the painkillers weren't working. "Well, you didn't request any, so you haven't had any," explained what must have been the same team of nurses who had tended the dying woman.

Finally, coincidentally enough, Leah and I flew back to Cairo on TWA's inaugural New York-Cairo flight, another surreal experience, with flight attendants in Halloween costumes. Dragging stroller, diaper bag and baby, trying to nurse without resting Leah on my abdominal incision, I happily anticipated going "home" at last. How welcome was the mild Egyptian air! How welcoming were the stray cats roaming through the old airport! How familiar the squatting men in *galabeyas* and turbans. And how very, very happy I was to be home again in this lovely, magical, maddening, frustrating, alluring and enchanting land.

This spring is full of preparation and anticipation of two grand events, as you will see by the enclosed invitations. The first is my 40th birthday. Rather than keeping this rather dismal date under wraps, we are joining with a very good friend who's also reaching the magic number this spring—and creating a great occasion, an Oriental masquerade complete with belly dancer, Greek band and huge appliquéd tent under the stars. We've each invited forty people, and we daily have the joy of contemplating details—jasmine leis for each guest, rose petals scattered on each table and the dance floor, a palm archway. We've yet to find the ultimate surprise—we had thought of entering on a camel, but reconsidered. Frank will be a pasha, complete with baggy trousers and a custom-made fez. Our invitations, wrapped as scrolls in golden thread and gold coins, were personally delivered by Jared along with Karen's son Matthew, our five-year-olds dressed as little Mameluke slaves in embroidered vests, sashes and turbans—and sneakers! We had hoped for a bagpiper to accompany them, but couldn't make connections. *Insha'allah*, God willing, we'll have no sandstorm that night! We are doubly fortunate in that my father will be here from St. Louis for the occasion.

And our second and most joyous event will be Leah's baptism, planned for April 26 at Saint Catherine's Monastery, an eight-hour bus ride into the isolation and wilderness of the Sinai Desert to the foot of Mount Sinai, where Moses received the Ten Commandments. We will again be blessed with visitors—at last! Finally in our fourth year here, someone is coming to see us! Frank's cousin Madeline and her husband George from Chicago will join us and become Leah's godparents. The Bishop of Saint Catherine's has offered to officiate—even if the baby is a boy, he announced beforehand, and we are very thrilled at the prospect of joining our friends at the oldest Greek Orthodox monastery in the magnificent setting of the Sinai Desert with all of its history, as our daughter is baptized into the church. We haven't quite contemplated the logistics yet—taking all food and water and bedding for two days—and a busload of, most likely, tired, hot and squirmy kids. We're sure it will be a very special experience for all of us.

All of these joyful preparations are tinged with *kaimos*—how can I say it in English?—a sadness and longing to include our far-away friends who should share these special occasions with us. By filling you in on the details, we'll feel you are here in spirit, anyway.

Where is my friend? The old man who appears every few days with flowers (surely picked from someone's garden) saying to me, "Morning, sir. Morning, sir. Anything you like, anything you like (regarding payment). One minute, five minutes, ten minutes, OK." Everyone moonlights here to make ends meet. Our driver sells imported make-up ("facials," he calls it) and goldfish on the side. The last day of the month, numerous guards appear, checking car doors, sweeping sidewalks, receiving payment, only to disappear until the end of the following month.

Jared is tall, blond, speedy and inquisitive. He has cracked the phonetic mystery of the alphabet and sounds out beginnings of words—so will soon begin reading a bit, I think. He is fortunate to be one of the twelve students in Ma'adi's best nursery school (after TWO years on the waiting list!). He's very much a boy, climbing trees, marching, "shooting" guns, and roughly affectionate with his sister. We hope his "boy-sterous" phase will be short-lived. He is simultaneously sensitive and empathetic. He remembers the past when he was just a little boy and there were cavemen and dinosaurs.

Writing this in a sandstorm! Will you read it in a snowstorm? Our trees are beginning to sprout their spring blossoms—so soon. We've enjoyed a long, fairly mild winter, and I think the hot weather will be upon us soon. And now…back to party preparations!

Jenna, the egg lady, balancing basket of eggs on her head—one of a cast
of local characters adding color and magic to our daily life

Knight of Knights
and
Day of Days

May 1984

Leah is baptized, her mom is 40, and life is calm again…. The last letter was written in anticipation of the two grand events, my 40th gala tent masquerade *orientale* and Leah's desert caravan christening at Saint Catherine's Monastery in the Sinai Desert, the oldest and most unchanged Greek Orthodox Monastery, center of pilgrimage for 1,400 years. After three months of wild and madcap brainstorming and unfettered and exhilarating preparation, it is now all over, and life is back to "normal."

Knight of Knights

Karen and I had prepared for all contingencies for our magnificent tent masquerade, we thought—all except a deluge of more than Egypt's annual rainfall atop our tent that night, moistening and then soaking guests, flooding the dance floor, dampening everything except people's spirits, and eventually shorting the electric lighting system, causing a corner of the huge tent to catch fire till the rain drenched it—and even electrifying the tent so that any unsuspecting guest brushing against the magnificent 20-foot-high multi-colored arabesque hand-appliquéd walls of our rented funeral tent, which canopied Karen's entire backyard, received an unexpected and unwelcome charge—truly a *current* event. The party was none-the-less an unqualified success—"party of the decade…century," "what every party should be," etc.—as our eighty guests threw themselves into the spirit of the occasion by donning most brilliant, ingenious or humorous attire—truly a (k)night of oriental splendor.

Preparations had begun three months previously with the post-Christmas letdown. "Let's have a joint birthday party," we thought. "Why not a masquerade? An *oriental* masquerade!" Thus began our period of intense and exhilarating out-of-the-box brainstorming and execution. Each one of us prodded the other to new heights—and depths—of imagination. We hit the medieval bazaars in search of wedding coins, spices, fabrics... Back to the City of the Dead to commission glassware for each table to hold the "gold" coins to be thrown at dancers... We each invited forty guests, one for each year, and had eighty jasmine leis made, not anticipating that they would arrive so tangled and knotted that we had to abandon them in their basket—but then again, what could be more Egyptian? The local tailor was kept busy creating our various costumes. We even redecorated the gardener's outdoor toilet—with a toilet seat painted gold placed on the hole in the floor and an "adult" Indian scroll hanging from the showerhead. A brilliant red flowered size ZZZZZ Egyptian bra adorned a black leotard with the sign "I Dreamed I Danced All Night at the Knight of Knights in My Maidenform Bra."

Invitations, hand-rolled scrolls tied with gold cord and coins, were hand-delivered by two young Mameluk slaves, namely Jared and Matt, in turbans, gold-embroidered vests and hand-woven sashes. Pun-filled menus took months to perfect, with such courses as

- Hector of Nector—This Troyly delightful concoction Izmirly a prelude....

LAHORE D'OEURVES

- Dacca Dip with Vizier's Vegetables

- Ali Baba-ganou and Balady Bread

- Effendi Fool Dip—bean dip with cumin

- Devil's Dervish Dolmas—Caliph of Grape cunningly whirled round rice and mince

- Sinbad's Samosas—Seven Seas-onings to as-sail your Tung, served with chutney

- Ma'alesh Mashee—Bokra, Insha'allah...

ON TRAYS

- Pun-jabi Rice—saffron rice with sultanas, apricots, almonds. Ask for Moor!

- Khyber Pass-the-Curry—tender loin of *gamoosa* simmered in yoghurt with selected spices of the Orient

- Cholley—chickpeas in curry-tomato sauce

- Maharajah Raita—yoghurt of yak with grated cucumbers

- Eunuch Salad—a gay gathering of fruits for all seasons

- Balady Bread—served on-the-rack (and it was!)

SCHEHERAZADE SPECIAL

- Pasha's Delight—assorted oriental sweets

- Magic Carpet Coffee—with cardamom

- Turkish Coffee—mas-boot

- Tarboosh Tea—renowned for its heady aroma

- Spice Island Tray—anise - cardamom - fennel

Served by 1001 Arabian Knights
    Hindu Kush-ions for your comfort
      Music by our friends from across the Nile
        Special thanks to Pasha Frank and Jeff-Bey

Guests sprawled languorously on the cushions around the dance floor, watching the more adventurous engage in exotic dancing. Though our planned Greek band canceled the day before, we were blessed with two groups—one a *balady* (local) band of primitive instruments in aging hands of elderly robed villagers who crossed the Nile in a small boat and then walked to the villa—whose strident horns and rhythmic drums and twanging two-stringed instruments added an exotic air, transporting us to other times and realms. And even the belly dancer and her thirteen member contingent showed up unexpectedly just before midnight, for a cymbal-clanging, mesmerizing interlude, nearly bringing the tent down in hysterics as my once-dignified turbaned and robed father joined in with gay abandon, nearly outlasting the belly dancer with his *galabeya*-raising bumps and grinds and the St. Louis side-step. Even our exotic belly dancer dissolved into uncontrollable laughter, and my father received a standing ovation! Our pun-filled menus and wine lists adorned each table, along with 4,000 "gold" coins and flower petals to throw at the dancers. Five red-sashed Greek waiters enjoyed Zorba dancing with occasional interludes to serve drinks and food, and soon nearly everyone joined them, sloshing about the dance floor with a variety of steps.

Guests were arrayed in magnificence and great cleverness. Some, such as the Swiss artist Margo Veillon, went home to change into more brilliant attire, returning in a flaming red *galabeya*, with heavy and ornate Bedouin jewelry—and sat next to my urbane and witty father for the rest of the evening. Our Indian friends arrived, laden with gladioli, in flamboyant saffron silk sari and white military tunic with red turban. One clever gentleman wore a fez, fake mustache and a tux with a red sash and his daughter's swim meet medals pinned to his lapel, looking very official, indeed. Quite a few arrived looking as if they had just stepped off the set of *Lawrence of Arabia*. Several women borrowed their maids' or gardeners' family jewelry and veils—and were most splendid! One man cleverly wore pajamas, standard street attire for lower-class Egyptians. Our friend John Bell, the former White Father missionary in Africa, had a minor car accident on the way over…and was a most suspicious and fearsome character to passengers of the other vehicle when he stepped from his car, robed and masked and bearing sword, knives and large wooden-handled pistol! Jim Ringer came as an Ethiopian slave—in skullcap, blackface, black turtleneck and tights, wearing a vest and dhoti and carrying ten-foot-high reeds, which he waved over us as we danced.

Karen had prepared an exotic and gargantuan feast, as the menu suggests—and so we decided to hire, at great expense, a local chef to supervise the last-minute details of the food, freeing Karen to enjoy the festivities. But this is Egypt, after all. We, in our western naïveté, paid him in advance—and he and his crew absconded with all the expensive nuts for the pilaf, and not a little of the liquor, leaving us to heat and serve the nut-less and tepid Pun-jabi Rice at the last minute. (…And what was left of our many cartons of liquor was taken care of during the night by our friends' teenagers and their friends.) As we ate, raindrops kept falling on our heads—through the tent. The heavens opened, and we received forty days and forty nights' worth of rain for our forty years. Fatima, Karen's maid, had to keep wiping off and throwing rugs onto the dance floor.

Our six-foot-long cake, the Scheherazade Special, created by our Indian friend Neelam Engstrom and carried in by four waiters on an eight-foot litter—the disguised and dismantled slide of Karen's son's swing set—was adorned with two dolls of Karen and me garbed in full costume atop a mound, which Neelam intended to signify that we were now "over the hill," but which we prefer to think of as "at our peak." Eighty candles took a long time to light, and some had nearly burned out by the time those at the other end of the cake had been lit! Cut by a

South American machete slung with great gusto by a friend in gaucho attire, it was an appropriate conclusion to our evening of evenings. Fearful of the collapse of our water-logged electrified tent, we moved the cake inside for serving—and the torrential rains continued. We later learned that this is considered a highly auspicious occasion—to be blessed with a downpour of rain amid the parched Saharan landscape.

Now our turkey-feather bejeweled *punka* fans lie at rest, our Indian Punjabi thrones for the reception tableau are returned to their rightful home, and even our red carpets, commissioned for the occasion, on the walkway are faded to a whitish-pink in the rain. The huge garden is again just grass, flowers and toys—even the tent-pole holes are filled in now—and we can't quite believe that our oriental night of splendor really occurred. Most of the invited guests will be leaving Egypt this summer, so the memory of that night will filter to various corners of the world.

…and now—to keep us going—Karen and I every few days muse, "What will we do for our 41st?"

Leah is baptized in 4th century Saint Catherine's Monastery at the foot of Mount Sinai in "the wilderness," where we traveled for eleven hours, swathed in fabric like local Bedouin, in our caravan of cars

Day of Days

Leah Catherine Fotis is baptized (and she has survived, I am glad to report, having had my doubts at the time)!

After an eleven-hour drive (usually eight, but we were plagued with car trouble and required a push at every curve or slowdown), we arrived in late afternoon at Saint Catherine's Monastery. The desert drive in our four-car caravan was spectacular, leaving the rubble of Cairo, crossing under the Suez Canal through the new tunnel into the purity and barrenness of the Sinai Desert, first flat and sandy, later mountainous and colorful, a geological wonderland of upheaved crusted earth in all hues, looking as if the earth under our feet had just gurgled, bubbled and erupted the day before.

We left Cairo as westerners, all organized and well-provisioned and watered in our cars. A few hours later, we looked like a group of desert Bedouin on motorized camels—with towels and clothes flapping from each window, in futile attempts to block the blazing and broiling sun. We wrapped the windows, we wrapped ourselves, we became dizzy from fumes, and we strived to absorb any breath of coolness from the overworked air conditioner, sputtering out a few tepid breaths of stagnant air.

After a welcomed picnic stop on a sandy beach along the Gulf of Suez, the northern branch of the Red Sea, turquoise, cobalt and aquamarine strips of color blinding in the sunlight—reminiscent of all those wonderful Mediterranean coastlines in Greece—the first sign of life was a lone scraggly tree several hours later. The next, highly appropriate, I thought, a baby camel nursing from its mother truly in the middle of nowhere. We would occasionally pass Bedouin, on camel or walking alone, women in brightly embroidered black dresses with coin-laden face masks, men wound round and round in various scarves and headpieces. At last—an oasis! Truly a miraculous sight, the dark green of palm fronds against the beige-brown landscape—how lush and inviting! I have a new appreciation of the biblical references to "wilderness." It is a barren and mountainous desert landscape with no water but an occasional spring, no food but the intermittent date palm. How Moses and his tribe ever survived four days, let alone forty years, in the Sinai is mind-boggling. Strangely quiet and peaceful in its silent fierceness, the landscape does provoke contemplation and awe at the mystery of life—no wonder it is such a center for religious history and pilgrimage.

Saint Catherine's! At last around 5 P.M. we reached the tiny fortress walls of this oldest existing Greek Orthodox monastery at the foot of Mount Sinai where Moses received the Ten Commandments. These ancient walls encircle the fourth century Chapel of the Burning Bush built by Helena (Constantine's other half), the 6-7th century Church of the Transfiguration with its original brilliant mosaics and richness of interior, accumulated through the millennia, and where Leah was baptized; the monks' quarters; the pilgrims' wing (our eleven adults and five children stayed here); the Burning Bush, Jethro's (Moses' father's) Well, and assorted labyrinthine alleyways and chapels—a quite tiny place in all. Isolated in the heart of the mountainous southern Sinai, Saint Catherine's has for fourteen centuries been a center for pilgrims who braved "the great and terrible wilderness" (Deuteronomy 1:19) to worship here and view the great library of ancient manuscripts and the only existing sixth and seventh century icons, survivors of the Byzantine Empire's eighth century iconoclasm. In the spirit of that tradition, we enjoyed our reception and tea with Father Georgios, and later we gathered in a tiny kitchen, half of which was a huge stone arched oven, and spread around picnic wares for a wonderful communal gathering, joined by Father Georgios, who enlightened us on church and monastery history.

The monastery was ordered built by Emperor Justinian in 550 A.D. to protect Christian hermits, who had lived in the Sinai since the third century, from Bedouin attacks. These early Christian hermits tried to escape persecution and follow the example of the prophet Elijah and John the Baptist by dwelling in the wilderness. The monastery was later renamed after Saint Catherine of Alexandria, the fourth century martyr whose remains were discovered on a nearby mountaintop. Father Georgios also told us of the disappearance of the Sinaiticus Codex, the world's oldest Bible in Greek, stolen from the monastery by a German "scholar" who gave it to Russia, which later sold it to the British Museum where it remains today (one of Melina Mercuri's projects along with the return of the Elgin Marbles—good luck!).

We quickly adjourned at 10 P.M., as the monastery's electricity is on only 5-10 P.M. daily, and the ensuing PITCH blackness is enveloping. I can't envision Moses alone on the mountain in the bitterly cold night, void of light. One also understands how the early Egyptians thought their dead would return as stars—their presence is so real! Just a few hours later, it seemed, in the pre-dawn in-between netherland, I glanced out the door of our tiny cell to see a black-garbed monk with a humongous nearly two-foot-long key walk across the monastery courtyard to an ancient wooden door which he unlocked with his amazing key of indeterminate age. How many centuries had that ancient key unlocked that door? What dangers had it protected the monks from? Strangely enough, the Bedouin, originally a threat to the religious hermits, are now an integral part of the monastery—in fact, they have their own little mosque within its walls.

The hardiest of fellows, Frank and company arose at 4 A.M. for a 5 A.M. climb up Mount Sinai, physically taxing but mentally and spiritually exhilarating. They reached the spot where Moses received the Ten Commandments—the eleventh, they said, was "Thou Shalt Not Trip." They hobbled back four or five hours later full of life and ready for a gargantuan breakfast—however, the picnic basket was running rather low by then, as we had extended hospitality to all the monks, who were most appreciative of the large ham we brought them. My four-foot baptism candles were broken or bent by then, but we prepared for Leah's baptism, greeted other friends who joined us from a Sinai camping trip, and enjoyed a special tour of the grounds led by another monk. I did not go to the charnel house outside the monastery walls to see remains of all the resident monks through the ages, but was told that when Frank kissed the hand of the monk who drove up in a pick-up truck, "That must be the archbishop!" Archbishop Damianos had invited Frank to have his baby baptized at Saint Catherine's, a rare and cherished event.

One could tell by the red plastic bucket for the baptismal water that baptisms were not part of the standard rites performed here. I wonder who the last baby may have been to officially enter Christian life in these storied surroundings. The extremely long, ultra-traditional baptismal service began with everyone standing and holding candles while the godparents, Madeline and George Gelis, removed their shoes to present Leah and recite the creed at the door of the church, sunlight tracing multi-colored squares on the carpet through the stained-glass panes and the ancient doors. (We later learned that after they had obeyed the priest's instructions, whispered in Greek, to "take off shoes," he then barked, "Not you! The baby's shoes!" They continued the ceremony unshod until they found a brief pause to surreptitiously step into their shoes again.) Leah, unsuspecting of the ordeal to follow, slept through the recitation and the crossing. She awoke as I undressed her and was confused and beginning to worry when, unclothed in strange surroundings among foreign faces with loud chanting, she was lathered in oil, every inch of her. She became desperate when roughly immersed, by two hands twisting her head, pushing and holding her under water, it seemed to me until bubbles appeared—and then again—and then again! Even Yiayia had never seen such a forceful baptism in Greece. I was afraid Leah would drown as she was literally held under the water, head and all.

But I was thinking just of Leah, not of the history behind this place. The priests were acting, in the old tradition, to protect and preserve her from future trials and tribulations, to wrap her in the protection of the faith through three total—and I mean total—immersions in the holy waters of Christianity in this age-old fortress of the faith. The entire ceremony had such a feeling of power and forcefulness about it—it was truly reminiscent of what life must have been for early Christians who faced persecution, and what a step it was to declare their faith, to establish it with strength, dignity and courage. It seemed that we were traveling back through the centuries, through medieval ages and before, back to the early centuries of Christianity, to a harsh life in a desolate landscape where the promise of God's protection was a precious gift.

Our modern ways did not always sit well here. We couldn't cross legs, as I learned when I was chastised by a priest for modestly crossing my legs as I sat for a moment before the baptism. I couldn't understand the priest's Greek, but Frank's mom rushed up, motioned me to uncross my legs and told the priest, "She forgot! She forgot!" (I had never known that crossing one's legs in church was considered highly disrespectful. Imagine—the mother of the babe to be baptized desecrating the church!) Equally disrespectful was putting one's hands in one's pockets—fortunately my dress had no pockets, or I would have been doubly damned. We were instructed to remain standing throughout the ritual. The priest was giving me instructions, in very archaic Greek, I later learned, which I could not understand as I flustered and fumbled my way through the grandmother's role of dressing the child while standing up with no table, a box of Leah's new clothes, and an oiled baby. "*To pani*! *To pani*!!" whispered the priest, louder and louder with each command, as if increased volume would lead to my understanding. I kept offering him a diaper, which I had learned was "*pani*" in Greek. Each time, he waved the diaper away and commanded, "*To pani*!" As it turns out, "*pani*"—the standard word today for diaper—is an archaic Greek word for towel. Someone mercifully intervened and pointed to the new white towel we had brought along. Finally, Frank's mother and the godfather took pity on me and helped as a button popped off during the difficult dressing process.

Leah and I were both near tears. Before that, the priest had forcefully made crosses all over her body with the *chrism*, a special holy ointment in the form of a blue gel, during the Sacrament of Chrismation. This was Leah's introduction to exotic fragrances, as 57 elements combine with olive oil to produce this holy ointment which symbolizes the laying on of hands of the apostles at early baptisms and represents God's gifts to the newly baptized. At last dressed in her many layers, all new and white, Leah Catherine was returned to her godmother, peering around rather anxiously, but calmer at last, when Father Sophronios raised the holy water sprinkler (*aspergillum*) and splashed holy water in her face three times! Her remaining composure dissolved. And then he proceeded to cut three long and thick locks of hair, down near the roots from the top and both sides of her head, as her gift to God in return for His goodness—and the ceremony soon concluded. I don't know who was more traumatized—Leah or her mom. We were both unprepared for the intensity and fervor inspired, perhaps required, by these ancient surroundings where Christianity was preserved in its early centuries in this remote and desolate area of the Sinai.

Everyone was moved, it seemed, by the aura of timelessness in the ceremony itself as well as the other-worldly surroundings. When only the family remained, the archbishop instructed Father Sophronios to bring the holy remains of Saint Catherine. We gazed down upon a brown leathery hand, bejeweled and in a golden box inside another gold and jeweled casket. Where was the line between reality and the leap of faith? The moon landscape of the scene, the desert silence, the black-garbed monks of all ages, the ancient doors creaking open, the centuries-old stones and the lone green of the Burning Bush outside the door—all fused into a hazy unreality where old was new, new was old, and anything seemed possible. Father Sophronios later led us to the holiest place of the monastery, the Chapel of the Burning Bush where we, correctly this time, removed our shoes and went to kiss the spot beneath which the roots of the Burning Bush lie. Outside, we touched the Burning Bush itself (one of the group—who shall remain nameless—snitched three tiny leaves), supposedly the descendent of the original manifestation to Moses in the desert.

Now ready to sit and quietly relive the past few hours and look anew at the scene, we packed and began our long journey back. Poor Madeline and George, to bed at 12:30 A.M. and up at 3 A.M. to fly out again! And now that we look back, it all seems so unreal, like a step into a time machine for a quick visit to another age. We hope to return, savoring the Sinai landscape, and see Saint Catherine's again, this time slowly and thoughtfully and in detail, and to relive those special moments that passed so quickly. *Na mas zisi*! (May she long live!)

The Three "Rs"

◆

Relaxation, Recreation and Ramadan

June 1984

The exotic name conjures up visions of dunes and palms, blazing sunsets and Mediterranean sea breezes in the "oasis" on the northern coast of the Sinai, formerly the border with Israel during their Sinai occupation until 1982. And that's just what it is! Overlook the broken machinery, littered roadsides, hot dusty town of noise and rubble—and proceed directly to the newest Oberoi Hotel on an expanse of sandy beach—clean and palm-lined and seemingly endless, full of thousands—no, millions—of multi-colored seashells, an occasional sand crab scurrying about and frothy white breakers rhythmically lulling you into the scene. Never mind the "service" so poor that we had to clear our own tables and flip the tablecloth over (all the help are "waiters"—above it all—and none will stoop to act as busboys, leaving the customers to wipe down their own tables). Never mind the food so noxious that we were stuck with the *prix fixe* buffet at $11 per person—and ate mainly bread. Never mind waiting under the wing of the prop aircraft (the only shade in sight) and hoisting baggage through the window of the mini-bus where the baby and I always seemed to sit in a jump seat next to a chain smoker—or that we (and others with babies and children) were always seated next to the emergency window.

It was all worth it—just to wade or plunge into the incredibly warm Mediterranean waves, super-salty and buoyant, the warmest sea water any of us had ever experienced. Frank floated on the waves for three days, Jared met some friends and also adopted his father's "broil and peel" method of tanning, and Leah had her first taste of sand and sea water. Had we known how lovely the beach was, we would have gone there long before now. Our one-hour plane ride had us arriving about an hour before those who made the five and a half hour drive. (We waited in the waiting room, we waited on the pavement, we waited over an hour inside the plane before takeoff....) The highlight of the journey for Leah was the cats inside the Cairo terminal. (There *is* no terminal at El Arish, just the landing strip…and the twice-weekly plane.)

RAMADAN—the month of fasting for Moslems. No food or water, cigarettes or sex from around 4 A.M. till 7 P.M.—when a white thread cannot be distinguished from a black one. The month-long Ramadan fast has noble aims: Hunger and thirst are supposed to remind Muslims of the suffering of the poor; it is supposed to enable them to practice self-control and to cleanse the body and mind, as well as lead to calmness and contemplation. Well, in reality tempers are short, drivers are *worse* than usual, if possible, and people come to work dead-tired and bleary-eyed after starving all day and partying all night. Local neighborhoods are strewn with special lanterns, and special foods are eaten. Only now during Ramadan is the butcher open every day instead of weekends only. Everyone follows the Ramadan rules, and everyone is in a daze, it seems. Leah had a doctor's appointment today, and the doctor, an articulate multilingual fellow, couldn't remember why he'd asked us to come in or what medicine we were supposed to take. And he had three hours to go! Just imagine, not a sip of water all day long in the withering dry heat of summer. I sneak into the kitchen and consume gallons of water while the maid is not looking. Someone driving the wrong way down our one-way street hit my car, which was parked in the driveway. When we summoned the police, we were told that as it was Ramadan it was therefore perfectly understandable for the other driver to drive the wrong way down the street ("It was faster," he explained), and so that was that. We paid for the damage ourselves, and learned a lesson about attitudes during Ramadan.

Each year Ramadan, the ninth month of the lunar Muslim calendar, is ten days earlier, and I'm sure it is a relief to everyone when it finally rolls around to winter with the shorter days instead of summer when everyone must be desperate for water during those long endless hours of summer daylight. Regardless of when it is, the women cook and cook and cook, without tasting, for the "breakfast"—break the fast—in the late evening when the white thread is no longer distinguishable from the black. Originally planned as a time of thought, reflection, repentance and spirituality, Ramadan has transformed into long late-night parties full of food and festivity, stretching late into the night, so one can imbibe and ingest a final drink and bite to carry one through the long day to come.

Farewell to Grandpa

September 1984

Hello again from our flower-filled tiny Villa Isis in Ma'adi. It's so good to be home again! For the first time in five years we missed our Cairo July 4th ceremonies on the American school grounds. It's always a grand occasion, with nearly every American in Egypt (and many British pretending to be American to get a free hotdog!) there to enjoy the imported authentic American hotdogs, beer and soft drinks. The last few years an enormous tent was erected, adding the color and beauty of Islamic artistic tradition and craftsmanship to the already festive activities and games. The first year we were here, as I remember, Frank somehow was listed in the program as one of the early American patriots in the play *1776*!

Our July 4 this year was restful and lovely, though we were the only Americans we saw! We donned our red, white and blue in Switzerland, where we cruised the beautiful icy green lakes, rambled through medieval quarters of beautiful old cities, took *four* successive cable cars to reach the Paz Gloria of 007 James Bond fame at the Schilthorn, rode every horse and carriage in sight from Interlaken to Innsbruck (a concession to Jared whose preconception was that Switzerland was one giant riding stable just waiting for him), and generally enjoyed the "niceties" of life—tablecloths, cleanliness, flowers, service, freshness and tranquility…which we needed before our hectic first week of doctor appointments in the U.S.—two or three each day and always on opposite sides of Boston. Our motel's phone system was out of commission the first few rainy days and the phone booth was outside, so between laundry, phone calls and doctors we spent a harried few days. We then moved into our very generous friends' showcase house while they were on vacation—but made it a point to leave early, return after both kids were asleep and confine ourselves to one room. An active five-year-old, inquisitive toddler and Architectural Digest setting are mutually exclusive! It was wonderful to see some of our old friends after a year's absence, however, and we planned to return after our Midwest travels.

First to Kansas City to see 93-year-old Grandpa, who had slowed down a bit but was doing remarkably well, considering his blindness and infirmities. He would always ask, "Where's Jared?" as his memories of him from infancy were so vivid. We most fortunately had our very good friends from Cairo living in Kansas, so we stayed there and Jared enjoyed playing with his old friend David again—they cooked up many new tricks after a year's separation!

Then on to Chicago where Leah's godparents, Frank's cousin Madeline and husband George, got a first-hand glimpse of the joys of transporting young children who were off their schedule. Our one shopping morning went from bad to worse—from upsetting a glass shelf and getting smudged from a make-up display case, spilled milk (only the *other* child was crying over it), culminating in a "leisurely" ice cream at the Ritz, with every third person informing us that Leah had lost her shoe, to losing Jared behind the huge indoor fountain, and then his mistaking the linen tablecloth for his napkin to wipe his fudgy mouth. Well, at least the orchids on the table *were* lovely to behold....

After a stop in St. Louis to see my father and Dorothy, we returned to Boston for food and clothes shopping, Frank's office "visits" ("not work"—just can't keep him away) until Frank's imminent departure to Egypt. A reservations mix-up and my cold feet about handling two kids, six pieces of luggage, car seat, stroller and rented car alone found us back in Kansas City for two days for another quick visit with Grandpa, this time filming him on our new video camera. And *then* back to Cairo, thankfully all together, where we happily settled into our little house and coped with the ravages of jet lag on four people with different schedules. It seemed that whenever the adults were sleepy, the kids weren't—especially around 2-4 A.M.!

Leah's first birthday!! Could it be so soon? A small garden party capped the event with Leah's ten-month-old girlfriend Sarah and Jared's Ma'adi cohorts to enliven the scene. Our video camera was busy, and we can now relive that happy night. Life's happiest moments are sometimes followed by life's saddest. We received news that night of Grandpa's hospitalization with pneumonia, and an urgent telex the next morning had us packing and preparing a hurried return to Kansas City. Our trusty travel agent friend performed miracles and somehow got us on filled flights—twenty-six hours and four legs of flights with four of us in three seats, not even together during the last two legs—but we arrived! And we had one last day with Grandpa. He tried to say "Hi, Jared" and greeted us through his hands and feeble responses in his last hours. We were so happy he *knew* we were there, as he had always thought he would die alone, with his family so far away.

So Grandpa left us the morning of August 26, 1984. Typical of Grandpa, even in his last stages, he had cheered the nurses and made an impression on them. They all stopped to say how special he was—as we knew… Grandpa left with dignity and grace—a gentleman to the end. A very beautiful small memorial service was held at the John Knox Village Chapel with a few special friends, someone from his early days, Chillicothe neighbors and—most appreciated by Grandpa, we are sure—Jared and young friend David in bow ties like Grandpa's adding a spirit of liveliness to the occasion through their hoarse stage-whispered questions and wriggly little bodies—and of course Leah toddling about, trying to croon with the hymns. We can't recapture the beauty of the service, the haunting spontaneous comments unrecorded by the malfunctioning tape recorder—perhaps it was meant to be…a special time, not meant to be held, re-circulated, relived.

From Grandpa's service: "He was Clark to his family, Henry to colleagues and John Knox Village friends, Grandpa to family and numerous young friends around the country. Henry's death seems the end of an era. He grew up with horse and buggy and saw jet travel and men on the moon. He gracefully adapted to these tremendous cultural and technological changes of his lifetime with poise and a sense of adventure.

"He was a true gentleman in the old and best sense of the word—he was dignified and articulate, scrupulous and moral, yet full of charm and wit. His adventurous nature grew with his age. He began his world travels at 79 years old—and always said that life begins at 80. Among the red-stockinged, booted, wool-jacketed climbers at the base of the Matterhorn in the Swiss Alps was an 81-year-old gentleman in suit, Hushpuppy shoes, straw hat and the ever-present bow tie—Grandpa Burnham—keeping up with all the well-equipped hikers. He was equally at home discussing the stock market with financiers in Paris or crops with a Brussel sprout farmer in the English countryside.

"Grandpa Burnham's great zest in life—his spirit and sense of humor—made the best of all situations. He never complained, and he bore the blindness and infirmities of his final years with grace and dignity. At his death, a friend observed, 'Henry always did everything right. And this, too.'"

And from the *Villager Inn* by John Harding: "The Inn's senior citizen emeritus, 94-year-old Henry Burnham, passed through the gates of his elderly place in history last Sunday. A distinguished and articulate retiree of the Missouri legal profession, this grand old man battled the ravages of old age and blindness, the past later years, with cheery and witty words tinged with courtesy and politeness, portraying a gentleman of intellectual demeanor. Henry's dress always displayed a suit and stylish bow tie of which he had quite an assortment. He will best be remembered for a favorite expression when on the way to his apartment, 'I'm on the way to Heaven!' Certainly, Henry Burnham has gained that sacred place."

The family, neighbors and Grandpa's best friend proceeded to the funeral home for a short prayer before departure on the five or six hour drive to St. Louis the next day. There we saw Grandpa as we had always known him, in his brightest red and white checkered bow tie, which coincidentally he is seen wearing in happy photographs from Jared's baptism in Lexington, where we remember his speech on the changes during his lifetime and remember also his dancing. His flowers were bursting with life, vitality and cheer—red and white like his tie, punctuated with purple stattice—a wonderful huge arrangement glorifying life, love, adventure, color—and Grandpa. How appropriate! Leah kept blowing kisses in a last farewell. To this day, when we say "Grandpa," she looks around and sends a kiss. Jared touched Grandpa's hand and said, "Don't cry, Mommy. Why are you crying, silly? God is taking care of him now."

The next day's long drive to the burial in St. Louis was a fitting finale for Grandpa's life in Missouri. He never wanted to leave the state he grew up in, learned in, and spent his professional and retirement years in. He was taken first past his old beloved apartment in the Villager Inn, and then on a glorious summer's day, sunny and breezy, across the fields, hills and valleys of rural Missouri, from Kansas City, where he'd been born nearly ninety-four years ago, to Saint Louis to join his wife and only child in the tranquil beauty of Memorial Park Cemetery where other segments of his long and productive life were represented—his old friend's widow, his daughter's closest friend's husband, two of his sister's children and his wife's sister's grandchild and great-grandchildren, his son-in-law—and the four of us. So from one end of Missouri to the other, from family, friends and neighbors, we bid adieu to Grandpa, Uncle Clark, and Henry—as we knew him. The entire proceedings were blessed from above, we are sure—from our unexpected return to Kansas City and filming Grandpa on video so the children can see him again, live and colorful, and hear his voice, to our incredibly (in Egypt, at least!) speedy return for Grandpa's last day, and the beautiful farewells across the state, including the family gathering after the burial at his nephew's in Saint Louis, which he would have heartily enjoyed. ("Ah, but he *is* here enjoying it," corrected my father.) So now young Jared is "the Burnham" of the family, symbolized by the bow tie he wore at Grandpa's memorial service and burial.

And now we are truly back in Cairo again and happily in place in our little home. Jared is enjoying his entrance at last to the big American school in kindergarten, and he and Frank enjoy evening swims in the pool there, after waiting four years for the privilege—in spite of the movie *Jaws* running on the large screen by the pool. Leah is back on schedule and now walking with glee. We are all very happy—as must be Grandpa, too.

Ma'a Salaama, Masr...

October 1984

Ma'a salaama, Masr...Farewell to Egypt!

Sadly, we look around us at the flowering trees and bushes, herds of goats prodded by Bedouin girls on donkeys, long-robed and turbaned pedestrians passing by our gate. In a few days Frank will be off to Bangkok, an exciting new assignment, and the rest of us will follow after packing up and shipping out just after Thanksgiving.

We came to our little Villa Isis just over a year ago with a 4 ½-year-old boy, and now we will leave with a big six-year-old kindergarten blondie and a year-old "strawberry brown" beauty who totes her brother's cars and trucks against her ruffly pink dress with a gleeful smile. We've been very happy here and are rather sad to leave—though it's really time, as most of our good friends are already gone, and Frank will enjoy the stimulation and challenge professionally after nearly five productive, but exhausting, years here.

And now, in the last minute scramble, there's suddenly so much to do and so little time. Leah has never been to the pyramids! I'm still re-ordering items for the fourth and fifth time after numerous errors, and each re-ordering requires reserving the car and driver and taking a day to go downtown. You can't "let your fingers do the walking" in Egypt!

And I think of the places we've never been—the oases, Tunisia and Morocco, Mersa Matrouh, the "gem of the Mediterranean coast," Tell el Amarna, the short-lived capital of Egypt during the brief reign of Akhenaten, its only monotheistic pharaoh, and so many other hidden corners of this ancient and exotic country. And even here in Cairo are several museums I've never managed to visit during proper hours, whenever they are. And the pictures I've never taken—I'm somehow too embarrassed to photograph people directly, but I'd love to have captured some of the local characters on film: the purple-turbaned knife-grinder, the black-robed lady on white donkey...with a cigarette in her mouth!, our barefoot gardener with his many sons, the strawberry man, the egg lady, the old man who appears every few days with a bouquet of straggly flowers from someone's garden, saying, "Good morning, sir, anything you like, anything you like (to pay)," but if it's not enough, "Tomorrow, tomorrow."

On the other hand, I can't wait to get out of here because there's (from the embassy grapevine) a red bomb alert (the next level of alert is *after* the bombing), as some crazy Iranians have slipped into the country and are expected to stage a major offensive against Americans, as they did in Beirut. So I wish we could leave today! Evidently, CBS aired a TV program three weeks ago about the lack of security for Americans in Cairo—pinpointing all the weak spots—even after the Cairo desk at the State Department pleaded with them not to jeopardize the safety of Americans in Cairo by showing it. So we're sort of sitting ducks here. That's the other side of the coin in exotic international assignments.

Our house is upside down with baby and household items to sell. Everything is wanted and needed here due to strict importation duties and general misman-agement. We had a garden sale with several friends last Friday at 9:30 A.M.—found strangers lounging in our garden furniture at 7:30 A.M. and a huge crowd outside the gate by 8:30. Several hours of hectic haggling later, we were exhausted…and also pestered to death. Our gardener, for example, keeps after us to sell him our aluminum table with eight-foot umbrella and seven chairs—for $15! This, after he sneaked in, dug up and stole *eighty* rose bushes, two and three at a time, to sell to his other customers. When asked about the missing plants, he would always reply, "Sick, Madame! Very sick!"

"Well, they looked healthy to me," I countered.

"Sick under the ground, Madame—cannot see."

We discovered that two big boxes of baby and household items had been left inside the house—by the very gardener who was supposed to carry everything outside. A rather sad observation at the sale was the pathetic and bedraggled appearance of two young British women dragging infants and toddlers, obviously married to local men—but not in the best of circumstances. Their lives must have been very difficult, as well as quite restricted. So sad to see them so excited about acquiring our children's outgrown items…. Another oddity was the request of so many people to buy any nutmeg that we had on hand; when we looked for it, we discovered that every single nutmeg had mysteriously disap-peared! Evidently nutmeg is a powerful hallucinogen (a tablespoon of ground nutmeg can kill you, so I'm told, so a little goes a long way), and so somebody out there is having a good time tonight.

Halloween! This occasion is indeed a big production for Americans in far-away places to preserve national traditions. Jared is the Lone Ranger this year, as his present craze is horses, horses, horses! He thinks he will have one of his very own in Bangkok and will name him Buster! Leah is unadorned as yet, but has a lovely Asian-Indian children's outfit from a young friend. My supply of American candy carried back this summer has dwindled to nearly nothing, as various household occupants have searched the recesses of our freezer.

Our weather now is ideal: naturally and continually sunny, now with balmy breezes and a hint of evening and morning chill. We'll never live in such a wonderful climate again, I'm sure!

From desert to flood plain, Islam to Buddhism, Middle East to Far East, paucity to abundance, chaos to (we hope!) order, it will be so interesting to greet a new culture. Already we're mentally disassociating ourselves from here, not by choice, but a subconscious drifting away to ease the sadness of departure from our home for nearly five years—the only home our children know. Jared will have to trade his smattering of Arabic—to become tongue-Thai'ed. Goodbye to my—at last, after so many repairs—trusty ole Mercedes, a touch of class in spite of its vandalized hood ornament—at 3 P.M. right in my own driveway! And to the lovely tree-lined streets of Ma'adi, in spite of the rubbish, with blossoming foliage for each few weeks of nearly the whole year.... And to the hoopoe, my favorite exotic long-billed and crested bird with brilliant striped wings and a faintly professorial look. And we'll miss especially our charming little Villa Isis on its triangle of land with an excess of doors and unnecessary corners, which adds to its appeal. We hope the next family will be as happy here as we were.

Our address will remain the same—so please remember us at Christmas—in a hotel in a new environment without old friends and familiar surroundings. I'm taking my Christmas ornaments, hoping to find a tree to smuggle into the hotel room.

One last note: Grandpa always sang, "I'm on my way to Mandalay. Beneath the shelt'ring palms I want to stay. I'm sentimental for the oriental..." ...and it was one of Jared's first solos, as well. So we feel we really must journey into Burma, just next door to Thailand, heading for Mandalay and all four of us singing Grandpa's song! How he would have smiled if only he'd known, all those times he sang it, that we would actually put those words into action.

Hoping to hear from you in our new home—

Ma'a Salaama, Masr…

Bangkok-Bound, Singapore Fling

January 1985

Happy New Year! And happy it is for us in the land of orchids, gilded Buddhist temples, klongs, exotic food fare, gentility and refinement. After an exhausting departure from Cairo, a brief respite in Greece, and a traumatic introduction to our new land of residence, we are at last beginning to settle down and enjoy all the niceties of life in the Orient.

A very good friend in Cairo once said, "You'll love Asia, Mary Ned—it's so civilized." And now I'm beginning to understand what she meant. Somehow we of the West assume we're superior culturally because of our technological advancement. How wrong we are! We can't even begin to understand the complexities and refinement of life here when our impressions are based on how well the phones work and how clean the streets are. Do you know how much beauty is hidden in a common carrot? Yesterday at a kind of Thai Sturbridge Village we saw demonstrations of various Thai handicrafts, one of which was carving vegetables. A basket of beautiful and exotic tropical flowers turned out to be just common carrots and tomatoes intricately pared and carved into fantastic flowers. I think life here will be like that. We can either see the carrot on the surface or seek and enjoy the beautiful flower that lies hidden inside, if we only look.

Well, the carrot was certainly easy enough to see on our all-night journey here with the children. Sometime in the middle of the night we stopped in Dubai (or was it Bahrain? One of those hot and humid emirates, an island in the Gulf with an incredible duty-free shop which we had five minutes to explore before the long process of re-boarding), and then on to Bangkok for heat, stairs, lines, stairs, forms, stairs, customs, stairs. (You can tell I was pushing the stroller loaded with hand luggage.) And then for our introduction to Bangkok traffic on the long ride into town on an extended flat Route 9, an endless thoroughfare of ugly buildings punctuated by an occasional Buddhist monk in brilliant saffron robes and the equivalent of American used-car lots—where row upon row of miniature Buddhist temples, gilded and sparkling in the sunlight, stood elevated on posts (must be above head level for proper reverence), rather like having a small-scale Taj Mahal for a birdhouse.

Anyway, now on to the flower! At last, arrival at the spacious Siam Intercontinental with its pagoda-like roof and twenty-six acres of palm trees, orchids, fountains and canals with a roving band of swans, geese and ducks (they eat the snakes!)—and our suite with its potted orchids in both rooms, fruit basket, amenities and welcome to our interim home. This hotel is nirvana to us, coming out of Egypt, though not so extravagant as the famed Oriental, or other newer luxury hotels which vie to outdo one another in the service department—including one hotel that irons its guests' newspapers so they can read the words in the fold! We are learning how to respond appropriately to Thai civility. For example, NEVER say "no"! The word does not exist in the Thai vocabulary. When a housemaid knocked on our door asking if we wanted the beds turned down, I replied, "No, thank you"—and she nearly fell over from shock. Frank informed me that I should have said, "Yes, please…perhaps tomorrow." We have a lot to learn!

Alas, on our very first day Leah was severely burned all over her face by a pitcher of "warm" milk, necessitating daily visits to various hospitals during our first two weeks for first degree burns and three third degree burns. Our rush in a hotel taxi to the emergency room of the first hospital occurred during the period when I couldn't hear due to a severe ear infection. Between the young doctor's soft voice, his strong accent and his limited English, I felt lost—but when he conveyed that his treatment was to pull off the scabs from little Leah's face EVERY DAY for weeks, I decided that we needed to find another hospital. Finally we located an old English clinic in a crumbly, but clean, tropical-style building where rooms are divided into small interior cells and larger outdoor areas. There we were attended by an elderly Danish doctor who agreed that she did <u>not</u> need to have the healing scabs removed daily—and that time and some ointments would suffice. Whew! Little Leah is just now recovering, and we hope that her permanent blush will begin to fade in a month or so. (A visiting nurse from Zurich just informed us that the marks will begin to fade in eight weeks or so. Until then, we'll have to settle for curious stares and strange looks whenever we go outside.)

The rest of the time was spent house-hunting, an interesting but rather depressing task, as the market is limited now and I had to drag the children along on most visits. Imagine the three of us in the back of a non-air-conditioned Volkswagen, breathing in the diesel exhaust fumes of buses just for a whiff of air, stalled in traffic, on a broken seat, Jared complaining of the sun, and Leah crying. Such were the crying, trying first days. The first house I looked at greeted me with a four-foot snake slithering across the front door. "First snake ever here," said the little Chinese-looking landlord in white silk tunic and magnificent green silk dragon and flower-brocaded pants. He then called his two teenaged daughters who with expertise born of long experience proceeded to kill the snake with long bamboo poles. "Not to worry," said the real estate agent, "it's just a tree snake; they live in the mango tree by the door." Actually, they were green mambas, the fastest and most poisonous snakes in Thailand...nested in the tree by the front door! Now we've settled on a house at last, forsaking tropical gardens for urban concrete—snakeless, we hope—just off the main business drag but easy walking for me to the grocery store since private cars are prohibitive due to excessive duty—and I don't think I could manage this traffic, anyway! We've fortunately inherited the previous tenants' two maids, and fortunately or not, their two dogs. Our gated "compound" is composed of three houses, the other two occupied by turbaned Sikhs, whose long-haired little girl dressed in pink...turned out to be typical little Sikh boy.

Next time I'll write of the fabled golden temples, the floating market, the sights tourists travel half-way round the world for. We've yet to see them. We did make an unexpected journey to Singapore for visas—so had a three-day Christmas holiday in that island of contradictions—a tropical paradise lush with vegetation and inundated with rainfall, with average 95% daily humidity, impeccably clean and unlittered (with a $500 fine for littering, one can well understand), Asia's highest medical standards (which I took immediate advantage of, having arrived with a variety of infections from head to toe—my final farewell gift from Cairo), no traffic, everything shiny, new, efficient, yet with ethnic neighborhoods reflecting the 80% Chinese, 15% Malaysian, 4% Indian and one per cent "other" (that's us!) population. We visited the famed Raffles Hotel, rather dilapidated compared to the spectacular hotels of more recent origin. Singapore—"Lion City" in Malay—was founded only in 1819!

How fortunate we were to be there for Christmas, for though the country has a tiny Christian population, the celebration of Christmas was indulged in by all, and the Christmas lights on stores and boulevards far outshone anything I'd ever seen anywhere at any time in the U.S.. It was simply incredible—choirs singing carols on nearly every corner, magnificent displays of holiday illumination with all the tropical foliage ablaze with thousands of tiny white lights. We experienced the same degree of culture shock going from Bangkok to Singapore that we had from Cairo to Bangkok. A double-whammy in two weeks—it was almost too much for us! (In fact, upon our arrival at the Singapore airport, we were over-whelmed with joy to find not only a McDonald's, but even rooms with piles of Legos to play with! When we finally departed hours later, after enjoying each of these wonderful discoveries, we were stopped by security and asked why we had spent so much time at the airport before leaving. Suspicious characters, we replied, "But the Legos! The McDonald's! It's wonderful!" When he learned we'd been living in Egypt, he understood and let us pass....)

We also purchased a computer and now, my friends, you'll be spared the toil of deciphering my distinctive calligraphy. As we approached customs at the Bangkok airport, I dutifully described the box with the computer monitor as our "word processor." "Like type-iter?" the inspector asked. "Something like that," I replied. (The rest of the computer was carefully stowed in two new suitcases.) Jared, our beloved son, not yet asleep though it was nearly 1 A.M., piped up with a huge grin and look of pride, "NO! It's a C-O-M-P-U-T-E-R!!!" Well, that cost Frank another hour that night and most of the next day as well as a hefty customs charge. So Singapore gave us much to remember.

Frank is luxuriating in the two-day weekends here. Not only that, but to have Christmas holiday and the New Year's within the same week—it's just too good to be true. But he has certainly earned his rest. Right now he's outside our door at the swimming pool, Jared's primary habitat these days, also. And to top it all off, we had a glorious New Year celebration on the lawn last night amid all the lighted palms and flowers, balmy air, with a four-hour show (I began to get a bit worried when the magician whom Jared was watching from the front of the stage was followed by "Miss Cigarette," an Australian striptease act, but Jared preferred galavanting around with his new boyfriends) and then wonderful fireworks exploding directly over our heads, burning our faces and arms with their ashy residue.

1984 has been very good to us—to see so much of the world, to enjoy our beautiful children, to make this move, and to remember our good friends and hope to see them again. And more! Leah's baptism at Saint Catherine's Monastery by Mount Sinai, our Knight of Knights oriental masquerade, and our final farewell to Grandpa Burnham, who will always be with us—wherever we are.

Stay tuned for:

Touring the Klongs of Bangkok (local canals with stilt houses and markets)
Thai-ed Up in Traffic
Classical Siamese Dancing—or
  All and More Than You Ever Wanted to Know About Moving Your Fingers

Which is Hotter—The Food or the Climate?
How Low Is Too Low to Bow?
Worming One's Way Through the Silk Market
How to Adapt Camel-Riding Techniques to Elephants (by Jared B. Fotis)
**One Mother's (Unsuccessful) Attempt to Survive 1 ½ Months
    Without School** (anonymous)
1001 Helpful Hints on Distracting Mothers (jointly authored by Leah and Jared Fotis)

Settling In, in Siam

February 1985

A hot steamy night in the heart of "winter"! Frank just got the word that a pouch will leave the office tomorrow morning, so I'll try to whip out a brief epistle in time to catch our rather random mail service. Actually, I had written a great long letter full of first impressions, adjusting to our new house, the children's activities, etc.—all you need to know about the Fotis'. Unfortunately, one finger just accidentally and so very lightly touched an unknown button on the keyboard and the whole letter was wiped out! I haven't had the courage—or desire—to attack the computer since then.

We are happily "installed" in our new abode—albeit without furniture, toys, most of our clothes, any dishes or kitchen articles. Our air freight, which was supposed to have arrived in two weeks, took quite a bit longer, but it really doesn't matter as we can't have it even though it's been sitting at the airport for weeks now—since before we moved in! Tape is red, regardless of the locale, it seems. Middle East or Far East—we still can't get our things till Frank has his work permit, which he can't get until we all get our permanent resident visas, which we can't get until.... But again it doesn't really matter, as our sea freight—the bulk of our furniture and appliances—hasn't even left Cairo yet though it was supposed to be here by now. Well, what's two months when Buddhists have a unit of time measured by how long it takes to wipe away a cubic kilometer of granite by giving one gentle swipe with the softest silk sari once every century? Now, that's slow!

Anyway, we're very happy to be in our large house, awaiting any prospective visitors. We're No. 1, Soi Sukhumvit, Bangkok 10110 (tel 258-5717), the first house on a side street off a very busy city street—but our house is set in behind another house off the road, so it's relatively quiet considering the location. Bangkok really has no suburbs. Everything's mushed in together—commercial areas, luxury housing, country-style houses, apartments, condominiums, slums, offices, shops, shops, shops, and sidewalk stalls and eateries everywhere. Just on our street in the few meters from our driveway to the corner must be ten separate sidewalk food wagons which bring chairs, tables and umbrellas daily, turning the whole section of street into a kind of shabby sidewalk café. (Is that where our resident rat comes from?) Food is grilled on tiny ceramic charcoal burners—and it looks wonderful, though I'm not brave enough to try it yet. Grilled chicken, all kinds of meatballs and exotic-looking concoctions, some wrapped in banana leaves, some somehow inside bamboo stalks, etc.

On to the supermarket just around the corner (one reason we selected this house)—a paradise we couldn't resist, coming straight from Cairo. All those foods we painstakingly dragged over every summer in our suitcases—here they are, at a price but nonetheless available. Peanut butter! Flour! Sugar! BROWN sugar! Corn flakes! And more—wonderful fresh fish—with no flies or cats! Fantastic shrimp, crab, scallops, sole! Beautiful meats! (Of course, one carrot is 50c and nearly that for a small potato, while apples are over a dollar each—but the local fruits should compensate for vegetables.) And now—the killer! Bunches of fresh orchids—plain or spotted, yellow or peach or fuchsia or maroon—at less than a dollar a bunch! By a "bunch" I mean eight to ten stalks with five to ten orchids on each stalk! (I remember how we laughed in Cairo after rejecting two dozen roses for two dollars as too expensive—we'd been there too long.)

The Bangkok street system is a true reflection of oriental circuituity (is there such a word? Well, you know what I mean), as there is no grid of cross streets by which to navigate. The old saying that "you can't get there from here" certainly applies—and even more so now that the government has instituted a complex system of one-ways (eight lanes all going the same direction on most major thoroughfares) for parts of some streets. We have to remember, for example, that on our major street, we can travel two ways till we get to the corner of Soi (side street) 21 at which point the traffic becomes one way all the way down to Frank's office and further to our one-time home at the hotel. However, returning to our house necessitates numerous side routes, most of which are also one-way but in the wrong direction—so a five-minute trip one way could become a 45-minute trip in the other direction. One always keeps in mind the one-ways when estimating travel time. We rejected a house much nearer to Jared's school because he would have had to travel miles and miles longer due to the one-ways. Oh, well, that's only a recent development.

The oriental mentality is further reflected in the overall street system in which there are major roads with sois—or side streets—on each side. These sois have sub-sois, or side streets of side streets ad infinitum. But they don't necessarily connect. In fact, they nearly always don't. So to get to a neighboring house behind yours, you would have to retrace your steps out to the main road, go down to the next soi (providing it's the right direction on the one-way street; otherwise you'd have to go literally miles out of your way to get there) and then go down the next sub-soi till you came to the property abutting on yours. So you don't really know your neighbors here—at all! And to add to the confusion, all the sois on one side are odd-numbered and those on the other are even-numbered. Sound sensible? Soi 44 is across from Soi 71; we're Soi 33 which is between Soi 22 and Soi 24 on the other side. Some blocks are nearly half a kilometer long. I took a walk to a "nearby" house—only two sois away—and it took over half an hour. Of course, a large portion of that time was devoted to crossing the street. Even at the pedestrian crosswalk, no one stopped for me and between the gaseous buses, speeding cars and daredevil motorcycles appearing out of nowhere, we were lucky to make it across in that time. Local jokes concern hit-and-run drivers on our street. Oh, yes. To add a little more flavor—and confusion—to the street scene, buses go the wrong way on one-way streets, so you must always take care in turning, etc., to clear the empty lane on the right, for a bus may come charging along out of nowhere. All this, and driving on the left side of the street, too. Frank's driving like an old pro now, but I haven't attempted it yet—and don't think I will!

The children are—*al hamdulellah!*—doing very well. Jared's face and figure have become well-known on the campus, as he is the proud owner of a sports trophy as the kindergarten boys' champion in the mini-marathon, and he has also won the 300-meter and the 30-meter races in kindergarten field day! He's busy with soccer two afternoons a week, baseball practice late one afternoon, and is bored to death on his "empty afternoons." Consequently, we've rented a TV and plugged in our portable video until our air freight is finally cleared for delivery, whenever that will be. Jared seems very happy and well-adjusted in his new school, although the class size threw him for a loop in the beginning—from thirteen in Cairo to twenty-six here! We all get up at 6 A.M. and stumble zombie-like through our morning routine to get Jared out to the bus stop shortly after 6:30 A.M. I am told we will be thankful for the early hours when the heat begins. (BEGINS??) Our church service at the international church begins at 8 A.M., and we've all cleared the sanctuary by 9:15. Again, the approaching heat is responsible. Actually, it's quite nice to attend a service also attended by the resident wrens who perch atop the cross and cheerfully and gracefully dart from side to side in the long sanctuary with all its sides completely open—like being outside under a roof. How thankful we'll be for those gentle breezes, even though there are ceiling fans above us every few pews apart to keep us from expiring during the service.

Leah enjoys our bit of "garden" (yard) with its two shaggy dogs, Doh and Kim Leng, courtesy of the servants. Our recently-delivered "No. 1 maid" (maid-cook), Am Phai, has just assumed her duties today after a month's recuperation from childbirth. Am Phai suggested that we hire her older sister Dog Mai as "No. 2 maid" for laundry and household cleaning. (She also suggested we hire a "No. 3 maid," but enough's enough!) Houses here (apartments, too) are built with separate living quarters for servants. We have a separate semi-attached building with two bedrooms, kitchen and bathroom for Am Phai, Dog Mai, and Am Phai's husband, a former monk from the countryside, now a security guard, who is respectfully addressed as "*maha*" (honorable). Leah's facial burns have nearly faded away, for which we are thankful. She's a beautiful and bright little girl who already has the maids giggling at her early language attempts and constant mimicking of behavior. She pulls up a stool, squats down and pretends to wash clothes. She's happiest in the shower where she is content to stand, wet the soap and rub it on her stomach for hours on end, regardless of whether or not she is clothed. Her first sentence was (in the true family tradition of canine-feline enthusiasm) "GOGGIE EAT! EAT, GOGGIE! GOGGIE EAT!" "Goggie," of course, is "doggie." Her first word, actually, was "kiki" (kitty), which is still one of her favorites. She thinks everyone is supposed to clap when she says "gak" (clock) and injects it into any conversation that might be bordering on the dull side. She's currently struggling with "clown," which usually comes out as "keeow" or "noun." Her wobble is verging on a tottering run now whenever she spots an animal.

Frank is very busy at the office, having instituted so many weekly meetings (eight full morning or afternoon ones) that he's practically inaccessible by phone. The new receptionist says only "He busy" or "He meeting" and hangs up! Nevertheless, he's reveling in the return to the human five-day work week, and we're all glad to see more of him. We've begun occasional "Jared Days" on Sunday afternoons when we three leave during Leah's nap for an adventure. One afternoon we attended an antique car rally where Jared sat in a beautiful array of antique sports cars and even saw an early king's crank-up limousine! Last weekend we took him to the crocodile farm where we escaped being bitten by any of the 30,000 inhabitants, and Jared rode yet another elephant. Frank expanded his photographic menagerie, this time having his picture taken with a tiger and then later his second photo with a long and heavy python draped around his neck. I finally succumbed, having bowed out in Singapore and a local temple here, and let the enormous creature be lowered onto my shoulders, amazed at the weight of the thing and at its slow sinuous movement—not at all damp and creepy-cold as it looks—saying, "Take the picture quickly! Hurry up!" Yuk! as Jared would say. He could not believe seeing his beloved parents encoiled in the spotted creature and would come nowhere near for a photo (smart boy!).

Bangkok's enterprising and active foreign community offers so many activities that one is always disappointed at what one's missing, regardless of what you're involved in. Frank and I are taking a Buddhism history and study group which meets at the school one night weekly with a wonderful instructor whom I'll call the "Frank Smith of Thailand" (Frank is the Massachusetts Teacher of the Year, a well-deserved and long overdue title), a former Californian and Buddhist monk whose enlightening and entertaining lectures are a highlight of every week. Last night, as soon as we were seated, he dragged us all outside to see the rabbit in the moon, Southeast Asia's version of our man in the moon. I saw the rabbit immediately, but struggled to find the man! The angle is a bit different here, accounting for the different interpretation. Next time you have a full moon, tilt your head a bit and find our long-eared rabbit! I have also joined the national museum volunteers (though the only thing I'm volunteering to do is go hear their wonderful lectures on Thai Art and Culture), an incredibly active and scholarly group of international women who give tours and lectures in a variety of languages. Frank is a member—get this!—of the Foreign Correspondents Club of Thailand (actually, nearly everyone we know is a member of this group, and only one of them is a correspondent) and during its annual ball (every group seems to have an annual ball—I've never seen so many tuxedos and long gowns) we were invited to a picnic at a weekend house of the wife of the brother of the present Queen Sirikit. (But will have to turn it down because of Jared's baseball game, and our turn to provide refreshments—oh well, royalty will have to wait!) The Thais are very reverential of their royalty—and there are lots of them. The fourth king of this dynasty (we're now on the ninth) had 82 children from 35 wives. Actually, they lose their royal status in the third generation, but that still leaves a lot of princes and princesses around!

Well, I'm still working on our long-overdue Christmas card, which Frank has suggested I turn into Chinese New Year cards—the next holiday on February 20. Stores still sporting Christmas reindeer and Santa Claus figures (I'm told they remain till April) are now festooned with red lanterns and Chinese characters in anticipation of the big event here. If I could just find out what the characters are, I'd convert my half-completed Thai Christmas card design into the Chinese New Year card as suggested....

Until the next pouch, whenever that may be, farewell from the Fotis'.

Here we are in our new home—a far cry from Cairo!

Coiffure à la Orientale

March 1985

The next time you're ready for a haircut, please come to Bangkok.

Here's why: You are first escorted to an area of raised beds, where you recline as if ready to sleep. Your head never enters the basin behind you, but rather rests on a vinyl cushion. Somehow your attendant manages to wash and rinse your hair in this position. If you are lucky she will even sneak in a little massage of your head, neck and ears, through the mass of foamy bubbles encircling your head. She may even wash out your ears, as mine did today! Just when you are relaxed and ready to remain motionless, it's all over. Up you go to another area with sparkling white tiles, wrap-around mirrors, and rock music blasting from all directions. There your head is gently patted, you are served ice-cold water, or tea or soft drink if you prefer, and then you are ready for the major operation. Your hair stylist may bow to you, with her hands in a gesture of prayer before her face; this *"wai"* is to excuse herself from the impropriety of touching your body's most sacred part, the head. Ordinarily, one would never under any circumstances touch someone's head here in Thailand. During the course of the haircut, you may be offered Q-Tips for any water lingering in your ears from the shampoo. At the conclusion, you give your thanks and your tips, receiving a gracious *"wai"* from each recipient. (Of course, your hair is styled in a sleek fashion, so becoming to thick straight black tresses of the East but a bit off for our wispy Western locks, but *"mai pen rai"*—never mind.) Now isn't just the experience worth a visit to Thailand? Please come and try it!

My hair usually looked terrific whenever I left "Gemie's" (they are trying to spell "Jimmy's") in Egypt, but my body needed a recovery room after Jimmy's grabbing and stretching, pulling and slashing, neck-snipping and ear-singeing style of hair-dressing. However, the results were impressive, as Jimmy was truly an artist in his field. Before touching a hair, he pulled this way and that, grabbed here and there to ferret out the in-hair-ent waves and sworls that he would then so masterfully subdue and shape into magnificent creations, giving us all a bit of oriental mystique in a masterful upsweep or majestic crest. No wonder he won the first prize in the world hairdressers' competition in Cannes. And no wonder we had to wait sometimes two hours or more just to see him (with a bit of groveling thrown in).

Out onto the main street with my locks shorn—I'll be cooler now for a few weeks—and by great good fortune, just the bus I am waiting for pulls up. And it is practically empty—most unusual—so I can actually sit down for the 20-25 block ride back home! This is one of the five baht (20c) buses as opposed to the normal two baht fare buses, because it is air-conditioned, not enough to notice but not so humid and clammy as the others, and primarily because it is therefore LESS CROWDED. After nearly five years in Egypt and trips to Hong Kong and through China, I feel fairly well-adjusted to the crowd syndrome, but what a pleasure to have one's own body space. The lumbering bus, I've discovered, is by far faster than a taxi or the office car with driver, because it gets to drive the wrong way on all one-way streets. So we coursed through the stagnant traffic in our one reserved bus lane, angrily honking at and nearly sideswiping drivers with the temerity to infringe upon it to speed up their own slow progress. At last my stop appeared, and the driver courteously slowed down while I grabbed the railing and hopped off onto the moving ground beneath. Turning at the corner of Soi 33 past a group of motorcycles whose drivers all wore bright blue vests numbered like football players—at first I thought they were a motorcycle gang and was not thrilled to have them all appear one day on our corner and settle in; later, I discovered they were motorcycle taxis—I wended my way on and off the sidewalk through all the food vendors with their portable tables, stools and awnings till I reached the welcome gray gate of No. 1.

Thus ends another morning of errands filling in the time between my 7 A.M. Thai class just several blocks from Frank's office and the bus stop, and my eventual return home. The class is a wonderful way to find oneself out in the world at its conclusion at 8:15 A.M.; otherwise, I'm sure I would still be at home stuffing scrambled eggs into Leah's mouth and wondering when, if ever, I would ever get out. My studies have dwindled considerably, but my attendance is near perfect!

High Road to China

May 1985

An overstuffed panda, laboriously hauled throughout China's major cities and verdant countryside, an assortment of fierce mounted warriors glaring down upon us from our own walls, the crocheted jacket I don for my daily round of errands, and a silk-bound journal exploding with unglued cards, unfinished reflections and a mass of data—historical, geographical, botanical, gustatorial—remind me that only two weeks ago I was juggling mementos, pamphlets and clothes in mad final preparations for our departure from China.

CHINA! Land of contrasts and contradictions, of endless avenues of brilliant green trees and dusty dry streets, towns and plains; of gray-garbed parents and purple, orange, green and red-wrapped babies, rouged and smiling; of masses of bodies, bicycles, trucks and buses, but rarely a car and perhaps, but not always, one dog spotted during an entire day; of palace walls and walks beyond one's wildest imagination in scale and grandeur and of endless buildings of one-room apartments for entire families; of stooped and grayed old women, hobbling along with canes, their miniscule feet, bound in their youth, bandaged and stocking-ed and filling only half their tiny slippers, sharing the sidewalk with exuberant youth in jeans and tee-shirts and an occasional daring young woman—in a skirt!

Was I really there? My still-aching muscles and rumpled boarding pass tell me I was. But my present pleasant easing back into my "real life"—with my children, home and husband—make it seem so far away, so long ago! Perhaps the following excerpts from my "High Road to China" journal will transport me—and you—back to The Middle Kingdom, as China has always called itself.

SHANGHAI—April 27, 1985

Arrival in the starkly white, efficient, oversized airport of Shanghai—devoid of color, shops, signs, stalls, food…a real contrast to the bustle of the Hong Kong airport we had departed from only two hours earlier. Ah, dreams of an evening stroll on the Bund, Shanghai's famous river waterfront with its graceful westernized buildings of the foreign concessions—architecturally like a European capital frozen in the early 1900s—and sampling some of Shanghai's fabulous shopping, for which I came prepared with voluminous maps and notes (carved mahogany chopsticks here, a tiny silk fan shop there, acupuncture needles at this address, silk nightgowns at that one...). Alas! We drove through Shanghai's "sub-urbs"—factory and shack complexes—endlessly for nearly an hour (spotting only one car for every hundred or so trucks and buses) until we reached our "hotel"—our initiation to our first night in China—a "new" (perhaps 15-20 year-old) steel mill "guesthouse"—multi-storeyed dormitory of single rooms with five cots each and a clothesline to suspend one's towel. Amenities here included numbered chamber pots and spittoons to match the number stenciled on the wall behind each of our beds, stenciled rubber slippers under each cot, and a tin basin for washing. A half-mile down the hall was the bathroom, consisting of doorless stalls for the shower and toilet cubicles sharing a tiled trough recessed into the floor—no footprints, even! One gigantic pipe in the last cubical served as the "master-flush"—like a torrent down the mountainside! ...And here's to those adventurous ladies on our tour, trying to shower or clean in the distant nether regions, putting the spittoon in the doorway to avoid mistaking a roomful of steel mill workers for ours. Now here we rest in our little rooms, listening to the hawk-ing (a more accurate word would be "trumpeting," as the elephant's call is the closest sound to it) and spitting of steel mill workers down the hall from us. (This sound to which we were so rudely introduced that first night stayed with us until the very end—in spite of all the "Do Not Spit" signs throughout the country, and I will never think of China without a red, white and green spittoon stenciled with pandas or peonies somewhere near my feet. I only wished they would change the signs to "Spit Silently!") Our dormitory hallways and starkness rein-force the mentality of commune-ism—no individuality. You're just a number stenciled on the wall behind your bed, or on your room's chair and spittoon.

Shanghai, city of tree-lined avenues and boulevards—mile after mile of trees. And amazingly, hardly a car! Buses, trucks, and bicycles prevail. I saw one skirt from the thousands of darkly-trousered figures, male and female. Thousands of housing units—high-rise or, more likely, one-storey hovels—were all one room per family, with bicycles squeezed in next to the beds. Fluorescent light prevailed, though some lacked electricity and many had a single bare bulb suspended from the ceiling. Shanghai, the largest (11+ million) and most Westernized city in China, main port and industrial center, is architecturally the "least Chinese city in China." Factories, construction, cranes, high-rises of one-room units surround us. There are few signs in English—even the calligraphy is rather straight-lined and harsh, not the graceful curves of older signs. Traditional Chinese garden elements are reflected in the "company garden" in front of each factory—a small landscaped area with the ubiq-uitous stone mountain and small irregular pond accented with bushes and perhaps flowers—a miniature Guelin (the mountain-and-river area we will visit at the end of our trip—the Chinese ideal of beauty in nature. In fact, the Chinese word for landscape consists of two characters: mountain and river).

The blue jacket abounds here. The occasional hint of color—usually on a baby—bursts upon your consciousness. Bedding is hung along the streets on clotheslines stretched between trees. Clothes are strung on bamboo poles sus-pended from windows. Shoes air out in baskets hung from windows on strings. Also, fish, fowl and all forms of animal life headed for the Chinese stewpot wait on rope, string or nail outside the windows. DRAB—the word that comes to mind—only the bright red Chinese characters of occasional signs add color. Multi-block-long lines wind about the train station to buy tickets—sometimes it's an eight-hour wait in line to purchase a ticket to Beijing.

In contrast to our dismay at our steel mill lodgings, we were delighted with our Sunday morning tour of the Shanghai Museum, crammed with treasures of the past—immense and beautifully decorated bronze vessels and drums, carved jade and cracked oracle bones for fortune-telling, delicate pottery and porcelain, won-derfully long and intricately painted scrolls of various dynasties, inviting us to lose ourselves in the details of scenery and household life of centuries ago. Flowers and animals—eternally fresh and vibrant—live on in these aging paintings. The museum had opened especially for us, the Bangkok Museum Volunteer Guides organization, with twenty-one travelers of nine nationalities, from a 73-year-old Israeli farmer to a 20-year-old Thai art student, my roommate. The tour was con-cluded with the first of many formal speeches and presentations of gifts and certifi-cates and lapel pins, a formality which I rather enjoyed in each city we visited.

Sunday—day off for many Chinese…and they were ALL outside enjoying it. Thousands of people were milling about, and we joined them as we pushed our way through the throngs to reach our various destinations. The babies! So beautiful! So colorful! Rouged cheeks, round and healthy, brightly quilted or layered clothes, colored shoes and socks, caps and hats—like little exotic dolls! And clothes split in the crotch, so no Pampers or undressing necessary. Little kids stand or sit in make-shift bamboo strollers, though most are carried and thus strike you in a blaze of color at eye level. We passed a family, obviously not city-folk, the wife wrapped in black velvet scarf and with long dress instead of the usual gray trousers, baby in col-ored towel and father with a long gray wispy beard—perhaps twenty long hairs coming to a point. "Oh, they're Tibetan," explained my companion.

Wheels of China—mostly I remember the hum and whir of millions of
bicycle wheels during rush hour, with an occasional truck or bus, but
very rarely a car

After a brief stop at the waterfront, the world-famous Bund, former center of all Sino-European commerce (during which brief stop a friend and I acquired a crowd of more than fifty, peering over each other's heads at us, pointed at and inspected like aliens out of a foreign world), we visited the first of many, many temples we would see during our two-week tour. Shanghai's Temple of the Jade Buddha—a huge collection of mammoth buildings, all with the traditional tiled and curved Chinese roof, smaller connecting buildings, a series of courtyards, upper and lower levels, a maze of ins and outs, ups and downs (never in anything Chinese—temple, palace, garden, home—can you view the whole from one place—everything is circuitous, labyrinthine, multi-layered, reflecting the mentality and society of Chinese as a whole). We were fortunate to be present at some Buddhist services—one with the female monks (yes, shaven-headed, too) upstairs. Some of us never realized they were female, but their high rounded and softened cheekbones lent a feminine air to their otherwise indistinguishable garb and bodies. As in the male monks' service in the adjoining building below, all nuns were lined up single file in rows facing the center of the room, constantly singing/chanting to the beat of a bell. At the conclusion, they marched back and forth among the numerous columns, hypnotically moving and chanting. The male service was similar, with increasing tempo of the drum accompanying them. Incense filled the temple, whose ceilings were hung with old lanterns and strips of red silk with brightly embroidered flowers and fringe. The walls were lined with huge gilded "soldier-gods" of protection, remnants of early animist religion pre-dating the advent of Buddhism. The back wall was filled with huge carved figures, gilded and painted. I was mentally comparing the grandeur of Gothic cathedrals to these Chinese Buddhist temples—both with an aura of mystery and awe, but the Chinese temples also infused with a sinister atmosphere evoking fear of the fierce, dragon-like gods towering above us, glowering down upon us...one even had dragons snarling at us from his kneecaps! The eeriness of the scene—black, gray and brown-garbed monks bowing and chanting, incense swirling, drums beating, and this pantheon of great gilded gods looking down upon us—was overwhelming. At the conclusion, the one hundred and twenty male monks all marched back and forth, back and forth across the courtyard, nicks in their shaven heads glistening in the sunlight. We left them still marching and singing.

All of China operates on Beijing time, leaving some places with midnight mornings and others with daylight mornings. Someone said that all China is up and about by 5 A.M. It certainly seems so. People already bicycling to work, an occasional mother with baby, old ladies with their omnipresent baskets of greens…but most especially the Taijiquan (Tai Chi)—traditional morning exercise routine engaged in by nearly everyone middle-aged or older. Especially graceful are these limbering-up exercises which stress opposites—pull-push, high-low, right-left. Like ballet, or martial arts in slow motion, the graceful movements (except for the "fanny-patting" seen from the rear of a group of women) add a softness and charm to the cold concrete sidewalks and street corners in the 5 A.M. chill. Some individually, others in large groupings lined up on sidewalks with a leader barking instructions and then crooning to each move, the Chinese begin their day in this peaceful yet invigorating way. Others more energetic practiced martial arts moves, and some, stripped to the waist, chased buses!

BEIJING in BLOSSOMTIME! Unexpected beauty of countryside and highways intensified by rows of flowering peach trees, backed by rows of poplar and now changing to rows of willow and then apple orchards, this brilliant early-spring green contrasted with the gray/tan arid landscape viewed from the plain. Straight stretch of road and trees into infinity… Everything symmetrical, even, in rows… Where's the traditional Chinese irregularity and balance creating harmony of scene and design? I guess the government can change that, too. Just our bus, the infinite green road and mules and workhorses pulling wagons… Deeper into China we go.

BEIJING

Beijing—the scale is immense! Man is dwarfed by gargantuan squares, incredibly wide boulevards, and large public buildings. Tiananmen Square, between Mao's mausoleum and the Forbidden City—palace complex of China's final dynasties, the Ming and the Qing—holds half a million people! Giant portraits of Marx, Lenin, Engels, and Stalin gaze down on the crowds. The city's five million bicycles cruise through the city's wide bicycle lanes during what surely must be the world's quietest rush hour! Only the whir of wheels and an occasional bicycle bell break the quiet. Nearly all the cyclists wear the ubiquitous blue trousers and jackets, with blue or green Mao caps with the red star. One's role as a tiny unit in a large society is reinforced architecturally and spatially in these wide streets and squares. But dwarfing one most of all—and incredibly so—is the Forbidden City!

THE FORBIDDEN CITY—so-called because to enter it uninvited meant immediate death—overwhelming in scale, design and detail…one is dazzled, amazed and nearly bored by the grandeur of it all! Gate after gate, building after building, each more grand than the one preceding. The largest palace in the world, covering five acres, it took one million workers fourteen years to build during the Ming Dynasty. Twenty-four emperors lived here and seldom went outside this incredible series of gigantic courtyards, yellow-tiled palaces, now stripped of their former opulent interiors, and "spirit ways," 250-ton marble ramps carved in sinuously winding dragons over which the emperor was carried while his bearers walked on cobbled sidewalks and steps to each side. Every grand hall had several entrances, every moat and stream several bridges, usually five, of which only the emperor could cross the central one, with various family and court members restricted to bridges and gates for their rank. No wonder such emphasis is put on the "classless society" now. I cannot begin to convey the immensity of it all. From each spot one sees only the next building across a huge courtyard, so one is overwhelmed time and again by this endless series of halls, each seemingly the final and grandest. I spotted an old grandmother hobbling along on her "golden lilies," feet bound in her childhood. People wandered, sat, photographed, spat nutshells.

And the names—so typically Chinese: Gate of Supreme Harmony, Hall of Preserving Harmony, Garden of the Palace of Compassion and Tranquility, Palace of Longevity and Good Health, Pavilion of the Rain of Flowers, Hall of Ultimate Principle (for business transactions?), Palace of Gathering Excellence, Palace of Gathering Essence, Hall of Pleasurable Old Age, and—my favorite—Hall of Exuberance, because it reminds me of our house when both kids are in residence! And many more...

I must say, if I were an average Chinese, one of the thousands roaming through the palace that day, I would be immensely grateful to whatever government abolished the unbelievable disparity between life in the palace and in the rice paddy. The excesses of royal life, just barely hinted at by the shells of buildings remaining, coexisted with a peasantry eating insects and overtaxed to support the royal lifestyle. Poetry through the millennia echoes this theme. The government was very astute to position its main buildings directly across from the Forbidden City, a constant reminder to the masses of what life was during the dynastic periods.

The Summer Palace—nearly as grand, but in a rural setting around a huge gracefully curving lake with delicate pavilions and covered walkways painted in intricate colorful designs—was occupied by the royal family and court during the summer months to escape Beijing's dry and dusty climate. However, my only memory of it shall be called "The May Day Mass-Acre," as we somehow ended up there on May Day with no other tourists but surely several million Chinese cramming, jamming every path, chewing and spitting their way through the expansive once sacred grounds of the Emperor. Enough palaces for me for the rest of the trip!

Tiananmen Square on May Day! A thrilling experience for five of us who left the tour bus that night at Tiananmen Square—the huge open paved area between the Forbidden City and Mao's mausoleum—to admire the lights and flags and to mingle with evening May Day celebrants on one of the biggest holidays in China. Many children were there, too—but with only one to a family, it was pretty organized and quiet. Everyone had a camera (WHO had mine? Both had been stolen in the airport a few days ago), and many prospective capitalists had brought along tripods and set up shop. All major buildings were outlined in lights; red flags flapped in the brisk breeze every few feet. Suddenly, for this day, universal drabness was transformed into a land of lights and red flags and lanterns—Tiananmen Square on May Day!

Temples! Temples! Temples! We climbed up, we climbed down, we walked all around. We saw enough temples to last a lifetime. All were similar in overall architectural design—a series of gate, courtyard, building, courtyard, building, on and on, each building larger or somehow more grand than the preceding one, each with various images of the Buddha, whether hundreds of gilded statues in rows or one immense figure towering above us. Some temples, however, really stood out in their uniqueness, and one of these was the Tibetan Lama Temple in Beijing. Lama? Llama? Odgen Nash enlightens us:

The one L lama is a priest,

The two L llama is a beast,

And I will bet you a silk pajama

You'll never find a three L lllama.

The most renowned Tibetan Buddhist temple outside of Tibet itself, this temple evokes the mysticism of Tibet. Incense, incredibly colorful painted eaves in tiers, bells hanging at every corner of every building, gongs, drums. Insides murky and misty with every inch painted in intricate designs. Creepy statues of various Hindu deities in various poses, giant carved boars, statues with multi-skull hats, black smirking faces, various garb. Ribbons hanging and flapping everywhere, some like polka-dot neckties, others exquisitely embroidered. Some huge Buddha figures—and one so tall I couldn't see its face! These Tibetan lamas wear brown robes with orange sashes—and have hair! One even sported a sports cap! Is there a revival in religion? Every temple we have visited has been loaded with native tourists. The government no longer opposes public practice of religion, seeing from Russia's example how religious oppression can backfire.

THE GREAT WALL

The Great Wall—endlessly winding through the landscape, thick, serpentine, graceful, STEEP and unending, it reappears at different angles on the various horizons. Known to the Chinese as the 10,000 Li (5,000 km.) Wall, it stretches from Shanhaigun Pass on the East Coast to Jiayugan Pass in the Gobi Desert. Work began 2,000 years ago during the Qin Dynasty (221-207 B.C.) or perhaps even 5th century B.C. when separate walls built by independent kingdoms were erected. Emperor Qin Shihuangdi linked these parts when he unified China to keep out marauding nomads. Ten years of hard labor and 300,000 men, many political prisoners, produced this astonishing structure, the only thing built by man that is visible from outer space, so they say. Most segments are of rammed (hammered) earth, but this restored segment, the Badaling Pass which we see in all publications, postcards and zillions of tourist photographs, is of brick and stone and dates from the Ming Dynasty (1368-1644).

Almond trees in blossom covered the mountainside, brushing the wall. Dusty air (bringing the earth of Mongolia to us), clear skies—and a few billion tourists, mostly Chinese. How steep it was in spots! People were clinging to a metal railing to avoid sliding down. A little capitalism was practiced surreptitiously as people sold fur army caps, old coins and statues. What an array of angles to view the curves, heights, depths, expanses, hillside of blossoms. Spring bees hovered, satiated from the profusion of blossoms. Again the Chinese ideal of harmony: old/ new, hard/soft, death/life, eternal/transitory, immense/miniscule.

The countryside near Beijing is flat, dry and dusty, with mountains rising abruptly from the plain, hazy and dreamlike in the distance. No wonder landscape painting was so popular. And now…The Steppes! The beginning of the Mongolian Steppes! We're on the far side of the Wall—and the land is in steps—small terraces for cultivation. The monotony of the tan landscape is relieved by the lovely blossoming trees dotting this most desolate-looking landscape. We wind in and out, through the valleys, up and down. Chinese landscape painting becomes real. Craggy, scrubby brush, jagged boulders—all the elements are here (except the water). I feel we're driving through a thousand scrolls. The mountainside ripples in terraces, every inch of desolate land in use; ancient castles crown hilltops, and mud and brick villages shadow the wonderfully craggy mountain outlines in the hazy distance.

I had been warned that the Chinese eat anything with four legs—except tables. I discovered that they don't limit it to four legs. During the course of the two weeks, my innards were exposed to every joint and organ of every form of life found in China—fish stomach, intestines of unknown origin, eel, squid, jellyfish, "100-year-old eggs" with black-green yokes and smelling of old fish, dark jellied mystery squares, rice gruel with garlic, pork and ginger for breakfast, cartilage in sauce, bones, fins, duck and pork skin, duck feet with their little webs still attached, and on and on. Chinese meals involve a variety of soups, most of which you don't want to know the origin. Usually the soup is brought out last and signals the end of the meal; however, in the more important restaurants, as in our dinner with our Radio Beijing hosts at the Beijing Duck Restaurant in Beijing, soups appeared regularly, one for each of the four tastes considered necessary to every Chinese meal—sweet, sour, salty, spicy. I enjoyed the rather bland creamy soup with grayish "mussels" which I later discovered were little duck tongues! Dessert for several of our meals was a pleasant sweet soup, served hot or cold, made of barley, tapioca, seaweed and tangerines! Every meal was an exploration into the unknown (except for the roadside greenery which appeared in various forms at every meal), aided by our trusty chopsticks at which we became quite adept after two weeks on the road. In China, one even eats a bowl of cocktail peanuts with chopsticks—one by one! (We were experienced, however, as a hotel restaurant, trying to cater to our western tastes, had served us peas, to be eaten—how else?—with chopsticks.) Foods vary according to region—Shanghainese food focuses on noodles—all shapes, sizes and textures. Schezuan food is spicy hot—you can pick out the really devastating peppers, but other tongueshockers lay in wait, camouflaged in innocent-looking sauces. Cantonese food is what we are used to in Chinese restaurants in the West.

Meals are very sociable affairs—ten or twelve of us around each huge round table with a large lazy-Susan in the center upon which is piled platter upon platter of edible/inedible matter, dishes and bowls pyramided unsteadily and rocking and weaving as we serve ourselves with our chopsticks onto the chipped saucer in front of each of us, which served as dinner plate. Beer, beer, beer—each region has its local brand—automatically brought to each table (tea was a special request—and we couldn't get drinking water, not for all the tea in China!). My favorite beverage was served twice during the two weeks—"High Energy Drink," carbonated ginseng! One meal at a dumpling restaurant in Xian was spectacular as we were served course after course (fifteen in all!) of dumplings, each with a different filling and each molded into a different form. It was so amazing that I catalogued them for the museum archives. From the "polychrome late Tang imperial yellow of uniform shape" to the "double-braided crescent High Hat" and "turtle longevity dumpling," we gorged ourselves on these delicious steamed creations, washed down with hot milky-white Chinese wine.

China is so overloaded with tourists now that there are not enough govern-ment guides to go around. Consequently, some groups are parceled out to vari-ous agencies. Our Bangkok Museum group, having planned its own itinerary, was "given" to Radio Beijing, and we were accompanied by three Radio Beijing employees through our two weeks, hitching up with Radio Shanghai, Radio Luoyang, Radio Xian, Radio Guelin, and Radio Guangzhou along the way. None of our hosts, of course, had been to any of the places we visited, so they let us off at the door with a "Be back here in an hour and a half." Some of us got lost and joined another tour group, happily listening to explanations and orientation missed by the rest of us. On the other hand, we were personally involved with our hosts, as friends, not just another group of tourists to be herded through the major sights. Our leader, Xu Meijiang, section chief of the English Department of Radio Beijing, translator of Chinese books into English, was a pencil-thin, proper and polite fellow, reading us our own previously written descriptions of what we would see. His stiff form encased in blue Mao jacket, he greeted us at the Shanghai airport with news of "unique accommodations"—the awful truth of which we later discovered when we were deposited in the steel mill dormitory. In Beijing Mr. Xu switched to our attire and was seen in tennis shoes, shirt and casual sweater the rest of the trip. He had worked nine years for Radio Beijing and was thus entitled to a bonus—two days off this year...in addition to New Year's, May Day and another holiday shared by all. He was very pleased. He lives, as does everyone else, in a one-room apartment with his two grown children, wife and in-laws. He is a sensitive, gentle, courteous and kind man who, when we toasted China on our final evening together, said, "To humanity." Embarrassed at buying yet another souvenir under the eyes of our poor but gentile host, I mut-tered, "...for my daughter. She doesn't have one." "Yes," he replied, looking at the $2 carved sandalwood fan, "you must buy it for her...and save it until her wedding day." I think I will...for Mr. Xu.

Nadia, our bright red-shoed Radio Beijing travel companion, was from a minority group in western China and was a modern woman complete with skirt and nylons, even joining us for a late night disco at the hotel. Mr. He (pro-nounced with gusto as if gearing up for a major expectoration) was the mystery member of our Radio Beijing hosts. In his late 20s-early 30s, shaggily attractive in faded blue jeans and deep-throated clipped British accent, he did not elaborate on his years as a Red Guard nor how he escaped exile to the nether regions, com-mon fate of most of that generation's Red Guard, who destroyed history, art, knowledge and lives with reckless abandon during China's Cultural Revolution 1966-1976. Even our gentle Mr. Xu was sent to near the Russian border for three years of forced labor. Many educated people did not fare so well. Mr. He, if needed, could pop open a suitcase lock in half a second with expertise. What else had he cracked during those gray and shadowy years the government now downplays? Many of our group felt secretly scorned by him—if conditions were different, his controlled polite façade might alter. Of course, the group's boisterous vacation demeanor and occasionally frenetic souvenir-gathering probably reinforced any anti-capitalist feelings. (Many of us felt that Mr. He, after two weeks of supervising luggage transferal with ease, had his revenge when he disappeared, leaving all our luggage on the sidewalk outside the Canton railway station when we were boarding for our return to Hong Kong. Fortunately, one of our group spotted the abandoned trolley, and we collectively raced back out through passport control and customs to claim our bulging bags and somehow propel them down the long railway platform and into the last car—where we fell into a stupor for the ensuing three-hour ride to Hong Kong.)

Low Road Through China

Fantastic travel! Our "soft-sleeper" deluxe railroad compartment for four has embroidered sheets and pillowcases and ruffles 'n' lace everywhere! A hand-knotted Chinese carpet whose original color one can only guess at covers the tiny floor-space along with four pairs of gigantic plastic slippers. Lovely lilting Chinese music wafts in, and the dusty dry countryside of the northern plains rolls by. Flat and sere, with patches of green crops, and every country lane bordered with towering poplars (Napoleon was here, too?), perhaps part of China's anti-erosion campaign. Occasional flocks of sheep, brick or mud houses, two lone farmers hoeing an endless field… Never, never a mechanized farm implement or machine—just farmers, oxen and plows. Our antiquated compartment seems a figment of the future by contrast.

LUOYANG—Capital of Peonies

Through the early-morning rain on our train windows, we wake up to a new landscape—low flat hills, grassless and brown, with numerous arched openings—cave country! An overnight journey to the southwest of Beijing brings us to Luoyang, capital of nine dynasties for 934 years. Built in the 11th century B.C., Luoyang lies south of the middle of the Yellow River in western Henan Province. Its primary claim to fame, aside from its long and rich history and present reputation as the peony capital of China, is its greatest art treasure, the Longmen Grottoes, caves along the Li River housing 2,100 Buddhist shrines from the 5th-10th centuries when this area was the center of Buddhism in China.

Over 100,000 Buddhist statues, from two centimeters to seventeen meters high, are carved into the cave walls of the sandstone cliffs overlooking the wide gray river—bas-relief Buddhas from the gigantic to miniscule, all viewed through a haze of rain. Our more photographically inclined tour members complained of the groups of Chinese girls with bright umbrellas intruding upon their compositions. I thought the contrast was perfect—bright pink soft round umbrellas against the ageless gray stone Buddhas...somehow very Chinese.

Shaolin Monastery! This is truly it! The aged crumbling monastery, a two-hour drive through spectacular eroded and terraced countryside lush with millions of newly planted trees in triple and quadruple rows and crisscrossed through every field of new wheat, is the home of Kung Fu, the world's most celebrated (through American TV and eastern movies) form of martial arts. Here Kung Fu was created as a necessary counteraction to the Zen Buddhist meditation practiced here in which monks sit for hours on end in a total trance, rigid and unbending. The extreme exertion of Kung Fu in its wild leaps and jumps is just what those stiff bodies need. We were the only western tourists, among thousands of Chinese making pilgrimage to the home of their cult heroes. What a mob! And not entirely friendly.... I guess their aggressive instincts were not inhibited here. Everyone was getting photographed looking very fierce indeed. Even the "darkroom boy" next to our bus, gloved hands in two holes of a black box swishing developing film before dumping it in a bucket beside him (Chinese Polaroid!), stuck his tongue out at prospective photographers—in a most martial way! Here at Shaolin, the four guardian gods, found at the entrance of every Buddhist temple in China, were even more fierce than usual, sporting martial weapons and poses, towering above us in gaudy colors. The weapons on display were indeed menacing, all shapes of sharpened metal atop long poles, surely designed to do the most damage. I saw one monk meditating, his short brown cloak over blue pants. Not a twitch! Perfectly motionless in spite of the mob milling about. I'm sure he would have liked to practice some of his martial arts on them! The few remaining very old monks—the real masters of Kung Fu—wisely were in seclusion somewhere. I had to get out my *National Geographic* to meet them.

At the White Horse Temple, first Buddhist monastery in China, built in 68 A.D. to house the Buddhist scriptures and statue carried from India on two white horses, I spotted, among the "ordinary" monks, two westerners with Nikes protruding beneath their flowing orange robes—"long-nosed" monks with shaven heads looking somehow so very vulnerable, pale fragile globes above their thin-robed forms.

XIAN

Another all-night train ride west to Xian, once the largest city in the world! Now the center of Shaanxi Province, Xian is one of the most ancient cities of China. Eleven dynasties ruled from here for 1,100 years. The famous "Silk Road" to the West originated here, beginning of the natural corridor connecting Central Asia with Northern China. And one can truthfully say that "Marco Polo slept here!" Xian competed with its contemporaries, Rome and later Constantinople, as greatest city of the world. Once one of the world's most splendid imperial capitals to which foreign merchants flocked to trade in silks, porcelain and precious stones, Xian now is a dusty and drab shell of its former self. However, recent archeological discoveries have made Xian one of the major tourist centers of China, for who would not travel thousands of miles for a glimpse of...

The Terra Cotta Warriors! Awesome! Inspiring! Overwhelming! Row after row of life-sized clay figures of warriors, still standing in their original positions as excavated in a field. We walk on ramps above them in a multi-football-field-sized building, peering down upon their dignified miens, intricate costumes individually adorned with buttons, scarves and knobs, each face unique. First discovered in 1974 by a farmer sinking a well, this army of over 6,000 life-sized warriors marching to the east to protect the nearby tomb of Emperor Qin She Huangdi, the first emperor to unify China as one country in 221 B.C., is one of three burial pits—most of which, along with the emperor's tomb, have yet to be excavated. Life-sized horses! I can't imagine the labor involved in shaping and firing these beautiful images. Warriors are in rows according to function—kneeling archers, armored foot-soldiers, and then horsemen, each with different clothing, hair-style and facial features—but all very fine, dignified. A tribute to this first emperor of all China, the nice fellow who had his wives and tomb laborers buried alive with him.

The fiercest of fighting, the most delicate and refined of arts—that's China, always a land of contrast. Old silks and slippers are sold outside the museum gates here by people who'll agree to nearly any price to get their hands on our tourist money (ours decorated with mountains, rivers, and sky while theirs has trucks, planes and buses!). The intricacy of design, the subtle coloration, the delicacy of each bird and flower on this tourist currency is beyond us from the West. Children's belts, hats and collars in multi-colored silk with bulging eyeballs, fringed whiskers, pearly teeth, shaggy silk hair and tails—unbelievable items, a Muppet fantasia—give us a glimpse of the brilliance and color of daily life in imperial China. Three-inch slippers are intricately embroidered to clothe the "golden lilies," bound feet of "respectable" women. Intricately embroidered silk ear-covers resemble half-hearts. Did women hide their ears as well as feet?

Anything would be anticlimactic after the terra cotta army, but the Neolithic Stone Age village of Ban Po was exciting—the most complete example of 6,000-year-old civilization anywhere in the world. As with the terra cotta warriors, a huge building was constructed over the entire excavation site. We walked on ramps around the village, peering into its granaries, burial pits, and remains of houses, including built-in ledges and windowsills! Raised thresholds against water and snakes and divided rooms were used even back then in this village of four hundred inhabitants. What wonders still sleep beneath China's fertile soil?

In a ridiculously-priced gift shop, I did find one real gem: a sign explaining transparent cloisonné: "Top-secret technical term of the SECRET COMMIT-TEE of the Ministry of National Light Industry." Now that's some secret!

We wandered through the Moslem section of town on our way to the Great Mosque—a mosque looking like a Chinese temple, but adorned with Arabic script. The Moslem influence in Xian is seen in women with towels or handkerchiefs on their heads in public—certainly not as severe as the cover-ups in the Middle East, but respectful to Allah, nonetheless. It's getting more like Egypt in other ways—sweet potato hawkers outside the bus, a crowd of nearly fifty staring in the windows at us. What a mixture of faces—Mongolian, Moslem, Tibetan.... China has thirteen million Moslem, 10-15% of its minority population.

GUELIN

What we've all been waiting for—China's most beautiful scenery—and a day of rest from climbing! A river cruise along the devastatingly beautiful Li Jiang (Peach Blossom) River. Towed along through the mountains of karst—water-soluble limestone—once a primeval sea, we wend our way through the humped peaks, rising abruptly from flat land, lush with brilliant green vegetation. Bamboo poles lashed together form the long narrow "boats" of local fishermen and those stopping to harvest river greens at water's edge or narrow islet strips. "Duck-herders" follow their charges as they waddle through the reeds. Water buffalo munch contentedly by the shore. Shoreline trees—like monster bonsai—capture the jagged irregularities so popular to Chinese sensibilities. One can easily see why this section of river is considered the most beautiful landscape in all of China—mountain, stone, water, contrast of soft/hard, wet/dry, green/brown, life/death, small/large. Silhouettes of basket-laden farmers move along single-file atop a mountain ridge. Cormorants are tied to a bamboo skiff—we're too late in the morning to see them in action, throats tied, bobbing in the water for fish.

Wonderful haze adds to the atmosphere—foreground in sharp relief against distant softened gray peaks. Rice paddies by the mountain—glistening fields of reflected water with people bent double planting the bright-green clumps of rice plants in the grid of terraced fields—yellow-green of fresh new life. From the wheat fields of central China to these rice paddies near Guelin in the south, people and dress change as do the crops. It's more like Thailand here, with an abundance of pointed straw hats.

Many of our group suffer from colds and sore throats (all those meals with communal chopsticks!), and so have purchased China's standard remedy, recommended by our Radio Beijing hosts. The more wary one who visited a physician was prescribed the same remedy: "Miraculous Effect Medicine," composed of six traditional Chinese medicines: pearl (and they looked like little lustrous gray pearly granules), two I didn't recognize, toad venom, etc. What lurks behind that nebulous "etc.," we wonder? These miniscule granules are taken—one for an infant and up to ten per adult dose—for sore throats and tonsillitis as well as tumors and "detumescence."

We were all a bit crazy at that last evening meal together—all excited at being so close to reunion with our families again. Our exhaustion after two weeks of physical exertion and mental assimilation of such history, culture and art was transformed into exhilaration as we celebrated, I in my black crocheted gloves from the gift shop, offered cigars by a Dutch girlfriend and a toast from a bottle of suspicious clear liquid with a huge lizard nearly as large as the bottle nestled inside! The Chinese! If they don't eat it, they drink it!

My journal contains farewell reflections in several languages, ranging from a poem:

Mary, Mary, not so contrary
How your shopping does grow!
With rolls of scrolls
And porcelain bowls
And twenty volunteers in tow!

to the lovely English of our host, Xu Meijiang of Radio Beijing:

"Your tour of China is virtually a direct experience of the landscape of an ancient land and the tempo of the people working for the benefit of humanity. Your warmth and careful observation will yield fruits shared by the Chinese and American peoples. You are leaving China physically but you will remain here as one of my best friends."

CANTON

Actually, Guanzhou. This is Hong Kong, not China. Still the crowds of bicycles and gray-garbed folk, but also skirts, color, European-style buildings left over from the old days of foreign concessions and international trade. A sense of hustle-bustle prevails. I had been forewarned about the brusqueness and commercialism we would experience here. My lunch companion spent the whole meal trying to get the waitress to smile—and finally succeeded—but after what an effort! Even the Cantonese dialect is rather brusque and lacks the polite niceties of other dialects, according to one of the Thai-Chinese girls on our tour. Guanzhou, or Canton, on the Pearl River, is the largest city in southern China, and, if one can judge by the local outdoor markets, dines primarily on turtles! Thousands and thousands of turtles of all sizes and shapes assault your eyes at every market corner. Civets hissing and lunging from their cramped bamboo cages are also destined for the dinner table. I hoped the same was not true of the fluffy white blue-eyed Persian cats caged next to them. We were now in transition to Bangkok as we perspired our way through the morning in this subtropical city…. A farewell to China at the Six Banyan Pagoda, where the spitting championship finals of China were held on the bench adjoining ours. These first sounds to greet us in China were our farewell as well.

Three hours and several centuries later, in Hong Kong, we saw what "the amazing Chinese," as Frank calls them, can do when unfettered by government restriction. Hong Kong's incredible wealth and glitter, every store window ablaze with priceless gems or an electronic paradise—and yet a hunched and graying cleaning woman with cart, sleeping on cardboard on the sidewalk.

The children's panda, one ear dangling by a thread, shed its black and white coat; my peony fan with my name in Chinese characters lies broken, wooden slats angled in all directions, and the sixteen rolls of photographs from the small camera I borrowed have arrived, gray and indistinct. But the leaves are still blowing brilliant green in the Chinese wind; rouged babies still ride on their parents' arms, bursts of color in the gray, and new ties of correspondence will soon develop, tenuous threads of contact between earth's oldest continuous culture and us brash newcomers from the West.

[And we did meet again. Mr. Xu Meijiang, our genial host from Radio Beijing, and the remaining members of our tour group reunited much later during Mr. Xu's surprise business trip to Bangkok. We gathered at a grand house, residence of an American diplomat and his wife from our tour. In the American potluck tradition, we each brought part of the meal. My "Great Wall of China" cake had a few blocks missing, but its odd angles and twists and turns, surmounted with a hand-drawn Chinese flag mounted on a chopstick, might remind one of the mighty Wall—after a few drinks, anyway. Mr. Xu, gracious as always, finally admitted to me that he was very confused. He had just come from lunch at a very humble Thai home, where everything was provided by the host. Why then, in this opulent house with servants and luxurious surroundings, could the host not provide the food? How could he allow himself to be humiliated by having guests bring food? Well, just as Mr. Xu had been our kindly teacher for two weeks, it was now our turn to teach him a thing or two about those crazy Americans.]

Meteorology and Magic

It's so HOT!!! Here is how we **try** to cope:

Days are rated by how many showers it takes to survive. A three-shower day is normal—a six-shower day is REALLY hot! After a few hours, one has to slip into the tepid shower, just to wash off the residue of "glow" that encases the body and fills the pores. Such a relief to step out of the shower and feel normal…for a bit, that is, until the welcome relief of the next shower.

Electricity is very expensive here, and so we cannot afford to air-condition our large house all the time. We settled into the routine of turning the bedroom window air conditioners on an hour before bedtime—just so we can sleep. As you can imagine, we go to bed very early here—just to cool off! And then, in the morning when we open the bedroom door, we are nearly blasted off our feet by the intense heat. It's like opening the oven door—and stepping in. We had friends from India as houseguests, and they were most surprised to find the Bangkok heat even worse than that of India! Now if you can make an Indian droop from the heat, that's something. Of course, Frank spends the day in an air-conditioned office, so he has only a few minutes at home in the morning and a few evening hours in which to suffer. I, on the other hand, am here most of the day. I shuffle around in the lightest of cotton clothes, resisting the lure of our inviting tropical garden, as it has its share of hidden delights: red fire ants, three-inch cockroaches, a resident rat nearly the size of a small cat, numerous lizards and reptilian looking things, not to mention any snakes lurking beneath the lush tropical foliage and sheltering palms. Well, at least we don't have a poisonous pit viper living in the bushes next to the children's swing set, as Jared's friend Matthew Morris does.

I've learned to adapt to this sultry and torrid weather in other ways. I quit wearing make-up completely—just an occasional brush of lipstick and then only if we were to spend the evening at one of the numerous balls held in Bangkok's splendid hotels by its many social and charitable organizations. (One of Frank's first priorities here was to have a tux made, and it's certainly getting a good work-out!) I have also forsaken jewelry, except for air-conditioned hotel events—it's just too irritating and chafing to have any metal, even gold and silver, touch the skin in this blasting heat. (What a shame…living in a land of sapphires and rubies and unable to wear them!) I've also learned to rise slowly before crossing the room—otherwise I become dizzy…and this is downstairs, where it's much cooler than the second floor. One learns to live one's life downstairs during the day. Traditional Thai houses are built on stilts over water, which provides a cooling effect. In the city, things become more complicated if the luxury of air-conditioning is unavailable or too prohibitively expensive. One must be inventive in order not to roast. Our church service, for example, is completely over by 9 A.M., and even in those early morning hours, with both sides of the sanctuary completely open from floor to ceiling (a unique design with walls like revolving doors swiveling open in order to catch some waft of breeze) and with ceiling fans whirling around overhead, even then the congregation resembles a flock of drooping, sitting birds—in contrast to the twittering birds overhead darting to and fro, occasionally stopping to rest on the large cross over the altar—fluttering away with a variety of handheld fans.

The rainy season is still hot—ALL the seasons are hot—but with the added aspect of torrential downpours daily, with earsplitting cracks of thunder and illuminating shields of blue-white lightning. Jared always loves these times. He says the thunderstorms "relax" him. I think they're pretty scary myself. And when it rains, it RAINS! One can't see more than ten feet. A wall of shimmering gray separates you from the rest of the world, and it seems as though it will never end. But it always does, and fairly quickly, too. For the rains come every day, but they don't last that long, and I must say, it is most refreshing, though extremely soggy, after the rain. We always like to go outside, as everything smells so fresh and clean—well, for a short time before the rank and rotting odors of overripe vegetation merge with and eventually conquer the refreshing post-deluge scent. And then, back to the relentless heat.

As if water all around you in the air is not enough, there are the floods. The traditional Thai society, built on stilts over water with primarily water-borne transportation, could cope. But the new Bangkok, a city of concrete, paved streets and sidewalks, and cars and buses, was not designed to accommodate truly major deluges, one of which we experienced. We were used to minor floods—just donned our flip-flops and continued on our way, hoping to avoid any slithering reptiles temporarily evicted from their waterlogged homes. But the flood of '86 was really something. We later learned that it is considered the worst flood in Bangkok history! The unexpected monsoon raged from Thursday night through Saturday, dropping 280mm (about eleven inches) of rain in one 24-hour period alone, and was compounded by rising tides in the Chao Phya River running through Bangkok. According to *The Nation*, Thailand's English-language newspaper, the all night rains "turned Bangkok into a lake" and were caused by a depression originating in the Andaman Sea and then traveling west of Burma along the coast parallel to Thailand. Bamrung Saragganonda, director of the Weather Forecast Bureau, described the causes of the three-day torrential rains and noted that "the rainy season will **start** in about ten days"!

It was the wettest day, according to *The Nation*, in five hundred years! This was the eighth major flood in Bangkok since its founding in the early 1800s. At least this one would subside within the week, with the public works department pumps chugging away. Earlier floods had lasted for months at a time. Newspapers with dramatic headlines ("DELUGE!" "Worst in Thai history!" "Bangkok paralyzed!" "Tales of woe all over!") were full of photographs of taxi drivers sitting on the roofs of their semi-submerged vehicles, miles and miles of cars, trucks and buses stalled on highways in up to four feet of murky water, people wading through the waters holding their pets (under umbrellas!), and an unfortunate fellow who had fallen into a ditch, up to his neck, right on our street. People made their way through the waters holding their shoes at shoulder-height; women tied their skirts at their waists but were still dripping wet as the water sought drier territory and wicked its way upward through their garments. Five people were electrocuted, one in his own house when he slipped and accidentally touched a live wire. (All this, and it's *still* a month until the traditional Thai New Year, Songkran, during which people inundate each other by pouring buckets of water on passersby in a very wet street festival. Well, as April is the hottest month of the year, I guess a surprise drenching is usually welcome, but will it be *this* year?)

Several of our friends had to evacuate the lower levels of their homes. The guests of honor couldn't make it through the flooded streets to our farewell party for them, and so we telephoned and had all the guests bid them farewell by phone. I'm not sure if they ever did receive their going-away gifts, as they had to be transported down their flooded soi on a buffalo-drawn wagon and then to a hotel near the airport in order to make their flight the next day. Boots and galoshes were useless, as the water was too deep. We sloshed out onto our street, which was full of happy Thai children, frolicking in knee-to-thigh deep waters. Water, water everywhere and—truly—nary a drop to drink, as it was chocolate-y brown in color, full of twigs and leaves swiftly floating by, and actually quite dangerous, as we were warned by hand gestures of passers-by to slide our feet ever so slowly and test before each step—to avoid coverless manholes in the street. That took the edge off our excitement, and we drew our gleeful son back into the safety of our compound, where there were only floating fire-ants and lizards to contend with and no open manholes.

There are many distractions here, in addition to floods, to take one's mind off the intense heat. Thailand's meteorological phenomena are matched, if not surpassed, by its magical temples, colorful people and distinctive customs. Golden *wats* (temples) and *chedis,* bell-shaped towers which usually contain a relic of the Buddha or ashes of a king or important monk, dot the landscape along with dazzling pagodas, which glitter with millions of tiny tiles of colored glass mosaic capturing and reflecting the sunlight in a thousand directions. A gigantic 160-foot-long 40-foot-high Buddha reclines under a roof in Wat Po, the soles of his ceiling-high feet inlaid with mother-of-pearl in a graceful pattern of ascending sworls, rather like actual fingerprints. Here in this magical land gold leaf becomes commonplace after a while, and one doesn't give a second glance at an elephant wandering down a city street or a corner shrine whose elephant statue (Hindu gods aren't overlooked in this Buddhist land) is daily plastered with yet more gold leaf patches, as a way to gain merit, sometimes with black smudges of opium rubbed near its eyes for a little extra merit. Little caged birds for purchase and release, another means towards the goal of earning merit, obediently return to their cages and wait to be sold to the next devout visitor who will send them on their short roundtrip to freedom. All this is overlaid with a multitude of colorful flowers and leis and little "wristlet"-sized garlands of odorless white seashell-like flowers (the Inverse Flower Law—the more flamboyant in appearance, the less fragrant) punctuated with brilliant reds and purples.

One of my favorite architectural touches in Thailand is the humble but ever-present *chofah*, a carved finial usually in the elongated shape of a bird or antelope head at the end of roof gables. I do wish there were some way to incorporate this exotic architectural detail into our westernized buildings at home. On temples the *chofah* is usually in the form of a *naga*, a mythical serpent that, according to legend, sheltered the Buddha while he was meditating. Many buildings have receding rooflines, and so there are often two or three or four of these mystical birds or serpents resting on each corner of the building. On the more extravagant temples, they are gilded, but I prefer the modest hand-carved birds sitting on the roof edges of houses along the *klongs* (canals).

Another very commonplace but very enchanting sight is the spirit house, looking very much like a tiny temple atop a pole, found outside nearly every house and building in Thailand. These miniature wooden houses are carved from teak in the style of traditional Thai houses or temples, with peaked roofs and *chofahs*, and they provide a resting place for benevolent spirits, enticing them to stay nearby and to offer protection for the household or business and its occupants. They are a holdover from a more distant time, before the advent of Buddhism 2,500 years ago, when animism was the principal religion of the region. (Buddhism is very accommodating. It is considered a way of life, not a separate religion, and so one may be a Catholic, a Jew, or Muslim or whatever else and still be a Buddhist. At least, that's the way it is with traditional Thai Theravada Buddhism, the earliest and purest form of Buddhism, still practiced in Thailand, Burma and Sri Lanka.) Offerings of food and flowers are made daily to the friendly spirits in the spirit houses, although I must admit that ours suffered a bit as I had to trudge through an insect- and weed-infested area to reach it...so I left the chore to our maids, and our spirit house languished. Generally, it is so cheery to come across these little spirit houses, resembling fantasy birdhouses, adorned with flowers and bits of food.

And now on to larger houses for the spirit—Thai temples. The golden brilliance of spires, pagodas, *chedis*, statuary of lions, dragons and elephants, as well as the omnipresent Buddhas, fountains, enormous drums, sacred umbrellas, all surrounded by encroaching tropical vegetation and saffron-robed monks, is ever with us...and really too overwhelming for description. So....I won't. I will, however, advise on temple etiquette in case any of you decide to visit this magical realm—then you will be prepared. Naturally, as elsewhere in the world, one must be modestly dressed—no bare shoulders, knees, etc. And, as in some other areas of the world, one must shed one's shoes and approach the temple in bare feet. Just remember, "bare feet and blossoms" (it helps to bring flowers, if you're fresh out of gold leaf) and you'll be all set. In addition to removing one's shoes, one must be VERY CAREFUL to sit in such a manner that no one, particularly the statues in a temple, can see the soles of your feet. This necessitates a rather odd position of sitting on the floor. You can't really sit cross-legged, as someone could see the bottoms of your feet. And so you kind of sit on top of your feet, which is respectful but can soon lead to a charley-horse.

One is also bent and cramped in the long and narrow klong boats, seated single-file in what appears to be a very long kayak or canoe, powered by a tiny but extremely loud motor at the end of a long pole raised and lowered into the water by the "captain" sitting at the rear. These infrequent forays into the backwaters of Bangkok and its environs were among my favorite activities. We snaked (word well chosen) in and out of narrow water alleys, under huge drooping banana leaves, past endless one-roomed houses built on stilts. People stood on the ladders leading up to their quarters, some semi-submerged with hair full of suds as they bathed in their watery "front yard." Others cooked on small grills, squatting in the constricted confines of their tiny homes. Although the water was muddy and murky, the people were gloriously colorful, with brilliant batik sarongs in a blaze of color and design. Children shrieked and frolicked, not yet constrained to the soft-spoken civilities of adulthood. This was truly a water world of wonder to me. Commerce proceeded at a different level here. Many canoe-like boats laden with produce—a coconut boat, a mango and pineapple boat, and yes, even a real live "banana boat"—drifted by, paddled by their "proprietors." They were dressed in the ubiquitous dark blue shirts and the unique straw hats whose interior system of woven reed struts and supports keeps the hat itself from touching the sacred head and also allows air to circulate, a clever Thai solution to forestall heatstroke. As they bartered and then lifted and handed purchases to housewives squatting by their open doorways, I wondered if these poor women were permanently curved into a crouched position, as every interaction with their outside world requires them to stoop to do business with the passing floating merchants. In one boat selling poultry, the boatman wielded a rather terrifying knife to dismember fowl on a huge cutting board which stretched across the width of his boat. Other boats sold liquor or bread—even hardware. Every need of families in the stilt houses was met by these floating mini-marts. I wondered when, if ever, the inhabitants walked on land.

This country with its magical temples, lush landscape and colorful people makes a fine setting for the thriving Thai movie industry. I responded to an ad for *farangs* (foreigners from the West) who wanted to appear in a Thai movie. However, it was Frank they were really after, as the first question they asked was "Does your husband own a tuxedo?" So the deal was made and we headed for a private British club for the filming of Frank's cinema debut. It was most interesting to observe the Thai method of production. Since the celluloid film itself was expensive, a scene was never shot twice. Each scene was rehearsed over and over, with a Thai speaking the words in Thai for the foreigners to repeat until they were close enough for a lip sync to be substituted in the film. The scene for this comedy, starring Thailand's most popular young star, a glamorous young actress, was a wedding reception, and Frank was cast as one of the *farang* guests. He certainly looked the part, and he mimicked his Thai lines quite well. The only problem was that the guests were supposed to eat the mayonnaise-laden banquet food, which was becoming quite warm after hours under the strong overhead lighting. With each bite, each time the scene was rehearsed, I prayed he wouldn't end up with ptomaine poisoning. The shoot went on and on into the wee hours of the morning. What they had promised would be a two-hour assignment (volunteer, of course) became nearly eight hours, and it was halfway to dawn when they finished. And their reward? Returning to the same banquet table for a bowl of noodle soup! Unfortunately, we have never seen that movie, as it came out the week after we left. But I'm told that it was quite amusing. How could it be anything else, with Frank Fotis in it?

From pyramids to pagodas, Mary Ned and Frank adapt to local ways

Manila & Malaysia,
Via the Land of Headhunters

August 1985

Back in Bangkok!

We're all so happy to be home again after our two-week excursion to the Philippines and Malaysia—and just in time, as Jared is now in the middle of his first LONG DAY as a first-grader! From summer lounging around in pajamas watching "The Cisco Kid" and "Lassie" re-runs on the video to a very full day—from the 6:40 A.M. bus pick-up to 2 P.M. dismissal—Jared will be a tired cowboy when he straggles through the gate today. Usually he scales the six-foot iron gate with ease after school each day, but I have a feeling he'll be sagging by the doorway for a few days till he adjusts to his busy new schedule.

We juggled baby stroller, diaper bag, various hand luggage, two children, and an immense load of sprays and sprays of seven kinds of Thai orchids through the airport, down the three flights of stairs, onto the bus out to the plane, up the steps, down the aisle, and finally into our seats. Anticipating a pleasant three-hour flight from Bangkok to the Philippines, we settled into our three seats and began to relax—until Leah, perhaps affected by change in air pressure if not possessed by an alien spirit, was transformed into a screeching, thrashing, inconsolable and very strong little creature, her feet pummeling the orchids so carefully wedged between seat and floor for minimum damage. We had always been pleased that our children were such good travelers—however, this trip brought us down to earth. Leah outperformed herself on each subsequent leg of the journey. Howling and thrashing for at least forty-five minutes till she fell into a stupor, she reduced the rest of us to glassy-eyed zombies, staggering off the plane with a by now sweetly smiling little innocent getting admiring glances from any passenger who didn't recognize her as the source of all the earlier commotion.

Reunited with our good friends of Cairo days, Karen and Jeff, and their son Matthew, Jared's old playmate and co-culprit, we proceeded through the rainy night through Manila streets to Makati, the financial district and suburban area for successful Philippinos and most expatriates. Blessed with a beautifully-land-scaped, neat and well-ordered gated neighborhood of contemporary homes tucked into tropical foliage (a kind of flat Beverly Hills), they now reminisce upon their years in Cairo with disbelief.

What an interesting blend of culture in the Philippines—a kind of Asian Spain…or Spanish Asia. Our drivers were Domingo and Orlando, the maids Isabelle and Vivian, the street Sampaguita—all the names seemed Spanish; the churches looked Spanish, the songs were Spanish, and the language sounded like Spanish—almost. It is Tagalog (tah-GAH-log), which seems to be a mixture of whatever the original languages were, suffused with a heavy dose of Spanish. Even the people look Spanish, if there is such a thing anymore these days, but with just enough of the oriental eye structure to produce an exotic mixture of East and West, and many very beautiful women. The people, according to the literature, are primarily Malay with a sprinkling of Spanish and other influences. One of the native dances is a form of flamenco, yet others are similar to the Thai bamboo dance where dancers jump in and out of long bamboo poles beating together and on the floor to increasing tempos. The people, as in Thailand, are exceedingly polite and gracious, and follow the oriental tradition of avoiding open disagreement and saving face at all costs. This is very lovely, but unless you can read between the lines and figure out how they really feel (probably the opposite of what they say), you risk offending unintentionally. And—nearly everyone speaks English!

Many people are very, very poor, pay levels are very low, and most seem rather depressed about the economic future. Everyone, it seems, wants to go to the U.S.. Living is incredibly crowded for most Philippinos, several families and country relatives often sharing two rooms. In fact, all of Manila seems like a boom town that stopped in the sixties. It has the usual crowded Chinatown found in every Asian city, and a Moslem section which we never located, and a lovely long palm-lined boulevard along the seafront to the graceful old Manila Hotel where MacArthur had his suite. Huge old cathedrals abound (and a lovely small one with lights of translucent seashells and an organ of bamboo pipes producing a haunting lilting tune), and an old fort. And that's about it.

Except, of course, for the jeepney factory. Jeepneys are a unique Philippino product—converted jeeps with extended backseats of two benches perpendicular to the driver's seat. They serve as the main form of public transport, each one covering the same set route. Passengers enter and exit, hopping up from the rear, and pay by the kilometer. The glory of the jeepneys, however, is in their individuality of décor. Most are laden with multi-colored lights, flamboyant murals, signs of "Supreme Joy," "Charity," "Magnificence," "Faith in God," "Queen Eppie," etc. Painted in bright reds, yellows and blues, their *pièce de résistance* is their hood ornamentation (one of which Jared is now the proud owner of)—foot-high metal horses, three, five or seven of which are bolted to the hood and carry the jeepney proudly forward to meet any adversary (the traffic). An occasional variation is the metal rooster mounted on springs on the bumper, daring any oncomer to encroach upon its territory. Now who wouldn't be proud to ride upon a vehicle such as this?

The lush and lovely Philippino countryside is a total contrast to the sooty and crowded city. Banana and palm trees, lush vegetation nearly obliterating the steep descent into scenic gorges, fields or crops or meadows of grazing cattle or buffalo, roadside nibblers of goat and sheep, garrulous chickens, lazy dogs, old women with banana-laden baskets for hats, roadside stalls of huge avocadoes, pineapples, papayas, lemons. The boys happily rode horses on a hillside overlooking the Taal volcano, inside a lake which is the crater of another now extinct volcano. We were immersed in a cloud, and then slowly returned to the sun, watching the cloud's shadows sweep across fields and water beneath.

Several days at two beach resorts several hours south of Manila were Frank's idea of an ideal vacation—just a sandy beach to get burned on and the lapping or crashing of the waves to listen to. The poor fellow had an undiagnosed case of gout and could hardly walk, and how he howled when I accidentally trod upon his affected foot. (However, his foot did improve considerably afterwards, so I—accidentally again—gave him another treatment the next day, but he was not so appreciative.) Jared and Matthew reveled in their choice of activities, swimming in the sea a few minutes, then the pool, then ordering a jeepney to the stable for bit of horseback riding. Never mind the twelve-year-old following us to our quarters with a machine gun—was it for rebel guerrillas or one of the several yard-long lizards we encountered by our door?

Our Manila-Kuala Lumpur flight was not the simple three-hour nonstop we had envisioned, but rather a five-hour odyssey with an unexpected stop, where we debarked, temporarily, over the blazing tarmac to a tiny concrete bunker which turned out to be Kota Kinabalu International Airport. We had no idea where we were and were still shell-shocked by Leah's airborne antics, so any escape from the scene of our distress and intense embarrassment was welcome, even a sweltering concrete room under the broiling tropical sun. We later learned that we were in, of all places, Borneo—land of the headhunters! (Wonder if we would have so eagerly deplaned had we understood where we were?) Had we even had an inkling of the performance Leah had in store for us, we would still be in Manila today. We feel we should get the passenger manifest and send notes of apology to all the other passengers. We are now the people we never would sit next to before. Leah outdid herself, and by the time we landed in Borneo, I was in tears, Frank was fuming, Leah was howling and thrashing, and Jared was on the floor (four of us in three seats).

At last, what seemed like several days later, we arrived at Kuala Lumpur's clean and modern airport, a real joy for us—no steps, buses or other impediments to our easy arrival. Kuala Lumpur, capital of Malaysia, a fairly recent country, is composed of thirteen, or seventeen, sultanates. Malaysia has a king, one of the thirteen or seventeen sultans, elected by the others for a five-year term; then it's another sultan's turn. Personally, I think "sultan" sounds much more exotic than merely "king," and goes much better with the golden jewel-laden turban he gets to wear. When we were on Borneo, we didn't know we were on Borneo, because it's merely the name of the island comprising three countries (Malaysia, Brunei, and Indonesia), so the countries were listed, but not the island. Only after we arrived in K. L. (as we pseudo-Asians call it) did we discover that we had set foot in exotic Borneo, land of the head-hunters...and escaped.

Kuala Lumpur is an architectural wonderland—a sort of historical Moorish Disneyland of turret and arch, minaret and dome which must be seen to be appreciated. The lovely graceful old buildings, the lacework railway station, the old public buildings are wonderful to behold. The modern mosques and business structures in Islamic style are very interesting as well—stone in lacy patterns of stars and geometric intricacies, mosques of immense scale with tall pillars and sunken marble pools accentuating huge expanses of marble terrace.

Malaysia is the world's primary producer of tin, and therefore boasts of its quality Selangor pewter. It is also known for batik, although the Indonesian is by far finer and more intricate. Malaysia, I believe, is the world's primary source of rubber as well. (It also seems to have a corner on the scorpion market.) There are some beautiful products of Malaysian silver and buffalo horn. All in all, Kuala Lumpur was an exotic and interesting stop for us, and we were now ready to fly (not again!) to Penang, Malaysia's prime resort area, an island off the northwest coast noted for centuries as a world center of trade, piracy, and intrigue.

Malaysia is the most pronounced of all the "melting-pots" we've been to, especially obvious from our visit to Penang. The mixture of faces, dress and custom is so immediate and overpowering that the impression remains vivid. Indian, Chinese and Malay are the three groups intermingled, and I guess the mixture is so noticeable because it's actually NOT a melting-pot, but rather just an intermingling of cultures. The Chinese are VERY Chinese ("They're not really Malay," said our Moslem taxi-driver) and run most of the businesses; the Indians are very Indian in saris, long braids, and the *tika* or *bindi* (dot) painted on foreheads; the Malay, brown and lean and batik-clad, are devoutly Moslem and with names so familiar to us from our years in Egypt. Actually, if it were a melting-pot, the cultures would blend, and the differences be less obvious. Because of the Hindu influence, most cattle are for dairy only. We see them roaming through gardens and temple grounds, tended by blackened old men in dhotis. I suppose the Hindu eat mainly vegetables, while the Moslems eat mainly vegetables and beef or lamb, while the Chinese will eat anything.

The island is full of dragon-laden Chinese temples, glaring bright red and pink in the sunlight. The Indian Hindu temples are perhaps the most exotic-looking of all, covered with statues of intertwined animals and people, brightly-clothed and colored and bursting with life. The copper-domed mosques with tall minarets seem to fill all corners of the land. What a mixture of style, belief, history and culture!

One unique blend of cultures is found in the Baba-Chinese, descendents of original Chinese immigrants who left their families in China, took local, probably Malay, brides who converted to the Chinese religion and customs in most ways, but left traces of their language and culture in this group of Baba (father) and Nonya (mother) Chinese. Their dress is Chinese with Malay overtones, their language a mixture. Now this group is rapidly disappearing through assimilation into the pure Chinese through intermarriage.

Fortunately, I was the only one who had to cope with the Penang pangs of some tropical illness. The rest of the family fared better, as Leah learned to love the water and gaily watched the waves come crashing over Frank and her. Jared has transformed into a "mer-boy" during the last year and was in the water more than out. So our few days on the beach in Penang were a fitting conclusion to our two-week R and R, which substituted for our annual home leave this year.

The Elephant Round-Up

November 1985

There we sat, all day on the American Women's Club tour bus on our way to Surin in the northeast of Thailand, 30 kilometers from the Cambodian (I suppose I should say Kampuchean) border, on our way to the annual Elephant Round-Up! The flat soggy countryside rolled by, mile after mile of rice paddy dotted with the occasional tree. Small villages of houses on stilts shaded by coconut palms and banana trees appeared with regularity. Clean children with round dark faces peered at us from their brightly colored plaid shirts. Water buffaloes were everywhere, strolling by the roadside or half-submerged in the flooded landscape. Geese, ducks, scrawny roosters completed the scene.

An unexpected treat ensued as we stopped briefly (after six hours) at the ruins of Phimai, a thousand-year-old Cambodian temple perched on the only hill for miles around. Climbing, climbing up in our bus and then on foot, we passed groups of bright saffron-robed monks, barefooted, and adding life to the multi-colored stone blocks in graceful rounded pointed towers with delicate carvings over the lintels. The arch had not yet been invented in this ancient Cambodian culture, and we marveled at the beautifully earthen-hued blocks joined with care and then carved in delicate tracery of flowers and tiny figures. The gods seemed calmer here than in Nepal—certainly more chaste! They lacked the ferocity and gaudy coloring of Nepal's painted deities glowering down on us. The beautiful stones, each a different shade of beige, brown or red, soaked in the sun's warmth.

Grass sprouted from joints of stone blocks, and a lone violet lotus floated in one of the four square ponds in front of the impressive structure on the hilltop overlooking Kampuchea. No river or range of hills delineates the border, adding confusion to an endless series of border fights. Jared, his friend Matthew, and assorted boys, freed from a day's confinement aboard tour buses, leaped and lunged over the silent ancient stones, life and action amid the ruins.

Buddhist monks were silhouetted against the earth-toned stone walls, brilliant orange, sharply outlined in the afternoon sun…and, happily, no snakes in sight! A long stone road led to the temple mount, which we climbed along with groups of young monks. The buildings were long and narrow, cool and dark inside, with the glaring sun piercing the interior solitude from each doorway. This temple is aligned with Asia's most magnificent ancient temples grounds, Angkhor Wat in Kampuchea, and with other impressive ruins in Thailand, thus facilitating a system of communication (somehow!) among these bastions of ancient Buddhist civilizations—early Asian telecommunications in action! It was a beautiful and serene spot, architecturally exciting and historically interesting (and it was great to get OFF the bus!).

Sunset? It escaped us, as night in the tropics falls quickly with no dusky preview. We drove—and drove and drove—through the darkened night (no street lights here) and then—ELEPHANTS! The town, which we had entered in darkness, was FULL of elephants! Like cows on the sidewalks and streets of Kathmandu, they sauntered around the town, more at home than we. ("Watch your step!" echoed a voice from the back of the bus.) Elephants all over the town—all sizes! All ridden by their "*mahouts*" (drivers) and many carrying passengers about.

This was THE weekend of the year in Surin. Sidewalk eateries, the usual open storefronts, small spirit temples lighted everywhere…. Bicycles, cycles, forges, ovens, dogs, dishes being washed—all shared the sidewalks. Some elephants were actually taller than our huge touring bus! 6 P.M. in Surin: The bus stopped while the Thai national anthem was played. The entire country stops in its tracks for the nightly anthem—except for cosmopolitan Bangkok, whose traffic is congested enough already without an additional daily standstill for the national anthem.

I'd never seen Jared so excited about anything. Eleven elephants—some absolutely towering!—were milling about in the darkness outside our hotel entrance, waiting to take people on rides. Probably the *mahouts* made most of their yearly income on this night. I backed out at the last minute, after ascending a huge wooden platform from which to mount the elephants' teak "*howdahs*," carved wooden seats with teak spokes—Frank and Jared's *howdah* wobbled so violently with their entrance that I feared we would all plunge onto the concrete below if I attempted to join them. So, I backed down the wobbly aluminum ladder and watched my family ride off into the night. Coward!

The elephants were absolutely huge! I'd never seen any of such size in any zoo. A mother elephant gave rides with her baby attached on a chain, her long bristly black hairs on leathery gray skin, actually sensitive enough to be bothered by mosquito bites, and mottled fringed spotted ears. The *mahouts* direct their charges with their bare feet behind the big flaps of raggedy ears, pushing and prodding, jiggling and jerking. What a grand scene—elephant after elephant appearing out of the darkness to line up before us! All these elephants are, of course, Asian elephants, extremely personable and intelligent. They are trainable, while their African cousins, larger (if possible!) and with large billowy ears, are not.

November 17, 1985   The stadium at last—after a long bicycle-rickshaw ride of wrong turns past temples, stores, houses, white-robed Buddhist nuns, groups of monks, lotus ponds, men in sarongs. Silent streets jammed with traffic, producing only the hum of thousands of bicycle tires, occasionally intruded upon by a monstrous tour bus or noisy motorcycle.

At last in our stadium seats (on the shady side—hurray!), we watched as 102 elephants milled about, getting organized for the grand elephant parade. The 3- and 6-month-old babies received special awards (young elephants bring good luck), for which their mothers took a bow. The youngsters, nuzzled under their trumpeting mothers' legs, raised their tiny trunks in mock indignation, and their mothers learned with disappointment that the prizes were inedible. A hundred dancers in pink tops over orange plaid silk sarongs, and others in bright blue, turquoise and yellow, danced gracefully down the entire field in classical Thai style, fingers elegantly extended, accompanied by weird wild music of strings, bells, and drums, escorting a dragon-float, some kind of fantastic painted and gilded barge, which turned out to be a real rocket, which they decided not to detonate this year due to accidents and injuries in previous shows—we were grateful. Several of the dancers were blonde or black, Amerasians left behind by their American soldier fathers stationed nearby during the Viet Nam war. We understand that their lives are very difficult, as they are so foreign in appearance to the native Thais.

The Elephant Round-Up—we learned that this was a great exhibition of local elephants and their skills, not an actual round-up, which would occur in the jungle at night and would be too dangerous for viewers. So we enjoyed a demonstration of round-up techniques, with some elephants chasing others while riders perched on their backs held a long roping-pole with which they lassoed the unfortunate elephant's rear foot with a 100-meter rope three inches thick and then tied him to a tree to tame him through temporary starvation. The actual elephant hunt is a very religious and mystical affair, held only on an astrologically auspicious night, with riders allowed to speak only a special "language of the elephant." Wives must follow certain rituals far away at home, or the entire round-up could be jeopardized. Elephants are amazingly fast, running at 25 m.p.h. in spite of their tremendous bulk. They appear quite light on their feet!

There followed numerous demonstrations during this four-hour spectacle of elephants gingerly walking over men, pulling two-ton logs with ease, racing through obstacle courses, and then another Thai dance with a cast of hundreds and several "ankle-crushers," bamboo poles rhythmically beaten together while dancers stepped in and out with alacrity. Then our favorite—the Tug of War in which a 65-year-old elephant who entered the stadium to strains of "Exodus" easily pulled sixty, then eighty and finally one hundred strong young Thai soldiers tugging the massive cable.

Elephant soccer! A long game in which the green team, appropriately adorned, contested the red team over a two-foot diameter leather soccer ball, adroitly maneuvering down the field with foot and trunk. The *mahouts* sat or stood on their charges' backs, vigorously directing them while the crowd's tremendous boos and cheers suggested that they all had money riding on the outcome.

And the grand finale—the Parade of War Elephants, adorned in spectacular costumes of all colors, sporting lances and arrows and costumed attendants. (The most important attendant is the guardian of the feet, an elephant's most sensitive area, as an elephant with an injured foot could go mad and wreck the war party.) The general's elephant was painted in gold from forehead to beginning of trunk. The general himself was arrayed in gold, perched upon his mount under a multi-tiered golden umbrella visible from afar, with two tall feathered poles by his side. Banners of all colors were paraded before the elephant cavalry. Red brigade, green brigade, blue brigade. Scouts on elephants, flag bearers, and wild horn music from somewhere back in time....

At the other end of the field lay hundreds of enemy troops, blue-plaid saronged infantry in a long line, rifle smoke hazing the air above them. An occasional cannon burst forth, filling the air with echoes and smoke. The "Thai" infantry advanced and the clash of color was the clash of battle. Elephants, troops, horns, smoke, confusion, silver scabbards flashing in the air. The Thais won—of course! I see now how battle, terrible as it must have been, could also be invigorating, rich, colorful, exciting. Surely this is how epics are born. And with the thrill and ecstasy of survival, the battle must seem even more exhilarating. One can see why a Thai king wrote to Abraham Lincoln offering to send Thai war elephants for help in America's Civil War.

At last I took courage and mounted a small—by comparison—elephant, swaying front and back high in the air. Just a little scary being on one of a hundred elephants, all giving rides on the field at the conclusion of the performance. The *mahouts* were generous with their sharp-pointed prods behind the elephants' ears and not a few elephants had dabs of blood oozing from their necks. A thrilling performance, an exciting weekend out of Bangkok, and then—off through the Thai countryside, half-flooded, with water buffaloes cooling off in the murky brown waters, we began our eight-hour ride home to a peacefully sleeping Leah and memories of our weekend of elephants.

Jared exchanges camels for elephants

Journey to the Top of the World

November 1985

Our first hint of the exotic venture ahead of us was when the sari-clad stewardess with diamond in her pierced nose and red "*tika*" third eye on her forehead bowed to us as we boarded the Royal Nepal Airlines flight from Bangkok to Kathmandu. From that moment on, our lives for the next five days were immersed in an incredibly diverse and fantastic culture of demons, Tantric Buddhas, pagoda temples and spires from the middle ages set in the temperate-to-tropical Kathmandu Valley nestled in the mountains at the base of the majestic Himalayas...and populated by the most colorfully-garbed and adorned people we had ever encountered.

Our aircraft carried a mixture of backpack-laden tourists ready to commence their Himalayan trekking upon disembarking, some sari-and-sweater Nepali women, an assortment of mustachioed gentlemen in layers of wool of varying pattern and color, high-ankled boots and Nepal's standard male headgear—the *topi*, an intentionally lopsided cloth hat of varying geometric designs woven into it, which is rather like a cross between a turban and a baseball cap without the visor. And then there was Frank—the only fellow in suit, tie and business shoes, ready for an afternoon of business calls.

We first amused ourselves with the "Flight to Enchantment" menu, and then admired the swiftly changing landscape beneath us: Thailand's flat emerald jungles and flooded rice paddies; Burma's muddy rivers and brown swirls of floody plains alternating with green jungly high spots, then its huge expanses of water and the incredible Irrawaddy River (wider than the Mississippi—and muddier, too) which we at first thought was a bay; and then over alternating breadths of water and land, equally wide, as if the earth couldn't decide whether to be firmament or sea. This, it turns out, is Bangladesh, which is water much of the year, just at the end of its monsoon season. But where were the Himalayas? We were due to land in 15 minutes and had not yet had a glimpse of the world's highest and most remote mountain range, even though we had selected our seats on the right-hand side of the aircraft with care. We suddenly realized that the fluffy white cumulus clouds spreading from beneath us to the horizon had tiny pointed peaks in the hazy distance—and then, slowly coming into focus, peak after peak of white and gray, endlessly dominating the horizon—the Himalayas! Glistening in the bright afternoon sun above the clouds, they inspired awe among us. Beautiful, quiet, cold and spectacular. "Everest? Where's Mount Everest?" No one peak was more grand than the others, as eight of the world's ten highest mountains were right here—in front of us. Everest appeared as a grayish pyramid surmounting white peaks beneath it. Actually it appeared shorter than its immediate neighbor, Mount Lhosa, as Everest is further away, behind the other peaks, striding the Nepal-Tibet border.

And then the landscape became even more incredible, if possible. As we descended into the Kathmandu Valley, we hovered over the most incredible display of terracing I have ever seen. The mountains seemed to ripple beneath us, the effect of thousands of narrow strips of mountainside farmland steps—absolutely unbelievable in their beauty, each a different shade of green or beige, each seemingly an impossible feat of earth-moving.

The Kathmandu Valley! Mystical mountain-rimmed strips of brown villages, fields of haystacks (we forget in eternally green Bangkok that it's harvest time in much of the world now). Pagodas, stupas, bricks, bricks, bricks! Grass sprouting from rooftops. Wooden doorways of all colors, old crumbly carvings… Bricks and dust. Dust and bricks. The rainy season is over and dust reigns till the onset of the next monsoon season. What a muddy mess this must be for half the year! Wonderful countryside of autumn golds and muted greens, figures in bright sarongs bent over the fields (men supervise here, as in much of the world). Rooftops sprout grass—houses need haircuts. Even temples are occasionally shorn of their grassy locks. Cows loll in the warmth of the midday sun, sauntering through the traffic, lazing on sidewalks.

Waiting under a tent for transportation in the super-sunny brilliant cool crisp air with local tribal people, we noticed right away how all Nepal seems divided between two kinds of people: Indian types from the lowlands to the south, masses of colorful saris, pierced noses, red dots on foreheads; and the more mountainous Tibetan hill peoples clad in homespun fabrics with brilliant chartreuse or orangey-red glass bead necklaces and large gold ornaments on the side of their noses, a different design for each tribal group. Women each wore a hip-length shiny black braid, the woman squatting in front of us (though there were empty chairs) with a terrycloth towel on her head.

You never know who you'll meet on the streets of Kathmandu

Yaks by the roadside, cows in the street. Wonderful carved wooden screens for windows, very like Egypt's *mashrabeya*! Even some rooftops appear terraced, with the Dutch zigzag borders. Bicycle rickshaws are painted in gaudy colors, their canopies torn and tattered. We walk by beautiful signs in lovely curlicue script, tile or corrugated rooftops and brightly painted wooden doorways reminiscent of Greek island houses. Occasionally, bare-backed men in loin-cloths squat cross-legged on platforms by the street—sewing? Oh! A glimpse of the brilliant orange-robed old fellow with waist-length blond beard, with bag, beads—right out of a movie. In fact, all of Kathmandu seems to be character actors in an other-worldly travel-mystical-adventure film!

Hard to believe that Nepal is the same latitude as Florida and Kuwait, even south of New Delhi! Imagine Mount Everest in Florida! Nepal is really three very different areas: to the south is the Terai, the northern part of the flat Ganges plain stretching from India, where most of the population and certainly the population explosion, exists. In fact, Buddha's birthplace is Lumbini, in the Terai. There the country abounds in elephant, tigers and rhinoceros. Next there is a strip of lower mountains to the north of the Terai. In these lowland mountains is nestled the incredible Kathmandu Valley, an odd mixture of terrain, climate and cultures. Is this the lost Shangri-La? Temperate crops of apples and potatoes co-exist with banana trees, orchids, frangipani and all those other wonderful tropical flora—all in the briskly invigorating winter air. Only here in the Kathmandu Valley do Buddhism and Hinduism combine to produce a religious and artistic tangle which is impossible to unravel. Erotic carvings adorn the wooden roof support struts of nearly every old Buddhist temple, though Buddhism aspired to go beyond the earthly and sensual world to a nirvana of the mind. Something went awry here. Meeting the plethora of Hindu gods, scary-faced creatures with numerous reincarnations, Buddhism somehow evolved here many years ago into Tantric Buddhism, reveling in the earthly, experiencing every imaginable sensation (in every possible position), as one can see from merely lifting one's eyes to the roof level of practically any really old building here! The proffered explanation is that the goddess of lightning was very chaste, so the profusion of incredibly erotic carvings served as a very effective lightning rod to protect the temples. Hmmm…I found that hard to believe.

Anyway, the third part of Nepal, and the one most of us think of, is of course the towering Himalayan mountain range, from the Annapurnas to the west to Everest to the northeast. Eighty per cent of Nepal consists of these tremendous mountains, clear to the border with Tibet. The Himalayas block the monsoon moisture from reaching Tibet, so though they share the mountains and border each other, Tibet is high, dry and dusty, while Nepal has a variety of seasons from hot muggy summers of torrential rain to the more pleasant fall trekking season, cold (everything unheated) winters, and cloudy cool spring. The country lacks a road system—who would even attempt it? So the air schedule is frequently interrupted as aircraft are commandeered to attend to needs in outlying districts, as we discovered after our long wait for a flight around Mount Everest. It was cancelled, as about 50% of the flights are.

The Royal Nepal Telecommunications Central Office—wonderful! An old brick and wooden house whose wooden walls inside are shades of green and blue. Tile, carpet and linoleum vie for floor space. Secretaries and receptionists wear heavy sweaters over their delicately flowing saris. Fall's brilliant golden chrysanthemums line the balcony; curtains cover doorways in an anti-draft campaign. We sat in a small green wooden room with high-beamed ceilings surrounded by sweater- and jacket-clad men in their multi-colored topis, the Nepali national hat. A wonderful long white-bearded gentleman with cane in thigh-thick knee-tight white pants and tunic under heavy black-wool Nehru knee-length overcoat seated himself next to me and commenced chewing nuts. Frank's laughter echoed from the managing director's office next door. The "gentleman" across the room tested his ballpoint pen on the blue and green patterned slipcovers. Satisfied with the black streak it produced on his chair, he progressed to paper. Every room, every wall was a different color, different texture. Indian-style music played in the background of this new language of unfamiliar sounds (like a choppy Slavic-Italian) written in squiggles and swirls with a horizontal line through the center of each word. Creaking doors and muffled footfalls broke the silence. Grimy photos of the King and Queen adorned the outer wall, while the bright red plastic wastebasket was the room's focal point. My goodness! The managing director's office! Egypt seems cosmopolitan by comparison. But I like the oldness, the sun, the chrysanthemums on the balcony, the general worn-outness of it all.

"Don't expose your knees here," advised Frank as I glanced at my protruding white kneecaps between my conservative blue knee socks and my conservative blue culottes. I stood up in order to veil the offending joints. One never knows what part of the body will offend (or arouse) in other cultures.

Telephone service? The assistant hotel manager's vacant expression when Frank inquired about placing a local call should have clued us in earlier. When we later asked again, she said, "Oh, it is always like this in Kathmandu." No one expects to call, because they know they can't. So Frank's planned afternoon of business calls to set up appointments was transformed into a series of taxi rides—much more efficient! No one seemed to mind his appearing unannounced; it seems to be the mode of operation around here.

So Frank interviewed while I sipped typical Nepali tea—like hot chocolate, only tea!—thick, whitish and sweet, with tea, milk and sugar all boiled together Nepalese style, just the thing for a long afternoon in a drafty unheated government office. This was the first of many such teas we were to consume during our days in Kathmandu; our other favorite beverage was "lassi," a sweetened yoghurt drink with which we began every day (along with my breakfast of curried potatoes in a giant crispy crepe to be dipped into a hot grated coconut dip and chased down by an even hotter lentil-cauliflower soup). The yoghurt did its job very well and neither of us was plagued with the "Kathmandu Quickstep."

Nepal's offices and shops open at 10 A.M., partially because one would freeze in the unheated offices before then and be unable to read in the early morning light (many offices have no electricity—in fact, only in 1982 did the country offer 24-hour electric service). Also, the morning is an important family time in Nepal, the world's only Hindu kingdom: Various family members apply the "*tika*" (red spot on the forehead) to relatives, daughters-in-law wash their mothers-in-law's feet (this is devout Brahmin practice), and everyone consumes a huge breakfast which must last them until dinnertime. (It was a bit confusing for us to set our watches to the new time, as Nepal in one hour and 15 minutes behind Bangkok. The 15 minutes is to establish it as a separate country from India, timewise if not otherwise.) Nepalis have extended holidays as well as shortened workdays; perhaps that's the secret of the people's general serenity, kindness and politeness—a surfeit of holidays! Hardly a week goes by without a religious (how many Hindu deities are there?) or royal holiday.

Our first day in Nepal ended in great success—we managed to track down the Maddens, our good friends from Egypt who were in Nepal on a three-month assignment, from these specific directions: "We're staying in a hotel on a hill on the way to a temple where there are many monkeys." Thank goodness there is only one major hilltop temple in Kathmandu, the Swayambhuhat, an incredible collection of structures whose gilt pointed roofs gleam in the sunlight from miles away and whose naughty monkeys grab any change or snacks one may have left after climbing up the hundreds of steps with alms-collecting monks seated on every third step. We found them in a wonderful place ("more of a cultural experience than a hotel" said our guidebook) of old bricks, wooden carvings, a library with its resident multilingual swami sitting lotus-like on a shelf in the lobby, swaddled in white cloth with wonderful white hair and beard coursing down his chest. Thus began four days of roaming the ancient old city squares and winding alleyways with Annita and three-year-old Aaron, while Frank interviewed telephone people and eventually joined us on our explorations of Kathmandu's rich and varied architectural heritage, crammed with people whose colorful garb would put peacocks to shame and full of exotic old and new wares beckoning us.

We began our adventures by heading for the old royal square of Patan, Kathmandu's sister city to the south, just over the river, the Buddhist heart of Kathmandu Valley, where we planned to stop for a few minutes before heading off in other directions. Four or five hours later, as the sun was setting, we dragged ourselves away with a promise to return the next day. Such faces! Costumes! This was the time of harvest, apparent from local people strolling by, with mountainous mounds of hay yoked on shoulders in baskets, to the stooped old women threshing golden grains of rice in one corner of the square, surrounded by ragged children, bare-bottomed. Purple saris! Green bridal-beads! Color! Life! Sunshine! Pure clear blue skies. Crisp breeze. Cows wandering at will, munching and snoozing wherever they chose, their foreheads adorned with a red third eye as well.

But the square itself—an incredible series of temples and pagodas, bells tinkling off roof corners, sunlight gleaming off *chedis* and domes, elephant sculptures, fiercesome orange gods protruding from building facades, wonderfully carved wooden roof supports (whose erotic interminglings I somehow overlooked in the profusion of impressions bombarding me), intricate wooden screens on balcony windows, tiled rooftops sprouting tufts of grass. Just too, too, too much to absorb! And all lovely! Sunken squares—huge—with marble fountains for people to wash themselves, their clothes, and to get water. Giant bells, twenty-foot-high poles supporting golden Buddhas with cobra-heads protecting them as umbrellas. Pagoda-style brick temples with wonders of art carved on each successive layer. Magenta-robed monks with bright golden-orange sashes. All this, and the Himalayan foothills in the distance.

Vendors! Vendors! I ignored them completely for the first several hours as I used up our entire supply of film on this first stop at Patan, "the town with a thousand golden roofs," as it as been known for centuries. Gaudy papier-mâché masks of Hindu deities for festival celebrations, Sherpa knives, religious paintings bursting with hundreds of miniscule Buddhas in all possible positions, prayer wheels, jewelry, brass Buddha statues, on and on and on—interspersed with vegetables and fabrics for the local market. We finally vowed to leave, but stopped to glance under one of the many flapping tent roofs to view the long red tassels to be woven into the single hip-length braid of most local women. These contrasted brilliantly with the profusion of tiny glass beads of all colors displayed beneath…well, several hours and many necklaces later, we gathered our strings and loops and ropes of beads all custom made to our specifications as we sat on the tent floor watching the beadmen's skill in looping strings round their calloused toes and fingers, transferring beads here and there and wrapping silk and cotton threads with a primitive lathe-type string-twister at an unbelievably quick pace. These brilliant bridal beads which I had so often admired on local women in the last twenty-four hours were now—in smaller ropes and subtler colors—mine! Local women watched us and admired our necklaces as we admired theirs. However, we would eventually remove ours—while theirs remain around their necks for life, not removed even during bathing.

That night all of us visited the second of what was to become our "golden triangle" of haunts we daily returned to—Thamel Road, a series of twisting alleyways of $2-4/night hotels and shops, Kathmandu's hippie-haven of the past, and now trekkers' hideout of used hiking and climbing equipment, tiny restaurants of surprisingly good and inexpensive food of all kinds, shops of hand-knitted sweaters in every color and design, colorfully striped local cottons and bright patchwork jackets (Frank ordered custom-made local shirts for $2 each!) As night fell, we found ourselves increasingly burdened—two large wooden masks here, some marionettes there, two thangkas (Tibetan religious paintings)…and at last Frank concluded his major purchase after four hours of on-and-off negotiating—a "singing bowl" and cymbals which look exceedingly plain but emit the most otherworldly ring which lingers long after most sounds fade and can be increased by running one's finger around the rim of the bowl. Composed of a mysterious mixture of metals, it surely reflects the mystical atmosphere we associate with Nepal and Himalayan Tibetan monks, mystics and religion—I can hear the sound echoing through the empty mountainsides from monastery to monastery.

Now one must superimpose on all the foregoing a most particular and pervasive odor, which lingers still on our Nepali purchases now at home in Bangkok and which rushes forth to assail my nostrils every time I open my Nepal journal. "Eau de Nepal" I had been calling it. I have now been informed by a Dutch Nepali resident that it is the smell of yak butter, which has endless uses in Nepal (and is surely smeared on the surface of every item I have purchased). I was never totally unaware of this pungent odor during our entire stay in Nepal, and it is the one aspect of the country that I do not reflect upon with nostalgia.

Kathmandu's Durbar (Royal) Square—a stunning collection of multi-tiered square-roofed pagodas perched upon tiered foundations of grass, stone and brick surrounding the impressive old palace (the new one in use now is elsewhere, resembling a surrealistic building from a 1960s James Bond movie) of numerous courtyards and overpowering buildings. Thirty? forty? fifty? wonderful old buildings, each one a work of art, appear as one rounds the corners through crowds of brilliant saris, mountain folk ablaze with golden nose florettes, silver coins, bright red and black clothes. Local daily life pulsates through these ancient walkways, and the age-old temples are still in use. The tiny corner Hindu shrines seemed the most popular, crammed with people with flowers, candles and esoterica. Incense, strange twangy music, crowds and crowds of people, too many vendors and potential moneychangers. Wonderful things for sale, probably most of them fake, flute-sellers carrying poles sprouting thirty or so wooden Nepali flutes from the top like a tiered umbrella with flutes for spokes. One corner of the square was roped off—the Las Vegas of Nepal—as men and boys played board games with crowds looking on. (In contrast, the major entertainment down the street in the "new city" was the local Kodak shop which always had a crowd of people looking in the window to see photographs roll out of the developing machine—a true moving picture show!)

One of the royal square's many old interesting buildings was the home of the Kamari, the "living goddess," chosen every few years from among four- and five-year-old girls who have never shed blood. Once the Kamari is chosen, she lives in this medieval house of wonderful carvings (with her laundry hanging out the window) and may not leave except for religious ceremonies once a year in which her feet may not touch the ground. She is then bedecked with jewels, and thousands upon thousands of people crowd the square to get a glimpse of the living goddess. The rest of the year she lives in relative isolation and reigns until puberty when the "impurity" of her first blood disqualifies her for this role which she has lived since early childhood (unless, of course she skins a knee or cuts a finger—then she is immediately dethroned). I've heard that "used living goddesses" have a hard time finding husbands—imagine living with one after a childhood like this!

Our other "find" of the trip was Pie Alley, a dingy-looking local alley with occasional pie shops operated by former cooks of foreign families who had truly mastered—and surpassed—the skills of producing scrumptious brownies and fluffy pies. We made this a daily 4 P.M. "must." Where else could you order three teas, a giant brownie and three gigantic pieces of pie for a total of $1? Our tips exceeded our bill each day.

So our only trekking was through the ancient royal squares and winding alleyways. We heard second-hand the tales of glorious mountain scenery and exhilarating treks. We hope someday to experience this other side of Nepal, to add to our already overwhelming impressions of this most remote, exotic, colorful and historic crossroad of peoples, architecture, and terrain which has so captivated us during our brief introduction to it. We *have* to go back—we missed the "yeti," Nepal's legendary abominable snowman!

Culture clash at the top of the world—an old woman threshes grain with her bare feet, with a young student in knee-socks in the background, as a western tourist—who seems to be wearing no pants at all—blithely photographs the surroundings

Our aircraft was abuzz during the return flight with tired and happy trekkers relating their various mountain routes, encounters and ordeals. We gazed again at the majestic Himalayas and sat silently as Everest seemed to linger in our porthole window…and then disappear in the clouds beneath. I tried to jot a few farewell impressions in my travel journal; then we all stripped off our layers of clothing, removing knee-socks from inside sandals, stuffing jackets and sweaters and scarves into bags in anticipation of Bangkok's sultry welcome. The diamond-nosed stewardess in sari bowed to us as we disembarked.

Heads or Tails?

Just as the head is regarded as the temple of the body in Thailand (because it is closest to the heavens), the feet are the lowest and considered the most unclean part of the body. That's why one would never think of entering anyone's house without first removing one's shoes. It's amusing to go to a dinner party and figure out who's already there by looking at the shoes piled up outside the doorway. The only time you see someone in shoes is in the street, stores or office—never ever, ever, ever in a residence. This is amusing also because the handmade shoes here are quite wonderful—in every design and material, carefully sculpted to fit your feet perfectly (a boon for me, with one foot larger than the other). So you buy these wonderful shoes, made especially for each individual foot, and to match whatever dress you like—and then you take them off before going inside to the party! Everyone stands around, cocktail in hand, shoeless. (You can bet no one goes out with a hole in his sock here!) And of course it's way too hot for nylons, so the carefully pedicured women are barefoot in their evening gowns.

It is also considered disrespectful to point to something—but not nearly as bad as showing the sole of one's foot, because the hand is not nearly as bad as the lowly foot. These subtle distinctions are taken into consideration in the curious protocol and regimentation involved in doing laundry. I was curious as to why our clothes were washed in such tiny little batches, leaving our large American GE washer practically empty with each of its numerous daily loads of wash. As it turns out, Dog Mai our maid explained, the clothes were washed according to proper Thai laundry etiquette—grouped according to the parts of the body they covered. All the above-the-waist items were washed together (I forgot to ask if they separated masculine and feminine attire), the underwear was in another batch, and socks were washed separately—probably no one wanted to touch them. The "bad" clothes from the lower parts of the body, and most especially underwear and socks, the most lowly of all, must never be left anywhere in a high position (so throwing one's socks and underwear on the floor is, I guess, an act of politeness and respect here). In fact, there are even two clotheslines, a high one for most clothes and a lower one for underwear and socks so they won't contaminate more respectable apparel by touching them while drying. In trying to ease

Dog Mai's burden, I think I horrified her by suggesting she just throw everything in together in the washer.

Well, this brings us to the right-left situation, as well. As in Burma, where one walks clockwise around the pagoda, always keeping the Buddha to one's right, right is GOOD, and left is BAD. Do good things with the right hand. Do bad things with the left hand. (I wonder what happens to left-handed people here…) One always presents and accepts a gift with the right hand (and one never opens it in the presence of the gift-giver). One eats with the right hand. One cleanses oneself with the left. But the worst—to me—is that the man must always sleep on the right side of the bed…and the woman on the left! (I reversed the curse—and insisted on inhabiting the right side of our bed. What must our poor maids have thought of these crazy foreigners who mixed "good" and "bad" clothes and slept backwards?) Also, a woman must not "contaminate" a monk by touching him, so if it is the woman offering food to a monk, she must first lay the food on a table, or even on the ground, and then the monk will pick it up. On the train to Chiang Mai in northern Thailand, my friend Karen and I saw a young monk in the last compartment (monks ride free). We tried to make some merit by giving him a banana, but I don't remember if we handed it to him (thereby canceling any merit we hoped to gain) or if we put it on the seat beside him. Let's hope we did it right and earned some Buddhist brownie points.

Nearly a semester of daily 7 A.M. Thai lessons—and I'm still tongue-Thai'd! I can master much of the grammar, and I enjoy the curvaceous "alphabet" (forty-four consonants alone!) with some of its letters resembling elephant prods and other Thai objects. I can even transliterate a bit from Thai writing to the English alphabet—but I can't for the life of me hear or reproduce the nine types of tones which define this illusive language. Thai children learn words in certain tones (going up, going down, staying the same, going up slowly, going down slowly, staying the same twice as long—and three other variations), so the tone is embedded with the word's meaning. Leah is learning from the maids and street vendors in this manner—she always says the same word with the exact same inflection. We westerners learn a word—and then use various tones to express feelings, such as anger, confusion or pleasure. (Thai's say each sentence smoothly and with the same inflection. To express emotion, they may add to the end of the sentence a word which means "said with great feeling," etc.) Here is a sentence in Thai: "*Mai mai mai mai.*" Some "*mai's*" go up, some go down, some are quick and some linger. The sentence means: "Raw silk burns slowly." Any Thai would understand this clearly without confusion. And any Thai would NEVER confuse one "*mai*" with another "*mai*," as the tone defines the word. Well, I had never considered myself tone-deaf before, but as far as the Thai language is concerned, that about says it. And so my attempts at the language resulted in unintended statements, as my voice went up where it should have gone down, or held a sylla-ble just a split-second too long or too short.

Also reflected in the language is the façade of politeness with which the culture is infused. There is no word for "no," as I learned during my initial stay here at the hotel when I replied "No, thank you" to the housemaid's offer to turn down the bed, in the process unintentionally offending her. Everything is smooth and polite. Everyone seems sweet and accommodating. Frank learned at the office, however, that this polite approach is actually more difficult to deal with than the headstrong and vocal Egyptian style of doing business. At least in Egypt you know where they stand. Here, one must try to read between the lines and all the "yes's" to decipher what they really mean. Since it is considered offensive and impolite (thereby causing one to lose face) to object to a suggestion or even to question something, people always smile and agree—and then do what they want to, anyway. A friend of ours who taught English at Thammasat University said the most difficult thing for her to overcome was the cultural predilection to polite acceptance of anything the instructor said. It was so difficult to stimulate class discussion because asking a question implied criticism of the teacher—that he or she was not explaining adequately. At long last, she managed to persuade her stu-dents to speak up, and they were most excited to participate in this novel form of instruction.

While everything is civil and agreeable on the surface, there is still "trouble in paradise." Since one's outlets for expressing disagreement, discontent or frustra-tion are mostly precluded by the culture, other more nefarious ways of handling disagreements are common. Nearly every day there is a newspaper account of a drive-by shooting, usually from a motorcycle. These articles usually conclude with the line: "It is believed to be business-related." Someone thought he was treated without respect and lost face—hence, another assassination in the streets. We knew a German hotel manager who had to flee the country because one of his employees was dismissed. The employee hired someone to kill the hotel man-ager, and when the plot failed, the police suggested that the manager "leave town" for his safety, as the employee couldn't regain face until the manager was dead. Finally, an acceptable solution was found which satisfied Thai cultural mores—and allowed the manager to live. Someone contacted employee's GRANDFATHER, who then forbade his grandson to kill the manager, thereby saving face for the employee—as it was unthinkable to disobey the head of the family. *"Jai yen"* means "cool heart" and that is the goal of this non-confrontational society, in which criticism or openly displaying anger or impatience in public is seriously frowned upon.

And so, never a voice raised, no emotion expressed (watch out for giggling, though—that is reserved for discomfort or embarrassment and is frequently a reaction to bad news). One can sometimes observe a Thai whispering *"Jai yen"* to another Thai when it appears that someone is becoming excitable, which in the eyes of a Thai shows weakness and lack of mental control. Those two little words will bring him down to earth, and everything will again be peacefully polite and civil. (Who knows, however, what is planned behind the scenes?)

In addition to being refined and polite, Thai society is extremely rigid in its classifications. One must always know how far to *"wai,"* or bow with palms together in front of one's chest, neck or face, depending on the relative status of the person one is greeting—the higher (or older) the person, the higher the level of one's hands. Within thirty seconds, most Thai's can establish who's on top in the *wai*-ing protocol through a series of questions. Since one's family, in addition to profession and domicile, is also important in establishing rank, much of the questioning relates to relatives. There is no one word for "aunt" or for "uncle." There are, however, separate words for the younger sister of the mother, the second younger sister of the mother, the older sister of the father, the younger brother of the mother...ad infinitum. Each relative is placed precisely in the line-up. From this, one can assess who's older and younger, who's related to the father or the mother...and therefore who has to *wai* higher or lower to the other one. This is very comforting, actually, as one can relax when one knows his rightful place and needn't worry about the embarrassment of bowing too low or not low enough—and NEVER to young people or inferiors, as this would be considered very foolish indeed. A simple nod will suffice.

King Chulalongkorn (Rama V), 1868-1910, the enlightened son of King Mongkut (Rama IV) 1851-1868 of *The King and I*, liberated his populace from the requirement, punishable by death if not obeyed, of lying prostrate whenever in the king's presence. I had always admired the many small carved figures of top-knotted Thai's looking up from their crouched position on knees and arms—until I realized that this was the standard posture for servants through the years. It's not too far off today, actually, as I learned from experience. How smoothly the young Thai women greeted the older woman I was seated next to at a private dinner. Their graceful dropping to their knees, so their heads would be lower than hers, was practically unnoticeable. And then I noticed that whenever I was served, the server slid to her knees before putting the food on my plate. Same thing for the beverage. But it was all so smooth—really quite amazing—that I was nearly oblivious to what was happening. The protocol of ascertaining and maintaining proper head levels is essential to Thai society. A friend tells of her husband's back ailment and how he lay down on the living room floor to relieve his back pain. It took them a while to figure out why the servants kept slithering and crawling across the floor whenever they entered the room—they were trying to keep their heads lower than his!

The head is considered sacred and should NEVER be touched. Not only is it the part of the body closest to the heavens, but it is the location of the *kwan*, the spirit which resides in the head and protects people from illness and harm. This spirit is protected by one's hair, so traditionally the hair over the place on a child's head where the skull bones don't quite meet was never cut during childhood, leaving Thai children with the trademark topknot seen in statues and paintings, and occasionally in real life today (again formally categorized, as everything else here seems to be, into four styles, ranging from a long thick braid to a simple tuft of hair tied in a knot). The pulse beat seen in a child's head where the skull bones meet is regarded as evidence of the presence of the *kwan*. Topknots are cut off in a special ceremony at puberty, although one would think that with the many problems encountered in adolescence, one would need protection for one's *kwan* even more! I guess that's where teenage long hair comes in.

I witnessed an assault on a royal *kwan* aboard our bus in Burma when someone accidentally touched the head of a Thai princess while retrieving something from the overhead compartment. This was not a major princess, you see, but one of the masses of lower-level but nonetheless bona fide royal progeny one finds throughout the country. "PRINCESS ON BOARD!" we were all informed at the beginning of the tour, so we would show proper respect. The brouhaha that ensued when her head was ever so slightly touched by someone trying to reach the overhead rack—well, it seemed as if all hell had broken loose, especially in this quiet-mannered society. The tour guide had to intercede and soothe, and we had to rearrange the seating on the bus to keep the culprit at a distance from the princess for the rest of the week-long tour. The princess had suffered the ultimate insult—and by a westerner, to boot!

Jared certainly doesn't bow to the young royal in his first grade class. A rather plump child, certainly raised with the privileges of his station, he is—I think—some form of prince. But then there are SO many semi-princes and people of rank around that it becomes very confusing. This is due to the many multiple wives of kings in earlier times. It takes a while for a title to be whittled away to nothing. Here's how it goes. There are five grades of inherited royal Thai titles in this most elaborate system of royal rank of any country in the world. There are three distinct ranks of Prince and Princess, but even within each rank there are finer distinctions which divide the members into different sub-groups. The first one is easy—the *Chao Fa* are the children of a king or queen. Then come the *Phra Ong Chao*, grandchildren of a king, who either have the word *Chao* repeated in their title or not—for example, "Phra Chao Vorawongse Ther Phra Ong Chao," which means Prince or Princess and Royal Highness, OR just plain ole "Phra Vorawongse Ther Phra Ong Chao," which translates as Prince or Princess and Highness—minus the important word "Royal." Next come the *Mom Chao*, the lowest of the royal ranks and the usual title of a grandchild of a king, except where raised to be a Phra Ong Chao. Here's where it begins to get tricky: in the case of a great-grandchild of a king who is a Mom Chao, then he or she is the child of a Phra Ong Chao prince, who is himself a grandchild of a king, and—as Yul Brynner would say in *The King and I*: "Et cetera, et cetera and et cetera...." The great-grandchildren of a king do not have royal rank but are entitled to use the title of *Mom Rajawongse,* which is not translated into English. The great-great-grandchildren have the title of *Mom Luang.* Subsequent generations in the male line of descent from a king have no titles—thank God, as this is getting VERY confusing—but they are allowed to attach an honorific to their name denoting the surname of the branch of the royal family from which they descend. I don't know where Jared's little friend fits into this system, but everyone is quite aware that he is special. (It didn't help him make friends in first grade, though. Children are naturally quite democratic!)

Yes, titles are very important here, and honorifics abound. I was instructed to *wai* especially low, with hands held especially high, to a *"khun ying,"* an older woman with a distinguished title which she received either for being related to the king—or was it for some service she had performed? Well, whatever the reason, it was most impressive, and one never used her given name...just "the Khun Ying did this..." and "the Khun Ying did that...."

Even the name of the city of Bangkok reflects the importance which Thai's attach to titles. Thai's call their capital Krung Thep (City of Angels), not Bangkok. The official Thai name for the city appears in the *Guiness Book of Records* as the longest place name in the world: "Krungthep Mahanakorn Boworn Rattanakosin Mahintharayuttha Mahadilokpop Noparatratchathani Burirom Udomratchaniveymahasathan Amornpiman Avatransathit Sakkathattiay-avis-nukarmprasit." This translates (move over, Los Angeles) as "Great city of angels; the repository of divine gems; the great land unconquerable; the grand and prominent realm; the royal and delightful capital full of nine noble gems; the highest royal dwelling and grand palace; the divine shelter and living place of reincarnated spirits." Notice that the plebian word "Bangkok," which comes from Bang Makok, meaning "Place of the Olive Plums," does not appear. It is not worthy of this majestic and magical city whose citizens must indeed hold their heads high!

On the Way to Mandalay

December 1985

BURMA! The Golden Land…Grandpa Burnham should have been with us, descending over the flat green landscape with occasional golden pagoda spires piercing the skyline. Grandpa, who always sang "I'm on my way to Mandalay," would have realized a dream (or perhaps dispelled it) had he been with us in our adventurous "barefoot in the dark" explorations of Burma's magnificent temples and pagodas, long-standing reminders of the wealth of riches and culture which this now poor and isolated socialist country accumulated over the centuries.

RANGOON—A city frozen in time, with all the trappings of the British colonial period—straight streets, squares, parks, wonderful old brick and stone arched and colonnaded buildings, tree-lined boulevards—all standing in a state of dilapidated grace, thirsty for a bucket of paint and good cleaning. As with Cairo, Beirut and so many other once wonderful cities, one looks around and sighs, "How lovely it must have been." But Rangoon is lucky—the buildings still stand (no new ones to replace them), the trees still spread their leaf-laden boughs over city streets, and the rust-red tropical sunset still silhouettes the great golden pagoda spires left from ages past.

It was fun to walk into another time-zone: the low white stucco airport—all one room with great heavy cane-backed teak benches which have supported many a straight-laced British overlord and prim colonial madam. Babies' and ladies' cheeks and foreheads are streaked with beige swipes of the dried thanaga bark powder which supposedly has a cooling (as well as beautifying?) effect. All men with the exception of soldiers wear *longyi's*, the national dress—an ankle length wide tube of fabric folded over twice at the waist and tied in various knots reflecting sections of the country. All men wear the same rubber-soled straw-bottomed burgundy velvet strapped thongs. "You'll love the temples in Pagan and Mandalay," said the British woman next to me, ready to fly off to Bangkok for R&R. "Do you like to climb hundreds of stairs?" queried her 10-year-old son, looking grimly prophetic. (He didn't add that I would have to do it all barefoot and with a viper awaiting me on one step.)

Outside into Rangoon proper, full of old fin-tailed American monster sedans and whiskey and cigarette traders assaulting us, and kids, kids, kids in search of anything they could get from these strange white long-nosed foreigners. Into an unbelievably old bus whose seatbacks rose to the middle of our backs, without knee space or air conditioning. Adventure! We drove on the right as in the U.S., but the bus's steering wheel was on the right, as in the UK—one way of asserting independence from their former colonial ruler—but it would help if the leftover vehicles cooperated. Our bus was adorned with a row of tiny bells hanging from a string across the entire windshield, surmounted by two peacock feathers over the rearview mirror. Developing countries' buses are always full of wonderful expressions of the driver's personality.

We drove through the wide tree-covered, palm-lined streets of Rangoon, full of old colonial-style arched and colonnaded buildings, gracefully decrepit. Barefoot monks walked by, heads lowered, food bowls pressed to their chests. Dogs abound, as they seem to in most Buddhist countries, looking just as pathetic here as elsewhere—and nary a cat in sight. Old villas, in fantasy style with thousands of tiny paned windows and large balconies all adorned with gingerbread, created a black and crumbly Disneyland effect.

SHWEDAGON PAGODA—a marvel of golden spired and tiered pagodas, gilded Buddhas and temple bells all resting on a fourteen-acre marble terrace of a hilltop sliced off millennia ago for the incredible 300-foot-high 2500-year-old golden pagoda encasing eight hairs of Gautama Buddha and topped with 2400 rubies, emeralds and diamonds, and then an orb of 4351 diamonds (1800 carats) topped by a single 76-carat diamond! All these were so high they were out-of-sight as well as out-of-reach. Amazing contrasts in this poor country. This incredible place, center of living Buddhism as well as a repository of thousands of years of faith, drew us back for every sunrise and sunset in Rangoon. How could we never have heard of this before? The Taj Mahal, which all western children learn about in school, pales into insignificance next to this majestic dome and hundreds of gold-spired shrines, each a work of art in itself.

Shwedagon! A magic word for our group. "See you at lunch." "No, I think I'll take a cab over to Shwedagon for a while." Like a magnet, this wonder drew us away from sleep, shopping, all other pursuits. And, unfortunately, I cannot begin to describe it, jut as all our photographs fail to suggest the grandeur, the immensity yet the coziness and warmth of a place where one sees only a tiny portion from any angle as one circumambulates this giant pagoda clockwise around the marble terrace.

Barefoot in the Dark! Much of our Burmese adventure was spent this way, including sunrises and late evenings at Shwedagon. Here, one removes shoes outside the temple grounds, so our shoes were always on the bus while we were mincing tip-toed over the gravelly streets, up the hundreds of temple steps (hoping that devout Buddhists had made merit by sweeping away dog droppings and red splotches of betel-nut expectorations before us), and onto the vast circular marbled terrace with robed monks and worshippers anointing Buddha images and offering flowers, paper umbrellas, fruit. We were truly transported into the scene, usually the only tourists at any site, as Burma admits few tourists—30,000 per year—and limits their stay to seven days.

Shwedagon is a vast assortment of hundreds of magnificent temples, shrines and spires, each one a jewel in itself, surrounding the great central pagoda, which was now scaffolded in a graceful latticework of bamboo for re-gilding. A hilltop was flattened thousands of years ago to accommodate the great marble terrace upon which these buildings now stand. Surrounding the great solid central pagoda, towering into the sky, are 68 small rust-colored arched and colonnaded squarish buildings with Buddha statues inside, *nats* (Burmese guardian spirits) of mirrored mosaic or bright colors, steps, two guardian lions—and of course topped by a glistening tall pagoda-shaped spire with golden umbrellas and thirty or so bells on top of that. Each little building represents one of Burma's 37 *nats* and so represents a day of the week with corresponding direction, planet, animal, personality traits. (It's important in Burma, critical I should say, to know the day of the week on which you were born. And there are eight weekdays here: Sunday, Monday, Tuesday, Wednesday A.M., Saturday, Thursday, Friday, Wednesday P.M.—in that order! One's name is chosen with regard to the weekday of the birth and bears no connection to one's parents' names. A Burmese meeting another Burmese could tell the weekday of his birth by the initials of his name. And under no circumstances would a Wednesday's child, for example, marry a Saturday child, as their corresponding animals are the snake and the rat, and therefore the marriage would be an unhealthy balance of temperaments, as the snake devours the rat. [How many Burmese Romeos and Juliets have been deterred from romance because of the days of their births?])

These little shrines are surrounded by statues on poles, Buddhas to be anointed, altars.... Around all this is a circular altar railing, hundreds of feet round, and then a wide marble walkway around which everyone walks clockwise, keeping the Buddha relics always to one's right (the good side in Asia—eat with right hand, wash up with left; man sleeps on the right, woman on left). To one's left, as one walks around the great circle, filling in the rest of the gigantic terrace, are hundreds of ornate pagodas of every style and shape and color, towers, glittering mirrored structures, old carved wooden ones...all open with arches and colonnades, all housing golden Buddhas in every size and mudra (stylized position, each of which signifies a different aspect of the Buddha, such as compassion or teaching).

Take this basic scene, fill it with incense, flowers, the hum of mumbled and chanted prayer, robed monks, the faithful all in ankle-length *longyi's*...and you don't even begin to capture the magnificence, the magic, the grandeur of it all....

Bells, bell, bells! Poe would be happy with the tintinnabulation of the bells, bells, bells of Burma! Huge bronze bells appear at every turning in the temple grounds. Tiny bells adorn royal garments in the museum. Our bus's windshield is strung with bells of all sizes. Stupas and pagodas and golden umbrellas over Buddha images are festooned with wires of bells, like streamers of a May Day pole, with thousands of bells tinkling and fluttering in the breeze. The spell of bells was with us, and our suitcase swelled daily with the addition of rectangular, round, oblong, circular, clappered, non-clappered, ball-bearing bells. The Bells of Burma!

The Strand Hotel—we were thrilled to complete the trilogy of grand old hotels in Southeast Asia. Having visited Raffles in Singapore and, of course, the Oriental in Bangkok, we were excited to check into the Strand in Rangoon, where Somerset Maugham and others spent many sweltering months in this high-ceilinged fern-filled grand old lady of hostelry. Of course, the ferns were gone (no frills in a socialist country), but the shape of our room with 15-foot-high salon and walk-in wardrobe swept us into an age of steamer trunks and prolonged voyages. Best of all, our mosquito coils worked!

Buddhism in action: A young girl stops to turn over a 4-5-inch beetle which has flipped onto its back. An old monk tries in vain to sprinkle powder on the huge bloody wound of a dog on the temple grounds. Faithful Buddhists anoint the hundreds of Buddha statues with water, cleansing the earthly dust from the statues' serene features. Some make merit by purchasing and then releasing small birds sold at the temple gates—Frank made some merit this way, and the little birdie promptly returned to its cage after a momentary flutter, awaiting the next opportunity to let someone gain merit by freeing it again. Flowers, fruit, the usual offerings are given in abundance. Our tour bus and a huge truck were both at a standstill on the busy street corner, honking at a tiny pup standing in the road between them. Neither hulking vehicle moved until a passerby rescued the pup and removed him from the road. Life is sacred to Buddhists, even animal life, as each life is a soul working its way to nirvana through accumulated good deeds and soul-searching in each of many existences. If you really blow it in one life, you might turn up as a lower creature in the next one. Accept one's fate in this existence, make merit, and you'll be on a higher level in the next life. This philosophy is possible in countries whose history and buildings are measured in millennia and whose concept of time spans millions of years. The most recent Buddha, Gautama, for example, has been the Buddha for this present age of about 2500 years. He accumulated merit in five hundred previous lives to reach this stage. And—he is the 28th recorded teaching Buddha that we are aware of. We know of many of these others—so time and history are immense here in Asia. People, by comparison, are so insignificant that it is comprehensible to think in terms of multiple existences and gargantuan time spans.

Just as everyone tells us that Bangkok is not Thailand, we can say that Rangoon is not Burma. A short flight on half of Burma's domestic aircraft (a Fokker Friendship prop plane) took us to the farthest limit any visitor can legally go, the border of Burma's Shan State, a rebel-controlled smugglers' paradise self-ruled mini-kingdom and center of lucrative business, the eastern tip of the Golden Triangle: the Shan (old Burmese word for Siam) State near the north-western Thai border, where sweaters, towels and blankets are wrapped around the hill tribe residents to stave off the chill of the mountain air.

The Shan Plateau was once a popular hill station resort area for colonialists trying to cool off from Burma's sultry jungle heat. They never came here in December, I am sure! I wore all my clothes (and half of Frank's) simultaneously and shivered through our short stay in Taunggyi, capital of the Shan State, which comprises most of the notorious Golden Triangle. The high altitude and European climate make this area ideal for growing poppies. The Burmese government has no control over the Golden Triangle. In fact, the Burma Communist Party controls the opium trade! The name *Shan* (*Siam* in Thailand and *Assam* in India) means "free people." Feudal principalities ruled in splendor until 1959, when the government jailed many of them. Now the "Shan Independence Army" wants to reclaim the area. The "Shan State Army" controls the Thai border and is in charge of the massive smuggling of goods from Thailand and of old Burmese artifacts and temple carvings into Thailand. The Shans are Buddhist, not animist like most hill tribes. Shans wear bath-towel turbans, both men and women, and we were to see many of these.

Typical Burmese houses of split bamboo woven into different patterns—plaid, herringbone—rested on stilts and cost $16-50, a lot when you consider the average yearly income of $88 and the lifetime of a well-built house at around eight years. They were lovely, like gift-wrapped boxes each in a different design, all in earthen hues. Huge white Brahmin bulls pulled bullock carts with wide wooden wheels. Children sported long green *longyi*'s (the long tube skirt), standard school uniform. Gorges wrapped in vines broke our ascent up the steep hillside through coffee and teak plantations. Tiny new teak trees looked weighted down by their oversize leaves. In the distance, fields of grayish-purple—sugarcane plantations—were interspersed with the brilliant yellow-gold of sesame fields.

Through the morning fog and chill, we descended the steep hills from Taung-gyi, passing most of the population which must have arisen in the dark, past a convoy of huge army trucks with fresh flowers tied to their outer mirrors and headlights—only in Burma! The weekly market! Into the crowds of bark-faced, towel-turbaned, cheroot-smoking vendors and shoppers we wove our way, past baskets of flowers, veggies, spices, cheroots, tools, fabrics—and found a wooden horse puppet for Jared, which we eventually bartered for with two cigarette light-ers. Burma operates on the barter system, goods being of a constant value (and hard to get, since Burma is virtually isolated from the outside world and imports nothing—legally), and the Burmese *kyat* (pronounced "chat") is subject to the whims of the government, which recently declared useless all 20, 50, and 100 denomination bills, resulting in our dealing strictly in multiples of 5, 25, and 75. Imagine calculating costs in the thousands, counting by 75s! So all of us came equipped with Thai fake Lacoste tee-shirts, lighters, lipstick, nail polish, ciga-rettes, and calculators. Changing money legally at seven kyat per dollar while the going street rate was 25, made Burma either the most expensive or least expensive place to visit, depending on where one changed money. We felt obliged to change $70 legally for the records of the Bangkok museum group with which we were traveling, but viewed it as a good will donation to the museum—otherwise it would have hurt too much!

Loaded with a bunch of fresh green cigars, Frank and I left the towel-topped men and women, beautiful young girls with various patterns of beige sandalwood powder on their cheeks and foreheads, and the world's scroungiest dogs (seem to find them in all Buddhist countries) for a three-hour morning cruise through the most unusual stilt villages and floating gardens of Inle Lake, an area of sixty square miles with 217 villages and 80,000 people situated entirely within and on the lake. When the Inthay people migrated to the Shan State hundreds of years ago, all land was taken, leaving only Inle Lake available for settling. So they built numerous villages on stilts in the 3-4 meter deep lake, and developed a prosper-ous weaving and gardening trade. Purchasing strips of soil on thatch-work 100 meters long and two meters wide, they tow the long narrow floating gardens to their spots, anchor them with long bamboo poles, put up flags and pots as markers, and proceed to grow luscious tomatoes, cultivating from their shallow canoes.

We cruised through this most amazing area in a long narrow motorized skull, each of the eight passengers sprawled sideways across the narrow boat, head hanging off one side, feet off the other—in alternating order—trying not to wiggle or hiccough for fear of capsizing. Our driver periodically stopped to change propellers, fetching his pliers and screwdrivers from inside a soft-drink can. Speeding through mile after mile of canal, actually lanes of water between the floating gardens, we entered a blue world of lake and sky, searching the distance for the famous "leg-rowers" of Inle Lake. Standing at one end of their narrow boats and rowing one oar with their ankle and knee wrapped around it, they somehow manage not to fall in and to get where they're going—rather quickly, too. Fishermen with huge conical straw basket nets, bigger than their boats, row by. Pagodas and thatched rooftops appear in the distant haze. Water hyacinth chokes all in its beautiful embrace. Violet water lilies add a delicate and graceful touch. Water spray droplets sparkle in the sunlight beyond my toes, and I am rudely awakened from my Burmese reverie when struck on the head by a clump of reeds. Amazingly ornate and elaborate temples and pagodas rise from the bunches of straw huts anchored in the water. Gold, marble, mirrored mosaics, old Buddha images distorted to golden lumps by application of gold leaf through the years—the immutable and the transitory, marble and straw, gold and thatch, eternal and temporal. One is dwarfed into insignificance in the overwhelming embrace of Buddhism.

MANDALAY!

Well, Grandpa, we made it! Mandalay, the "heart of Burma," site of its last royal kingdom, capital of Upper Burma, is a relatively new city, founded in 1857 on a hot, dry, dusty plain. Kipling, who wrote the famous poem extolling the virtues of mythical mystical Mandalay upon which Grandpa's favorite song was based, had never come here. I wonder how the lyrics would have changed if he had! Four hundred miles north of Rangoon, sprawled across the dry plains of the upper Irrawaddy rice district, Mandalay lacks Rangoon's colonial architecture and tree-lined streets and squares, but offers—in addition to its Italianate architecture—a glimpse of the grandeur of royal life in its three-meter thick 25-foot-high crenellated palace walls (under which fifty-four people were buried alive to ensure protection of the city—something omitted from modern blueprints, thank goodness!), each side two kilometers long, surrounded by a 225-foot wide moat, like a wide river running its square course through town, reflecting pagoda-tiered watchtowers in its wide blue waters. This wonderful structure encloses two square miles of old straw huts and romping children—where once stood the "golden city" of gilded carved wooden palaces, destroyed by fire in World War II, and now family quarters for the military.

Each city seems to have one central temple that draws us back again and again. In Mandalay, it was the Maha Muni. Numerous times our bare feet trod the gritty grimy floors of the Maha Muni, Mandalay's most important religious structure, not because of the grace or splendor of the temple as the Shwedagon in Rangoon, but to browse in the tiny shops tucked in alongside the temple steps—bells, marionette puppets, wonderful sequined hats and turbans, wooden carvings, gongs, workshops carving marble Buddhas and forging the delicate lacy tiered umbrellas of iron to be gold-leafed and placed on temple spires.

The Irrawaddy River—not exactly a household word in the West, but this mighty river is wider than the Mississippi (the Big Waddy instead of the Big Muddy?) and carries more silt, later deposited in the rice-rich delta of Burma. Where is the Huck Finn of Burma? Afloat on this mighty river, gazing lazily to the shore where women washed clothes in the river and each tree had a horse tied to it, we had survived our embarkation, balancing our way over a 15-foot-long teak plank over the waters with a bamboo pole held by one man on the boat and one on the shore for our handrail. Like cruising on a huge lake, waters swirling and bubbling, the river is immense! Under the gleaming steel bridge built—of course—by the British, the only sign we were in the 20th century, we encountered such a vast and magnificent scene that we were incredulous at the sight stretching before us—Sagaing Hill, site of one of the three nearby capitals of Burma before Mandalay. Stretching endlessly along the shore and up the tree-filled hillsides in the distance were hundreds and hundreds of magnificent domes and spires, temples and pagodas from a brief period as capital 1315-1364, each one perfect in design, sparkling white in the sunlight (whitewashed because Burma is now poor and cannot afford to replenish the gold leaf which originally covered every building here). One of three ancient capitals of Burma before Mandalay, Sagaing is the "living center of the faith" now. Reverberating with echoes of cymbals, gongs and pagoda bells, it beckons city folk to come for a rest on its wooded hillsides overlooking the Irrawaddy. Over 600 monasteries, hundreds of temples, stupas and caves house the 8,000 monks now residing here. Through the binoculars, flashes of red dotted the hillside, monks descending the long covered temple steps to the riverside. (Had I known the effort required to climb these same steps, I'd still be on the boat!) Covered walkways formed jagged zigzags in the landscape, tiered tiled rooftops of covered steps, so scenic from the boat, nearly our undoing in later explorations of the hillside. Pagodas! Pagodas! Pagodas! Ceylonese, Indian, early Burmese, intermediate Burmese, late Burmese—they were all wonderful, and now mesh together in my memory of many barefoot expeditions. (Frank, seeing a small wooden Christmas tree upon our return, said, "What's wrong with me? It looks like a pagoda!") We dutifully obeyed the "No Foot-Wearing, No Umbrella-Carrying" signs directed at the British colonialists who soured relations with the generally friendly Burmese by wearing shoes on sacred temple grounds (where not even socks are allowed) and pointing umbrellas at Buddhas.

It was peaceful under the big trees with horse-carts clomping past in the temple grounds (we couldn't wear socks, but horses could leave their offerings). Colorful women walked by with tall baskets on their heads and babes in their arms. An old woman puffed on her ten-inch long cheroot. Brahmin bulls, with huge humps atop their necks, lounged about, yoked together with a crude wooden log. Bicycle taxis transported people in wooden sidecars. Woven straw sacks, dogs, teak planks lay about among the banana trees. Sunlight stripened the dusty, hazy air. Men sat under trees in old bamboo lounge chairs. A woman walked by with hundreds of cookies on a plate balanced on her head.

We later walked across a 1.2-kilometer footbridge of wide old teak planks, some nailed down, some not, some missing, over a winter-dried lake bed where oxcarts plowed and lone monks meditated in the distance. This Uben Bridge, several hundred years old (would it last long enough to get me across?, I wondered) spanned Lake Taungthaman, a shallow lake which dries up in winter, leaving fertile farmland, plowed by Brahmin bulls yoked to primitive sleds and logs. This was indeed a highlight of the trip—the tranquility of this long unbroken walk with monks and villagers heading to their island village. Teak rest-houses appeared on the bridge every so often, some filled with young monks, others with cheroot-smoking women and young girls with sprays of tiny white flowers flowing down their foreheads. Thankful to break the hectic touring pace we had established, we savored our mile-long walk to a brilliant towering white pagoda with marble statues of monks in each window and real piggies on the lawn. This is elephant country, reflected in murals inside the temple. But we saw only dogs, pigs, roosters, bulls and goats. The smaller pagodas around were all plundered to supply Bangkok antique shops when Burmese art became expensive and fashionable, which explains the iron gates for nighttime locking of all huge Buddha images in all the temples we saw in Burma. We scurried quickly back over the long bridge, afraid of falling through a missing plank in the approaching darkness, and savored sunset over the farmlands and ponds of ducks, small boats and reeds. Sunset in Burma—a truly outrageous orange spectacle behind the silhouetted palms.

Chickens and chimes! Roosters crowed and Westminster chimes pealed at 6 A.M., reminding us that the sun always rises in Burma—and that the British haven't left entirely. Their chimes ring on—now replaced by the tinkling of temple bells, yapping of Burma's numerous pups—and continuous unwelcome presence of silent mosquitoes hovering about in a land where malaria and dengue fever are well known.

I was a Mandalay Hill drop-out. Perched on a wooden crate in one of the many, many open spaces housing Buddha images on the steep, stepped climb up the stairs of Mandalay Hill, I halted my barefoot-in-the-dark ascent halfway, while a few hardy souls—including Frank—continued barefoot in the pre-dawn on the cold clammy concrete steps. Up (we make this a habit, it seems) at 4:45 A.M. to see the sunrise from Mandalay Hill, the only bump on the flat Mandalay plain, a few of the more adventurous tour members had hired a tiny, open-aired jeep taxi which along with horse-drawn carriages and 40-year-old World War II vintage cars comprise Burma's primary transport system. Exotic music—bamboo xylophone and twangy singing—drifted up from below.

"Burma has the world's highest mortality rate from poisonous snake bites." That phrase from a guidebook hadn't particularly fazed me, not having encountered any of Burma's low life so far on the trip. But my blood did chill with the sudden realization that the coiled roll of thin brown rope next to my bare feet on the stone had a viper's head and struck at me, as I had awakened it from a chilly night's sleep. Caught barefoot on the smooth stone with the awakening viper between me and the temple steps, I pondered my fate. After a long period of indecision, I leaped over the still-chilled fellow back to the relative safety of the stairs, awaiting Frank to relate my "brush with death." I pointed to the yawning viper, stretching and slowly writhing itself awake in the morning sun, and some Burmese men laughed, pointed up the steps where Frank had disappeared and said, "Many more! Many more!" Frank returned half an hour later, mercifully unbitten!

Burmese marionettes stem from a medieval tradition—stock characters performing on elaborate sets or makeshift village stages, dancing and prancing to wild music. Horses cavort, enemies duel, ladies weep. Each two- to three-foot tall jointed wooden puppet is hand-carved by its puppeteer, all bodily parts complete even though hidden, and adorned in gaudy velvet, brocade and sequins. Numerous two-foot-long strings are untangled and held separately from the wooden handle to manipulate the marionette. Some say that the rather jerky traditional

Burmese dancing is an imitation of marionette movements. We loved looking at the variety of flamboyant puppets at temple stalls!

Mandalay's final wonder is "The World's Largest Book," Kuthodaw Pagoda, built in 1857—729 gleaming white spired pagodas, originally covered in gold leaf, each housing a marble plaque with Buddhist scripture in the ancient no-longer-used language of Pali. It took 2,400 monks six months just to recite the text! With a wonderfully tall graceful golden pagoda in the center, endless rows of gleaming white pagodas filled our eyes. And then, farewell to Mandalay, land of golden spires and white-washed pinnacles stretching to the sky. Palm trees and smiling faces, flower-haired women, goodbye.

PAGAN! (pah-GAHN)

What everyone had been waiting for—"the most amazing sight in Burma, if not southeast Asia," tempted the guidebook. Across forty square kilometers of flat countryside, in the middle of an arid plain stretching back from the Irrawaddy, stand thousands of temples and pagodas of all sizes, shapes, repair and history…those surviving the earthquake of 1975, that is. Only two centuries produced these buildings, now only 2,200 remaining of the 13,000 temples that once graced these now bare fields. Pagan kingdoms date back to times before Christ, but its "golden period" began in 1057. In 1287, Pagan was abandoned and overrun by hordes of Kublai Khan from China. Only two hundred years for such a wealth of magnificent temples! From the early style of rounded Ceylonese and thickset Mon temples with dark dim interiors for meditation to the later brightly-lit high airy Indian-influenced buildings, Pagan spans the development of architectural styles. One surveys a broad flat plain stretching endlessly with hundreds of towering stone temples and rounded crumbling brick pagodas, set among the cornfields and banana groves in isolated splendor. Only religious structures were built of brick and stone, so nothing remains of the once-glorious carved and gilded wooden palaces which shared these grounds with temples and bamboo villages.

Pressed against the rail-less heights of the 200-foot-high twelfth century temple, all agog with vertigo as we peered down on the tiny bullock carts on the red earth roads far, far, far beneath our feet, we awaited yet another sunset, this one over the Irrawaddy as seen from the highest temple in Pagan. Yet more lovely and interesting was the view from the other side, out over temple and brick mounds rising from surrounding cornfields. A few children joined us, then scurried over the treacherous steep and crumbly steps of the 700-year-old temple while we clung to each step with hands and feet.

Two days on the Pagan plain, heads reeling with pagodas, we divided our attention between the architectural wonders and our more mundane pursuit of shopping for lacquer-ware, for which the region is noted, under the watchful eyes of our local tour guide, a government agent of whom local merchants were afraid. Six months to produce a piece of lacquer-ware, applying, etching, drying the many layers of lacquer around a woven bamboo and horsehair framework—and two seconds to scoop it up in the hands of a buyer! Even monks' bowls are lacquer here in Pagan.

More than the magnificence of the temples, the variety of the styles, I will remember the disintegrating pagodas of crumbly bricks, warm in the sunlight, jagged in outline, silhouetted in the fields, one after the other, inviting speculation and solitude. (I will also long remember the temple where we tiptoed barefoot through the dark over mushy bat droppings while the resident bats squeaked above us as we tried to concentrate on murals and carvings and statues.)

Interesting temple trappings in some of the more frequented temples here: rows of small light-bulbs with individual switches which one pays to light up—contemporary temple candles (say a prayer and flip a switch); electrified round prayer wheels eight feet in diameter—write a prayer, put it on a wheel, and it will do the work for you.

Women tie their long braids in a thick knot halfway down their back—or wind the braid around a hand-carved sandalwood comb which protrudes from the knot of hair atop their heads. Flowers frequently adorn women's and girls' hair. One girl had two lengths of hair to her waist, each knotted halfway down—instead of pigtails.

"Psst! Rubies? Rubies?" Slinky young men in *longyi*'s followed us through the temple grounds, selecting likely targets for their "jewel-of-the-century" deals. Frank eventually turned the tables on them and would approach one of them, unwrapping his knotted handkerchief and asking in a loud stage whisper, "Rubies? Rubies?" Frank was the hit of the vendors as well as the bus!

Striking out on our own for lunch one day, Frank and I took a horse-cart, then strolled up Pagan's tiny dusty main street, ate a wonderful meal cooked over an open fire out back ($1 for both of us!) and acquired an old Burmese drum in exchange for some nail polish, used skin cream and a TWA courtesy shaving kit. Later, we walked through the plain of Pagan, viewing the sun-glowing bricks for the last time—through the goatherds, cactus and corn. Beautiful in the jagged outlines, elegant in crumbling plaster, rich in grassy crowns, they dotted the plain as far as the eye could see—unbelievable.

Last moments—finally found a newspaper that can be read faster than the *Egyptian Gazette*, and that is *The Rangoon Working People's Daily*—official government rag of government meetings, local individual sports competitions, and the weather: "During the past 24 hours weather had been fair in the whole country. Night temperatures were about normal in the whole country. Forecast: Weather will be generally fair in the whole country." No international news. Truly an insular isolated country!

And what better way to end our Burmese adventure? Return to Shwedagon where the magic of Burma captured us on our first evening. Sunrise at the magnificent Shwedagon Pagoda! Barefoot in the night among the many early-risers lighting candles, washing Buddha images, circumambulating the great golden dome, and offering flowers at the shrine for their day of birth, we watch silently as the hundreds of golden spires surrounding the central pagoda become richly warm in the first light of dawn. Pigeons cluck, temple bells suspended from the numerous gilded umbrellas surmounting each spire tinkle in the breeze. Worshippers stroll or sit or kneel, pigeons congregate on spires and *nat*-heads. All are barefoot. Monks carry their metal bowls. A group of young nuns (they're always such young girls—teens or younger) sits on the floor of one of the numerous small temples, clad in their regulation pink tunic over orange robe with brown linen-like folded towel balanced front to back over their shaven heads—receiving instruction and chanting—at 5:45 A.M.!

The incredible assortment of square tiered pagodas carved of wood and trimmed in many colors of gingerbread crowned the outer side of the marble walkway—a profusion of shape, texture and color to astound the eye. Full of golden Buddha statues among the mosaic mirrored columns and walls and painted metal grillwork, any one of these buildings would be a wonder. Here there are literally hundreds—with only a few feet separating each! Any bit of space is filled with a glistening white stupa, or enormous bronze bell inscribed in Pali or Burmese. Tucked into tiny corners are earthen water pots, whose rough exteriors have a variety of geometric designs, topped with conical straw "hats."

Daylight! The deep rose in the east was now the palest yellow and the spires became softest gold, not yet brilliant in direct sunlight. Pigeons and bells above, candles and flowers beneath. No books or photographs could even begin to evoke the enchantment of the scene. One must come to Burma to see—and we did!

Young Buddhist monks outside temple in Mandalay

It Was a Very Fine Year

January 1986

Happy New Year!!

1985 has been a wonderful, wonderful year for us—we are sad to see it pass, but look forward to more of the same: daily life in an exotic culture of palms, orchids, and oriental refinement (conveniently forgetting the three-inch cockroaches and ripe odors of the rainy season), travel to places we never dreamed of before, and watching our children experience the beauties and frustrations and excitements of early childhood.

We continue to enjoy life in steamy Bangkok in spite of its unbelievable traffic, the oppressive sultriness of most of the year, and neighborhoods of seven-foot concrete walls and heavy iron gates fencing us in. The year-round greenery is refreshing, especially now as we read of sub-human wind-chill factors in our various former abodes in the U.S.. Our houseguests are always thrilled at the variety of tasteful handmade items available in the local market. We are still stunned by the splendor of local department stores, where an antebellum-style McDonald's abuts Bangkok's original super-chic Gucci boutique, and by the magnificence of local *wats*—Thai Buddhist temples of multi-tiered rooflines, sparkling mirrored mosaic walls, and golden Buddha images. No mere gold Buddha for the King, however; the Buddha in the Royal Temple on palace grounds is carved from a giant emerald, perched high above our heads on an ornate platform, and is garbed in robes which are changed several times a year in a ceremony full of pomp and pageantry. Within these exotic confines we live our daily lives, and occasionally stop to marvel at it all. Frank's office window overlooks a popular Hindu shrine to Erawan, the three-headed Hindu elephant god, a reincarnation of Vishnu, or one of their biggies—and is packed from sunrise till midnight with people pasting gold leaf on the heads of the numerous large stone elephant statues, setting free small wrens to "make merit"—while four Thai classical dancers in golden headdresses and glittery costumes perform dances of expressive finger movements to the eerie echoes of bamboo xylophones. Bangkok also boasts the best hotels in the world, and we enjoy visiting them regularly, reveling in their architectural delights and repeating, "Were we really in Egypt just a year ago?"

Never certain just how long we will remain here, what with the labyrinthine government channels of approval for Phase II of Frank's project, we have—hesitantly and with great trepidation at first, and now joyfully with great expectations and enthusiasm— ventured into corners of Southeast Asia and beyond. And so we traveled with the children to Singapore, whose Christmas lights, decorations and corner carolers surpass anything we have seen anywhere in the U.S., to Hong Kong for ten rainy days in "shoppers' paradise" with two children whose only goal was to sit in McDonald's or the video arcades, to the Philippines whose lush countryside beauty and serene beaches contrasted with the crowded confines of urban Manila where many people survive on $20—or less—a month, to Malaysia, a Moslem confederation of thirteen sultanates occupying part of Borneo and the mainland between Thailand and Singapore, and whose old and new Islamic architecture of domes and arches was a joy to the eye. And then we tearfully, regretfully left the children for the first time (with five capable adults in supervision!) and flew past the lofty white peaks of Mount Everest and its Himalayan cousins into the incredibly beautiful terraced Kathmandu Valley for a brief excursion to Nepal, the world's only Hindu kingdom, and cultural immersion into this strange mélange of Indian/Tibetan, lowland/mountaineering, silk sari/homespun garb, whose medieval pagodas dominated daily life and our senses during our brief stay.

Invigorated by our Himalayan adventure and the survival of our children (and their caretakers!), we subsequently ventured with our local museum group into Burma, whose restrictions on tourism and trade have virtually isolated this former British colony in the past: 30-year-old American cars, Art Deco interiors on colonial architecture, bartering the primary mode of business (a Burmese jacket for two bottles of imported nail polish, etc.), and a smiling population, all in ankle-length tubes of cloth knotted at the waist, with children and women painting designs of sandalwood bark on their faces, and whose astounding collection of golden pagodas, domes, spires and temple ruins overloads the mind with speculation of the former grandeur and devotion of this strictly Buddhist country.

Our wanderlust was so aroused that we're off to India as soon as Frank returns from Singapore and Indonesia. Oh yes, I've omitted my solo travel—also with the museum group—to the Middle Kingdom: two weeks of ascents to temples and descents into tombs in China, adventurous encounters with primitive plumbing, and general stupefaction at the scale of monuments, countryside, work force, imperial lavishness—not to mention the captivating beauty of the rouge-cheeked babies decked out in purple, chartreuse and orange—simultaneously—beside their gray-clad unisex parents on black bikes. Frank's solo expedition was with a missionary group to the hill tribes of northern Thailand in the mountains of the Golden Triangle, where tribal folk still live and dress much as they have for hundreds of years—in brightly adorned costumes with glass beads, shells and feathers, and whose livelihood still depends upon the poppy. Queen Sirikit and foreign missionaries are trying to reduce the hill tribes' economic dependence on the opium trade by encouraging them to market their native crafts.

Frank has adapted to the eastern business climate where more is assumed than said, where eyebrows can carry more weight than reports, and where surface protocol and politeness prevail. (He's not here to edit my comments, so please don't hold him responsible!) He has with great difficulty adapted to oriental touches such as the proffered tea and cookies, sandwiches and even the orchid on his desk, replenished daily by the office's coffee-and-tea girl, Porn. Yes, that IS her name! Porn is a common name here—in fact, we once took a tour bus whose large painted sign running the length of the bus read "PORN CHUM TOURS." These little office amenities are in stark contrast to Cairo where the office menu consisted of sliced hard-boiled egg on sliced hard bread every day, and we now look back and laugh, remembering how Frank wouldn't drink anything all day in his first Cairo office so he wouldn't have to set foot in the "facilities." Office life here, however, can be stressful in its own way beneath its polished and polite surface. Outside of the office, Frank has been pressed into a more active community life here, serving several functions in our international church (thank goodness he wasn't counting the money the two weeks the church driver absconded with it) and sponsoring the Arthur D. Little Red Sox, Bangkok's Little League T-ball team which is about to embark on its first season. One of his delights this year has been his monthly culinary orgies as a new member of the Bangkok branch of France's Chaîne des Rôtisseurs—a SERIOU.S. eating club whose forays into local restaurants must be described in detail in future letters. Suffice it to say that he was initiated ("intronisized") in style, holding a sword, sworn in in French in front of the king's sister! He is indeed a fine advertisement for the joys of fine eating. His new tux is getting a good workout, from formal balls to his role as an extra in a Thai movie to be released this month!!

Jared is mumbling his way through the maze of introductory phonetics as he enters the world of the written word in first grade. I never realized quite how confusing our multi-rooted language is until I began trying to explain some of the rules, which invariably have more exceptions than examples. He continues to enjoy his various playmates (seems to have a Matthew in every country), and—unlike his sedentary parents—is a sportsman who enjoys racing, soccer and baseball. He is a dropout of the Korean martial arts program, which I feel reflects the finer side of his nature! (He still practices various chops, kicks and death-grips on his little sister, however.) Jared is more articulate than ever, his vocabulary surpassing the regressed state of mine ("Baby go here now?"), and it is more difficult to win an argument with him—he always finds the loophole (too bad he can't help us with our taxes). His supreme joy remains horses. I sit quaking through his weekly riding lessons as the horses become rambunctious and Jared looks so tiny in the saddle. We have a line-up of 3- and 4-foot-high wooden and papier-mâché mounts—with Egyptian saddles and Burmese stirrups attached—in front of the video from which he views his numerous old cowboy movies and reruns lovingly recorded and sent to him from his Granddad Ned in St. Louis. Jared is still tall and blondish, lanky and lovely in his toothless 7-year-oldness.

Leah ("Baby"—sister of "Boy") is nearly 2 ½ now, a tall little girl who gaily describes every activity within her view. I understand that "ahhh-beam" is really ice cream, "bidden" is medicine, vitamin and Christmas, and "bobbybye" is butterfly, while "tubbybear" is old Teddy. Her Leah-language is quite charming, if sometimes confusing. Important words are never mumbled, however—"McDonald's" comes through loud and clear, truly an international word. Leah is lovely, sprouting two tiny ponytails beside her expressive delicately feminine face. Her brilliant blue eyes still evoke comment, and she has learned to use them alluringly. Daddy becomes "Ee-ter (Mister) Potis, peeze" when we call the office, and she has learned the miraculous effect of those little words "uv-oo" (love you) when she has incurred maternal/paternal wrath, as she begins to do with increasing regularity as the "terrible two's" enter full swing. Our dining room chairs survived seven years with Jared, but are beginning to crumble after two weeks of Leah's attention. She disdains paper for her artwork, preferring the more natural elements of wood and plaster…and flesh. She is addicted to "Winnie the Pooh" on video—the same one every day—and cannot fall asleep without her mother's off-key rendering of "We Are the Church" and "Home Heng" ("Home on the Range"). She has inherited her mother's childhood attraction to all furry creatures, particularly cats, whom she caresses, and dogs, whom she tries to lick—a real concern here with the world's highest incidence of rabies. We are daily amused by her antics and language leaps, and daily frustrated by the sibling rivalry in our home! We love to ask Leah rhetorical questions which she answers with her high-pitched "yet!" Our nonexistent Christmas family photo this year consists of thirty attempted shots by a photographer friend of the four of us in local dress—we ended up with 29 shots of Leah in various stages of undress or tugging us out of the picture and one shot with my eyes closed. Perhaps next year?

Maybe next year...

"Prettydress" is one word in our house, and each day begins—and sometimes ends—with Leah's retrieval from her closet of yet another dress which she dons (sometimes over her pajamas) with glee. Her closet is full of wonderful little dresses made by young women working in a home supported by missionaries—and these are most fanciful beautiful little dresses whose yokes are painstakingly embroidered with English smocking in geometric or floral designs, or perhaps with little bunnies, too. Leah is drawn to the same dress each day (in fact, I eventually had to hide the dress from her view), her "boat in water" dress which she wore the day we took her to the terrace of the Oriental Hotel by the Chao Phya River. Now she thinks that if only she could wear that dress again, she'd get to return to the river, and so every morning she looks at her gaily hanging smocked dresses, first with eager anticipation and excitement, and then, realizing that the special dress is not there, with aggravation and frustration as she calls out, "BOAT IN WATER! BOAT IN WATER!!" Coincidentally, the famous (or infamous, depending on one's viewpoint) "boat in water" dress is a deep turquoise-blue, the color of the wine-dark sea, reflecting her Greek roots, rather than the murky brown of Thai river waters.

My time consists of various miniscule chores, such as orchestrating the above-mentioned Christmas photo failure and the failed Christmas cards prepared for the printer but somehow abandoned or lost—and keeping on top of the Fotis Family Foto Archives, an ever-expanding collection of excessive enthusiasm in photography of the wondrous places we've seen this year. I spend two mornings a week taking Leah to "baby-toy," rotating play-groups for two-year-olds, and one day helping out in Jared's classroom, having been shamed into volunteering for "room mother" when, after a particularly rousing assembly to honor mother helpers last year, Jared came home and announced: "Do you know why our school is such a big success? Well, it's not because of YOU. It's the room mothers that did it." I also spend occasional Sunday mornings tending the church nursery—and try to coerce Frank into helping out. I chair a committee for the monthly Hill Tribe Handicraft sales—which means I get to inventory thousand upon thousands of tiny beaded and sequined Christmas tree ornaments before AND after each sale, and must follow a bookkeeping system so complex that I often "buy" a lost sequined shrimp or Santa rather than record the loss in the cavernous complexities of forms I must submit monthly. (Sequined ornaments are not exactly the native craft I was anticipating!) I am very happy and contented juggling domestic life with exciting travels, and whole-heartedly resist Frank's every suggestion or innuendo about returning to teaching.

We have been blessed this year with houseguests—at last! No one seemed too anxious to traipse through the Middle East to see us, but we're glad that the Orient sparks more interest. We've just regretfully said goodbye to our cousins, Madeline and George from Chicago, who returned with a treasure of Burmese boxes, Thai silks, ceramics, carvings, baskets and Burmese tapestries. Our acquaintances, the world cyclists Roger and Betsy Kalter, whom we met in Cairo a year ago and who have been on the road nearly four years, have pedaled here and become good friends, brightening our Christmas holidays with their wit and good cheer. Friends from Cairo days have passed through and spent days and weeks with us in transit to Nepal and Bangladesh (and wonderfully brought a case of Pampers with them!!!!).

So 1985 has been a truly wonderful year of visitors, travel, hearing from friends at home, seeing our children flower, and absorbing nuances of life in Southeast Asia. We are truly thankful for this exciting year of rewarding opportunities and can only hope that 1986 will retain some of the flavor and excitement that has been with us throughout this year.

Mary Ned and Frank ride to IndiAH

Passage to IndiAH

March 1986

"IndiAH!"

It must be pronounced with the final "-ah," not the "-uh" that so easily rolls off our lips. And the "-ah" must sort of rise and then be cut off in the middle, left to linger in mid-air, evoking images of sound and color and mystique so absent from our commonplace pronunciation of the word. "Indi-uh" is present—"IndiAH is past, alive in the present. "Indi-uh" is grim poverty; "IndiAH" is grandeur. "Indi-uh" is crowds, dirt, beggars, questionable food, political turmoil—"IndiAH" is throngs of brilliantly sari'd women and turbaned men, raggedy holy men whose black marble eyes pierce your camera-laden façade and see something even you are unaware of, some essential core of you buried beneath all the actions and accoutrements of a busy western daily life. "IndiAH" is vegetables amassed in huge baskets, Moghul architecture so overpowering and yet beautiful and pure it stops you in your tracks and sticks an unexpected "aaah" in your throats, remnants of past glories we can't quite conceive of having existed, the nearly invisible exquisite detail on some tiny tool used for a mundane task hundreds of years ago. That's "IndiAH", but that's only an inkling.

"I'm not ready for India," I thought last May as I walked, reeling, out of yet another Chinese temple whose frightening statues and mural-laden walls seemed to swoop down on me. "I'm not ready for India," I commented in November, overcome by the masses of brightly-sari'd Nepalese swirling about me in Kathmandu's medieval royal square crammed with wonderful pagodas whose every inch was carved with Hindu gods and goddesses in every imaginable—and unimaginable—position. "I don't need India," I thought, in Rangoon's indescribable golden glittering glowing Shwedagon Pagoda: "This is enough to remember for a lifetime."

But India was always there—and always would be—in the back of my mind. Merely a vague desire for many years, and then an intense yearning after meeting my friend Ferriel from Bombay whose intimations of castles and palaces, hills and lakes, splendor and opulence, history and romance would not subside in my mind. And then my friend Karen in Egypt, who never pronounced "Pah-kee-stahn" as merely "Pack-uh-stan," robbing the word of its beauty and the country of its dignity, who always said "IndiAH" so perfectly, enticing me there with every pronunciation of the word evoking wonderful images—Karen said, before we ever came to the Far East, "You must go to IndiAH, Mary Ned. You especially would love it."

But alas, there was Frank, an Indophobe if I ever met one. Early business trips there had soured him on the whole country for decades. "They leave people sick in the streets! They don't help each other! They crowd you and give you no peace! It's dirty, the food is awful...." So I decided to leave Frank at home and take the International Women's Club tour of Rajasthan, India, so I wouldn't have to return to the U.S. and spend the rest of my life thinking, "I was so close and yet so far...." Imagine my shock when, after regaling him with the itinerary of converted island palace hotels and hilltop forts, and the Indian ambassador's fascinating introduction to India's peoples, cultures and religions, Frank said, "Well, I think I'll come, too"!

And thus was born "The Can-Can Girls and the Tuk-Tuk Cowboys" in which a tour-ful of Frenchwomen, two Israelis, an Egyptian and a Thai princess were joined in the final days of preparation by the Greek Typhoon and me. Ten days later, we all left New Delhi on our return flight to Bangkok, carefully looking behind to see if they had closed the airport and hung a new sign:

INDIA CLOSED FOR ONE WEEK
FOR RESTORATION AND RECOVERY

Our madcap tour leader, ex-Egypt Air stewardess Laila (married to mild-mannered American Chuck who with Frank and Frenchman Denis comprised the entire male contingent of our 18-member tour), forcefully established the tone for our nine-day venture by alternately charming and bullying the Air France crew for 23 bottles of champagne and leading French singing as we settled under a haze of cigarette smoke in our non-smoking section. I learned that nothing can stop the French when *"en vacance,"* and soon grew accustomed to local merchants and even passersby asking, "Are you with that Thailand group?" The brilliance of attire of vacationing French rivals the intensity of colors of saris and turbans; their continual chattering and loud laughter announces their arrival and lingers after departure. ("This is the worst group I have ever seen!" commented one scholarly local tour guide, used to conducting Germans.) And there we were—right in the middle. (Actually, we liked them all, and Frank was cracking jokes in French after a few days!)

NEW DELHI—There we were, but where was India? Broad tree-shaded avenues with an occasional car; walls, gates and gardens; an orderly grid of streets with large traffic circles full of trees and flowers; occasionally a pedestrian or two. Imposing government buildings in huge squares, high-rise lower government employee housing, low-rise higher government housing—this was obviously a government city! This green, wide-open, uncrowded, orderly city came as a shock—particularly to us from crowded, unzoned, unorganized Bangkok. Where were the people? (As we later discovered, they all seemed to be crowded into tiny Old Delhi, the more traditional India, while New Delhi, created and established as capital in 1911 by the British, reflected traditional colonial design and order.)

We shivered through New Delhi—too easy to forget in Bangkok's sultry winter that real winter is not so very far away. Delhi's ladies donned their "overcoats"—beautiful woolen shawls minutely embroidered in the northern state of Kashmir. Some of these elegant "pashimina" goat wool shawls cost as much as a fur coat! We soon had all purchased embroidered woolen scarves and shawls for our shivery frames. Wrapped and wound in wool, we met our first Indian tour bus—a wonderful house on wheels, like a gigantic trailer with separated glassed-off "cockpit" for the driver and his friends (with a bed!), and settled into curtained comfort high off the ground. Our bulky local guide, whose pierced nose and doubly-pierced ears glittered with diamonds, wrapped her elegant shawl around her, but her bare bulging midriff still challenged the chill. We settled into the singsong patterns of "Indian-English" ("So, you are having your first trip here. We'll be having a tour....").

Here we were at last in the world's second most populous country (800 million plus)—but where was everyone? We found some of them at a Hindu temple. One must commence one's plunge into India by plunging into Hinduism—and that we did at a rather gaudy marble and plaster Hindu temple dedicated to Vishnu, one of the Big Three deities. In fact, most of the thousands of Hindu deities are reincarnations of the Big Three powers: Brahma the Creator, Vishnu the Preserver, Shiva the Destroyer. (And with 840,000 rebirths for each soul, no wonder every god is a reincarnation of some other one.) To the eerie twangs and tootings of the snake charmer on the sidewalk outside, we proceeded past the marigolds roasting on an open grill in front of the deity, their powerful fragrance released through the heating, mingling with the red powder on trays, dots on foreheads.

Hot flowers, cold feet, bare on the frigid marble temple floors. Stained glass above, elephant-headed columns, swastikas—a cultural mishmash that left me dizzy (but then this is what India is supposed to do!). The temple was crowded with worshippers bowing, chanting, offering flowers, incense, enlightening themselves with the "third eye" on their foreheads. My favorite was the fellow in bright pink turban ("Pink is the navy blue of India," Diana Vreeland once aptly observed). India's early Hinduism assimilated the country's early animistic roots from the south (you can always tell a Hindu temple by all the brightly painted animal statues of the roofs) and later even managed to assimilate Buddhism which originated in India, as Buddha is now considered another reincarnation of Vishnu, and to our surprise, Buddhism as a separate religion is basically dead in India. Islam was never really assimilated into Hinduism—it's still alive and very strong in India with its 11% minority of 88 million followers; however, Sikhism, which was founded 550 years ago as a reform movement within Hinduism, incorporates many Moslem characteristics from the 17th century when Hindus were converting to Islam under the Moghul emperors.

Little by little we oozed our way into India that first morning in Delhi as we neared the crowded labyrinthine streets of Old Delhi—a world away from sprawling green manicured New Delhi next door. India's first mosque was built in 1193 in Afghani style of hundreds of Hindu columns, each distinctive and each with faces of the Hindu gods gouged out by the Moslem invaders. Arabic arches on the left, squat shops on the right. Indian commerce is alive. Huddled men enveloped in shawls (it's cold!) squatted by baskets of nuts on the curb. We passed under an old gate of crenellated stone with arches, rather lovely in its dilapidated way, and…suddenly it was green and spacious and New Delhi! We'd come a couple of centuries just by passing under the gate. We continued on in the early evening darkness past fields of sports-minded men playing soccer (excuse me, I mean "football") and cricket. The British are gone, but British habits remain.

And so farewell to Delhi—definitely NOT "the real India"—spacious, green, orderly, uncrowded, full of green midans with tree-lined avenues radiating from their grassy cores in New Delhi, whose colonial buildings form circular columned Connaught Place to the beautiful Parliament House with its towers and platforms, creating a New India as well as a New Delhi—where a middle class emerges, where government permeates all with numerous office buildings and workers' quarters. And to Old Delhi, a tangle of narrow alleys, mosques and bazaars, a 17th century walled city with city gates, capital of Moslem India for centuries, with its small shops, bicycle trishaws, street carts and people, people…and wonderful old forts and palaces and mosques from the heyday of Moghul rule.

RAJASTHAN!

"Flower in the Desert," land of old Moghul forts rising from the sands, literally "Land of Kings" (Raja's), Rajasthan is the second largest of India's 364 states. With "only" twenty million people due to its poor soil and therefore inferior agriculture, the state of Rajasthan is one of India's most sparsely populated areas, another surprise for us in this land of surprises. We had expected crowds everywhere. Southwest of New Delhi, Rajasthan shares a long border with Pakistan and is south of the Punjab, home of the Sikhs, which accounts for the incredible airport security we went through for every half-hour leg of our journey. With the Thar Desert on the west and little rainfall, hot winds creating sand dunes, the "Country of Death" seems more like the Middle East than our usual impressions of green and crowded India. These cities were on the old caravan route and now exist on camels, goats and sheep.

Rajasthan, the "Land of Princes," was formerly "Rajputana," "Land of the Rajputs," the only people in India claiming descent from the warrior caste of Kshatriyas. (Other castes are the Brahmins, the priestly—and highest—class; then the warriors; then the Vaisya, artisans and merchants, and finally the Sudra caste of farmers and peasants. Each caste has hundreds of sub-castes, and beneath them all are the "untouchables," whom Gandhi renamed the "Children of God," the Harijans. If a matchmaking advertisement states "caste no object," it means a wealthy person of low caste is looking for a mate.) The Rajput warrior clans controlled this part of India for a thousand years with a code of chivalry and honor similar to Europe's medieval knights. They were never united, however, and therefore never a real threat to the Moghuls. Famous for their courage and pride, they are the subject of many folktales—warriors would don their wedding clothes to ride into certain death, while women and children committed suicide rather than be captured. Under the British, Rajputana was a group of princely states, each with its own maharaja. With the coming of independence, however, India joined Rajputana and its neighbor Ajmer to create the state of Rajasthan. The magnificent cities of Rajasthan reflect the incredible former splendors of the ruling maharajas.

They say the men are taller here—and more handsome. Certainly it seems so. They all sport wonderful mustaches—actually, they are so wonderful that one must elevate the term to "mustachio." These men are tall and lean and they wear not the Sikh-like hard starched tight-fitting turbans, but wonderfully full puffy turbans of brilliant colors, plain or printed, wound and wound and wound about their heads in a most regal manner. Each town has its own style of turban-wrapping, some with a flap hanging from the side, some with a long trail down the back. Rajasthani men flash white teeth and smile devastating smiles—and they wear gold earrings. Yes, the wife wears the family jewelry, but she gets all the silver; the gold adorns the man. How wonderful to live with the remnants of this chivalric age in one's everyday life. No more jousting or combat on horseback; elephants carry only tourists up the castle ramparts now; camels pull carts of bricks or loads of pipes—but the Rajasthani warrior is everywhere, serving your tea in the hotel, punching your ticket in the palace museum, pouring his tray of ivories and gems onto the cloth before you behind closed doors of his shop, inspecting your bag as you enter the plane.

Rajasthan! A wonderful bumpy ride through the countryside from the airport to Udaipur. Sere thirsty landscape, stone walls dividing brilliant green irrigated fields from scrubby patches of brown rocky land. Cactus hedges, brown humps of hills in the background, alternating fields of green, yellow, chartreuse, brown, ochre and tan. Women are clad in brilliant hues with scarves from head top to ankles, backlighted with unearthly brilliance as they walk down the roadside, squat earthen water jars balanced on their heads. There is an aura of the Moslem in this—like a touch of Egypt in a Greek landscape with Hindu overlay. Men in dhoti loincloths walk next to others in shocking pink shirts, surrounded by children in red and gold with brass pots gleaming on their heads. How thrilling to bump and bounce through this beautiful and rugged countryside with its roving cattle and turbaned mustachioed men. Two men squat, side by side, in blue paisley turbans—each one a sari's worth of fabric wound and puffed out like an oversized Egyptian cabbage. True glory for the head! Even the most menial and insignificant head assumes dignity in such a turban. Crenellated stone walls climb up the brown hillsides in crumbly spurts. Two men appear in white pants, brown shawls and matching bright pink turbans. Long-horned buffalo stroll by....

After Delhi's orderly avenues, we were thrilled to enter Rajasthan and experience the same sense of joyful shock and wonder that we first encountered in Nepal. Each roadside vignette surpassed the one just before: woman all in fuchsia with large basket of red wool on her head, accompanied by woman draped in orange, crowned with a huge basket of leafy green produce. A camel pulls a horse cart just ahead of us. Buses and trucks sport fantasy decoration—true Third World. Matching printed saris make twins of girls. Women here wear large looped nose rings, not the delicate diamonds of New Delhi. A group of 20-30 women appears, all clad head to toe in various hues of fuchsia and chartreuse—nothing muted, nothing subdued. A barefoot man carries a mattress along the road. A steam engine in action! A girl in a purple sari peddles her bike

behind a man in a brilliant saffron turban. Our eyes are overwhelmed by the richness of color superimposed on the sere landscape. Cows loll in the center of the
street. Shocking pink ribbons and faded plastic roses adorn local horses. Curly-
horned buffaloes pull carts. Long-haired striped pigs run about. Hairy, hairy one-
humped camels pull heavy loads. A bullock cart passes, the bull's horns painted
bright red! A woman passes by in vibrant red sari with yellow shawl, the basket of
huge manure chips on her head glistening in the sunlight.

UDAIPUR—Nonsensical syllables before, now a word evoking our favorite
memories and images of our brief brush with India. Udaipur—city in the hills
surrounded by manmade lakes with floating palaces; white-washed houses
painted with fancifully-garbed elephants and horses set in twisting alleyways;
mysterious doorways and shuttered windows of all colors looking onto the narrow streets full of goats, wandering cattle, old women squatting, young girls tot-
ing their babies, children scampering about, women hidden by the huge
overhanging loads of hay balanced on their heads. Brass jars and earthen pots rest
on ledges behind small wooden shutters slightly ajar. Saris stream from rooftops,
fluttering in the breeze as they dry.

We walked through the magnificent stone archway, up the cobbled courtyard
through the maharani's (only Udaipur in all India has a maharani instead of a
maharaja—the elevated status because only Udaipur was never conquered by
anyone, including the Moghuls; the maharani was very diplomatic, it seems) palace grounds, around the corner and down the hill to the boat landing. These
buildings looked vaguely—and wonderfully—familiar; we later learned that the
winter palace through which we had just so cavalierly made our shortcut was the
exotic old casino-hotel where James Bond stayed in *Octopussy*, the most colorful
of all the 007 films, and the ethereal white arcaded fantasy palace just across from
us in the lake, inhabited by the beautiful girls of *Octopussy* in the film, actually the
Maharani of Udaipur's summer palace, was our hotel! Not a speck of land, just
the palace rising serenely from the waters—bougainvillea-covered colonnades,
scalloped arches, domed pavilions, marble floors, colored-glass mosaics, and formal garden inner courtyard in arabesque design with manicured bushes and fleur-
de-lis shaped pools—all in sparkling white.

We looked across the waters to Udaipur's other floating palace with its row of
huge white-washed elephants standing guard by the landing and its gradually
crumbling columns and arches hidden amidst the purple bougainvillea. Deserted
since the filming of *Octopussy*, its domed silhouettes further enchant these exotic
waters, and one is transported to the days of maharajas and sultans and emperors

who stayed here, gathering ideas for the culmination of Moghul architecture, the Taj Mahal. Now we could cruise by, pinpointing the location of various scenes from the movie. Frank was a bit disappointed to discover that none of the screen beauties had remained behind, but we all had a laugh when our guide explained that the final scene of the movie had to be re-shot, after all the actresses had departed. So next time you see *Octopussy*, take a good look at those heavily costumed beauties in the final scene, and you will find the youth of Udaipur, descendants of the great Rajasthani warriors, their muscles and moustaches veiled in flowing feminine drapery.

The view from our arched bedroom window could not have been lovelier—the hilltop winter palace of the Maharani of Udaipur! Actually a conglomeration of aging yellowing towering balconied palaces sprouting fuchsia bougainvillea from their cracks, blue ceramic tiled balconies and latticed marble windows, cupolas and domed pavilions, these 400-year-old structures were home to thirty-two kings, and are still occasionally resided in by the now-powerless but still extremely wealthy Maharani of Udaipur. Wonderfully ornate in a light-hearted fanciful way inside with glass, mirror and tile mosaics, painted walls, a huge collection of miniature paintings, for which Rajasthan and particularly Udaipur is famous, the palace grounds are quiet now, some geese, goats, cows, a few sitting men—and us—the only trespassers. The only discordant note, as Frank pointed out, and I have to agree, was the hideous flowery ceramic tiles donated by the Earl of Mountbatten.

As if Udaipur's natural beauty, set on the hills surrounding the lake, its history reflected through its wonderful hilltop and island palaces, and its folkloric charm in colorfully painted elephants and horses around each doorway were not enough, it is also a center of art—miniature paintings on silk, ivory, and old paper. Amazed at the dexterity exhibited in creating these miniature masterpieces, we viewed artists adding the tiny details with a brush made from one eyelash of a squirrel! Paint is composed of ground stones, except for the color yellow which is a mixture of buffalo urine and gelatin powder. All the paintings are copies of the old masters, with wonderfully intricate ornate backgrounds of carpets, foliage, ceramics, tapestries—and main figures whose subtly shaded visages reflect a variety of temperament through the fewest strokes of a brush. This is art I have always admired—and coveted—and now we look at our walls with their tiny graceful Moghul warriors and court figures in pleated skirts, beads, tiny turned-up elfin shoes and flamboyant turbans, and we wish we had been even more extravagant!

One afternoon's stroll through town found us down by the riverside—the most colorful place in town—where groups of people scrubbed and rubbed brilliant saris and other assortments of clothing and linens on the steps descending into the lake. This was a typical scene of India, where the river or lake is always at the center of all activity, whether the ritual morning Hindu wash in the river, cremation on the riverbanks or just washing the endless array of fabrics. We skirted past goats and geese, cows and a camel, past houses with huge palms of hands painted by the door (local fortune-tellers), a 400-year-old Hindu temple with elephant statues up its steep steps and clothes hanging out to dry in front, and squatting old women who must have been at the temple on opening day. The usual colorful cast of characters was in the streets—wonderful long-bearded old men with turbans and canes, green-horned cows, saris flying out from behind bicycles, horse carts jingle-jangling along. One three-wheel taxi streaked by with a man's arm extended on each side, a pair of men's undershorts drying in the breeze on each arm—so this is how they dry them after washing in the algae'd lake. We entered a puppet- and sari-adorned doorway, and Frank honed his bargaining skills on two old ivory and amber necklaces. ("You're not like the rest of the tourists!" the shop owner kept exclaiming.)

We met a "French Grandpa," a wonderful old man braving the lakeside chill in sockless sandals, beret and cane which he lifted into the air and burst into song whenever he encountered our group of mainly French ladies. *"Filles de mons pays!"* ("Daughters of my country!") he called, and regaled us with French love songs, while the rest of his geriatric tour looked on in horror or ignored the scene. We happily encountered him many times, in deserted temples in the countryside, in town and at the boat landing. I was reminded of Grandpa beginning his world travels at 80 and also the life of the party!

Frank and I escaped the group and took a boat ride to another island garden retreat, where we spoke to a young couple from Madras in the south who had to converse with local inhabitants in English, as their native tongue was Tamil, and the locals speak Rajasthani. Most commerce and communication in India takes place in English—with 545 small kingdoms in India before independence, each with at least one local language, what else can one do? Even now, with 1,050 dialects in India, there is no one central language aside from English. Hindi is widely spoken around the government areas of New Delhi, but not at all in the south. The girl from Madras was brilliantly arrayed in a striking red and black silk checkered sari with sparkling gold woven into the borders, with a glistening hip-length black braid down her back (of course, the baby blue sweater she wore on top did diminish the overall effect a bit). Other occupants of this 1-rupee local boat wore Punjabi suits, long tunics split up the side and worn over long pants with an ankle-length scarf, and the central parts in their hair were bright red with a carnelian dye, a sign of marriage (as if the omnipresent nose ring were not enough). Their henna'd hands and feet wore delicate designs of tiny leaves and flowers, both palms and backs, and on all fingers and toes up to the ankle. Were these painted on or tattooed? I don't know. Silver rings adorned ladies' toes, silver bracelets their ankles, diamonds and rings their noses and ears, gold and glass bangles their wrists.

Back on our interesting tour bus whose entire ceiling was fake leopard and cheetah fur, air-conditioned by six tiny fans mounted upside-down on the ceiling. Various colored lights alternated with the fans, and a silver panel with fluorescent lamps ran down the center. The numerous seat upholsteries were in shades of brown, while green and silver curtains shaded our eyes…and—the *pièce de résistance*—a large painting on glass of two tigers above the front door into the driver's cabin, for us to admire should the scenery tire us. This was one of the more subdued buses we were to encounter during our journey.

Through the countryside…wild peacocks crossed the road, large green parrots flitted about, and monkeys and large baboons eyed us from atop nearby walls. This bumpy path was "National Highway Number 8" to New Delhi! We stopped at a very old temple full of carvings, but I was so busy taking notes on the history that I overlooked the erotic entanglings that everyone was talking about later. Now I've forgotten—or lost interest—in the history, and wish I had taken a closer look at the carvings!

The most exotic place of the entire trip was next—an 8th century Hindu temple to Shiva, the god of destruction. This is the creepy god, entwined in serpents and rubbing ashes on his body, who was probably one of the original Dravidian gods of the early short dark residents of India before the Indo-Aryan invaders introduced Vedantism (early Hinduism) 5,000 years ago. We could not take our cameras inside, nor wear any leather products (belts, billfolds, etc.—certainly no shoes!). Our Thai princess was in a bind, as she was supposed to remove her pantyhose from inside her slacks—however, no one noticed when she didn't. "This is the real India!" we thought, but it was almost too much to take. Rows of squatting women vied frantically to sell their long marigold leis; the emaciated bare-legged, bare-chested wise men whose long matted chunks of hair fell beneath their waists and whose flesh was brightly painted in geometric designs, pierced us with their intense glowing eyes; children ran about the rows of shrines with carvings and huge marble elephant statues. Wonderful things, eerie music, bearded old gurus in pink turbans, or maroon with white dots, or orange, or….

Theatrical-style mustachios and bears, big and fluffy, incredible carvings everywhere, a room whose walls and ceiling were pure silver…. Some Hindu priests here, as well as all Jains (another ancient religion, offshoot of Hinduism), wear white cloths across their mouths—to avoid swallowing insects. Now that is what is meant by "strict" vegetarianism! Many age-old symbols finally became clear: the Star of David, which we saw everywhere in Nepal, combines the inverse triangles representing male and female, and thus represents sexual union; the swastika represents the four possible forms of reincarnation (god, human, animal, demon) in a never-ending circle of rebirth with nirvana at its core. Thus are Hindu temples always in tiers of carvings, the four levels of rebirth beneath the five levels of supra-godly being, with a flag at the top when the temple is open. Worshippers enter the temple, ring a bell suspended from the ceiling, announcing their arrival to the deity, and proceed to wash hands and sprinkle their faces with special flowered waters, bowing and chanting, then offer flowers and incense and receive the red "*tika*" third eye on their foreheads. All worship seems to be individual—we saw no group rites or services.

JODHPUR—The Blue City, to me. All in a haze beneath, white and beige boxy buildings, like Greece before the high-rises, with houses of an unearthly blue interspersed among them. India operated strictly on the caste system (with so many people, it simplifies who's who)—and in Jodhpur, only the Brahmin caste may paint its houses blue. I'm not necessarily in agreement with the caste system, but its architectural effects in Jodhpur are wonderful to behold—the blue-spotted city fading into the distant haze.

Jodhpur is known (aside from the horseman's trousers named after it) for its most spectacular fort—the fort to end all forts—built atop a huge rocky cliff rising from the center of the city. We were in Jodhpur on one of the only five days a year when the sun did not shine, but I must say, the dusty gloom of the atmosphere was an appropriate backdrop for this massive fort rising straight above us in this old Rathore Kingdom known as Marwar, the "Land of Death." The old city has a 10-kilometer wall with eight ancient gates, one of which has the handprints of widows who committed *suttee*—only recently declared illegal—the centuries-old tradition of jumping onto the cremation pyre of their dead husbands in a fiery suicide, supposedly bringing great blessings to those around (but what else to do? Their lives were worthless after the death of their husbands). Vultures soared through the air and nested on castle ledges, reinforcing the somber mood of the place. Stone walls rose 125 feet above us—and we were already on top of the cliff 400 feet above the town beneath. This place is surely impregnable! (And to assure that it would be, a man was buried alive in the foundation—a practice not unknown in Thailand and Burma.) The various palaces inside this 1459 A.D. fortress, of carved red sandstone with peacock-design latticework windows for the ladies of the palace to peek out of, have incredibly ornate carvings—how could anyone climb that high, hang on (avoiding the vultures) and carve such intricate designs on the exterior walls? Inside was even more ornate—but in a rather gaudy manner, lacking the delicacy of design of the Udaipur palaces. Displays of baby cradles like thrones, suspended by carved gilded angels (and of the maharaja's giant swinging cradle for when he felt like being "babied"), of maharajas' palanquins (the long-handled litters upon which they were carried), both "convertibles" and "coupes," of bizarre musical instruments of hundreds of strings and unexplained bulbous spheres, and of the most fearsome collection of weapons incongruously adorned with the most delicate birds, fish, and flowers—such were the displays in this memorable fort, all owned by the 37-year-old Maharaja of Jodhpur who chose to reside in the Umaid Bhawan Palace, his residence and our hotel, an immense hilltop structure of marble and red sandstone easily visible from the air, an extravagance built not too long before independence (possibly with a maharaja's business-like eye on future commerce and hostelry?) where tigers' heads and bears' bodies assaulted us as we rounded each corner, where gilt and velvet furniture was appropriately uncomfortable, and where we brought out our 23 little bottles of Air France's champagne for our ballroom dinner under the sparkling eyes of red-turbaned waiters and our tour leader's futile attempts to belly-dance to sitar music. The staid palace trembled a bit that night, as our tour leader somehow obtained disco music from somewhere and gathered the more adventurous members of other tours to join us in a night of dancing. Palace employees occasionally walked by and peeped in, wide-eyed and unbelieving.

By this time, our bodies were revolting against the rich Indian food, which is delicious and satisfying every few weeks, but impossible to consume three times a day. Rich buttery breads, mutton and chicken in thick sauces, spicy curries, numerous concoctions of vegetables—no wonder all those saris are bulging! For a change of diet, New Delhi is planning its first McDonald's, serving—what else?—lambburgers.

JAIPUR—Goodbye to the curly-toed slippers of Jodhpur men, a feminine touch in contrast to their wonderful turbans with train of fabric falling to waist or knees in the back. Over the increasingly brown flat landscape to the capital of the state of Rajasthan, gem center of India, the "Pink City"—Jaipur! Petra's description seems apt here: "A rose-red city half as old as time." Thanks to the ingenuity of

Maharaja Jai Singh II (1699-1744), a true Renaissance man—warrior, architect, astronomer—the city has a most unusual and orderly design. Wide tree-lined boulevards, so incongruous in India where crowded labyrinthine alleyways are the norm, lined with wonderful old buildings of pink stone with geometric designs etched in white, full or arched windows, old wooden doors, magnificent gates set in crenellated city walls—this went on for miles and miles. Add to the architecturally fascinating scene spice merchants, mystics, beggars, camel carts, bulls with painted horns, barefoot holy men with long matted hair, baboons scurrying over the rooftops and burro herds scrambling through the streets, black-garbed Moslem women, colorfully sari'd Hindu ladies, tribal women in bright colors and coins and beads, turbaned men playing some sort of checkers on the sidewalk...and you'll begin to visualize Jaipur, whose rose-red peach-rust walls have watched the progression of man through the centuries. Thank you, Jai Singh, for finding those old Hindu city-planning tracts and showing us how lovely the ancient designs are. When Moghul power waned, Jai Singh brought his capital down from the hills of Amber Fort, which we would ascend by elephant the following day, and erected his new capital here on the plain, a wide open city of pink terra cotta paint enclosed by beautiful pale rusty crenellated walls etched in white, a city whose minutest markets were organized back in 1727 to avoid the usual oriental clutter. Of course, Jai Singh is gone, and clutter and crowds have returned, but all are subservient to the beautiful original design.

The richness and brilliance of paintings, costumes, instruments and weaponry exhibited in the maharaja's palace contrasted sharply with the crowded street scenes and professional beggars whose tears flowed freely whenever a tourist bus approached. Evidently the government offers accommodation and work to beggars, but begging is an honorable family tradition which they prefer to carry on. One never becomes quite inured to deformities thrust into one's face, and the many begging children with their little tin buckets. ("We're getting closer to the real India—well, the stereotype, anyway.")

Jai Singh way back then was quite an astronomer, and he built the most amazing series of surrealistic walls, sunken marble hemispheres, and sets of stairs to view the stars and their varied paths through the heavens. Astronomy and astrology were very important back then—even the rulers' daily selection of clothes and jewelry was determined by readings of the stars. Frank and I ascended our Aries staircase and viewed the 100-foot-high sundial which accurately tells time to the second. Baboons surveyed us from the walls and occasionally took a daring leap onto someone's purse or bag. Between the baboons and the beggars, we sought the sanctuary of our house-on-wheels, another enormous Indian bus, as we proceeded to Jaipur's most famous site, the "Palace of the Winds."

The five-storey fairytale façade of pink sandstone carved with tiny niches, latticed windows, arches and cupolas, and etched in flowery arabesque designs in white, the "Palace of the Winds" is actually only a façade, an elaborate palace in front, a series of steps behind, from which ladies of the palace, bored with their riches and each other's constant company, could look out onto "real life," the street scenes beneath, as merchants carried their wares, common people strolled and quarreled, unknowingly offering amusement to the ladies hidden behind the latticed screens above. This ornate building, seen on nearly as many travel brochures as the Taj Mahal, stands idle today, its hidden stairways empty of costumes and intrigue, its rosy exterior changing in hue with sun and shadow. Wild-looking barefoot seers and visionaries, waist-length hair and beards matted or braided, with toothpick legs, sat twisted in their lotus positions, mumbling and chanting, sensing every glimpse from near or far, intense eyes eerily honing in on the unsuspecting viewer—me. Night fell, we left the bus and strolled the busy streets, occasionally stepping inside a shop, all of which have a raised platform, padded and sheet covered, where the merchant sits cross-legged, waiting to serve you as you take a seat across the narrow room.

Yet another incredible maharaja's palace, the Rambagh Palace, now a luxury hotel, gave another glimpse into the fabulously rich lives of the maharajas. Of course, the present Maharaja of Jaipur has numerous magnificent palaces—as well as a special license plate to compensate for his loss of political power at India's independence.

Amber Fort—the spectacular hilltop fortress which was Jai Singh's capital before he daringly descended to the plain to create his new city. The usual superlatives apply. By now we had seen so many overwhelming hilltop fortresses that we were more interested in the playful baboons which pestered us as we rode our painted and bedecked elephants up the old elephant ramps into this huge fort, constructed in 1592. The usual ornate palaces within sported the usual mirrored mosaic walls, transforming the light of one candle into a starry heaven above. (This was reserved for the king's "hall of pleasure" where he required many attendants to help him achieve his pleasure—one to hold the candle to create the artificial starlight, some for musical accompaniment, and at least one with which to practice some of the intricate feats displayed in temple carvings. But with twelve official wives and over 200 concubines, he never lacked a partner.) Frank and I were happily lost in the village, having taken the wrong set of steps from the fort down the steep hillside and enjoying the panorama of crenellated walls stretching to infinity along the distant hills, monkeys perched on housetops, winding roads of whitewashed stone houses with groups of giggling sari'd girls with golden earrings and flashing teeth smiling at Frank's bright printed turban which was so much a part of him that we'd forgotten he was still wearing it!

We loved our rides through the Rajasthani countryside, though the bumpy all-day trip to Agra nearly did us in. Green parrots flying across the road, camel carts, fields of yellow flowers, curly-horned buffalo and Brahman bulls in silver ankle bracelets, peacocks roaming wild through the countryside, baboons, spotted goats followed by sari'd shepherdesses, long bristly-haired pigs among the golden-brown haystacks on the unproductive dry red soil. Even so, India is self-sufficient in food!...and one of the world's big 10 industrial powers. Hardly any imports here—our guide, an educated man, had never heard of Seiko—he wore the local brand and drove the omnipresent Ambassador, India's tiny homemade car with a 1940s design, but surprisingly spacious and comfortable inside. Self-sufficient in energy as well, it appears, as we passed through village after village with buffalo and cow "chips" molded into flat round disks and pressed onto sides and rooftops of houses to dry, then artistically arranged in six-foot-high mounds in various herringbone and checkered layers. This recycled fuel appears to be a mainstay of the villages and graces the head of many a lovely maiden carrying her rich and fragrant load along the roadside.

An old man sat on his wooden chair in front of his mud house, surrounded by a brilliant red carpet of chilies drying in the sun. A woman in chartreuse walked on with large round earthen bowl balanced on her head—and a brass bowl balanced on top of that! On the roadside, vultures picked clean the huge red-stained white ribcage of a cow or buffalo, assisted by a spotted dog. Thatched roofs emulated the carved red sandstone peacock tail window of so many Rajasthani forts and palaces. Tree roots stood exposed where surrounding soil had been excavated for building bricks, creating strange mounds and bumps on the landscape. We had left Rajasthan's hills for the flat land of the state of Uttar Pradesh, southeast of New Delhi.

FATEHPUR SIKRI—Moghul ghost town! A perfectly preserved Moghul capital in the middle of nowhere built by the great emperor Akbar on the site where an old holy man correctly predicted the birth of Akbar's son. Occupied only during 1570-1585 A.D. and probably abandoned due to lack of water, this red sandstone city of courtyards, five-storey palaces, domes and pavilions, the "City of Victory" combines Hindu, Gothic, Egyptian, Persian, Buddhist, Islamic and various other styles of architecture in its elaborately carved buildings. Akbar, Moslem emperor, studied eastern religions, was tolerant of all beliefs and eventually created his own religion, a synthesis of all those beliefs of the various peoples he governed, which was interestingly reflected in the combination of architectural styles incorporating elements and symbols of all beliefs into his buildings. Even so, he amused himself with a huge human-scale marble chessboard in the court-yard, with enemy captives or slave girls as the chessmen. Now the courtyard was barren of carpets and silk canopies—just our raucous French group and occa-sional Moslem women, black veils clenched in their teeth, just like in Egypt. Akbar returned the capital to Agra after only sixteen years' inhabitance, leaving his beautiful ghost city to stand through the centuries.

The Jama Masjid ("Friday Mosque") just across the way was wonderful as are all Moghul Jama Masjids. The immense inner courtyard was filled with robed and turbaned worshippers—where did they come from to this abandoned former capital? The gates, walls and domes were magnificent, as usual. The usual crowd of 10,000 could easily be accommodated in the courtyard, all kneeling on their prayer rugs. One all-white marble building carved in intricate lattice designs held the tomb of the holy man who had predicted the birth of Akbar's son—even now, women come to pray for fertility, tying red threads of wishes into the lacy lattice screen walls.

Six great Moghul emperors ruled northern India (no one ruled both north and south until the British came along) 1386-1707 from Babar, Muslim descendent of Genghis Khan and Tamerlane, who came from Afghanistan and was called "Moghul" from the Turkish side of the family, died in Agra and was buried in Kabul, Afghanistan. The second, Houmayun, ruled 1530-1562 when he fell down the library stairs and died, resulting in the glorious domed tomb his wife had built for him in New Delhi, our first inkling of the grandeurs of Moghul architecture, after which the Taj Mahal is designed. Akbar of Agra-Fatehpur Sikri-Agra, "The Great," was known for his scholarship, tolerance and bravery in warfare. During his 49-year rule he built not only Fatehpur Sikri, but the Agra Fort, an impressive tomb and a grand mosque in Lahore, Pakistan—all in charac-teristic (meaning wonderful!) Moghul style. History gets hairy with the soap-opera existence of his son Jihangi (Salim)—the one he waited so long for—and his wife, lovers and relatives who ruled the country while Jihangi caroused, drank and smoked opium. His son, Shan Jahan, the fifth Moghul ruler, who built the Taj Mahal as a monument to his wife who died bearing their eighth (some say 14th) child and who planned to build a black Taj Mahal for himself on the other side of the river, was finally locked up by his fanatical Moslem son Aurangzeb to curb his building sprees. Ah, but the ones he left us…the glory of Moghul architecture resounds in his name. His son mistreated non-Moslems, lost the support of the people, and died in 1707. Everyone—Rajputs, Sikhs—revolted, resulting in the "birth of the maharajas," and then the British came in 1789—and that's it! Until independence in 1948....

AGRA—where yellowed old colonial houses crumble, where the 400-year-old Shiva temple is across the street from the Methodist Church—was the culmination of our journey. After a distant glimpse of the great white bulbous domes appearing over shanties in the foreground, we continued our pilgrimage to the famed Taj Mahal, masterpiece of Moghul architecture, which I had always thought was highly overrated in tourist publicity—until I walked through the courtyards, through the immense heavy arched gates, and beheld its misty-white ethereal form seemingly floating on its platform at the end of the long reflecting pool. None of its many photographs do it justice. ("Mine will," I thought, as we shot roll after roll from various angles in the changing light; but of course they didn't at all—they look like all the rest.) I think the magnificence is not in the white marble intricately inlaid with floral patterns of semi-precious stones, nor the marble terraces and minarets, but just the overall grace and delicacy of the Persian outline of domes and arches. How can something so heavy appear so light? The hard stone seem so soft and cloudlike? The stable structure appear almost to hover above the ground? We arrived late one afternoon, saw the last rays of the sun set behind one of the two elaborate twin red sandstone mosques rising from the bright green grass on each side of the gleaming white Taj next to the river—and best of all, we arose the next morning for sunrise in the mist, for just a few fleeting moments the best of all scenes as the Taj slowly took shape from behind the dissipating mist, and then stood in sharp clarity of detail in relief against a pale gray-blue sky.

Friday is free, the Moslem holy day, and we were fortunate to be there then, to see the Taj in use as a holy place. An old man sat inside, reading his Koran from the pale mote-ridden beams of light through the carved marble screen. Three camels waded serenely across the river in the early morning light. The lacy tracery of inlaid lapis, carnelian, coral and malachite suffused the central tomb of Mumtaz Mahal and the larger one of her husband Shan Jahan beside her, foiled in his final attempts to build a black marble Taj Mahal across the river, the lovers forever joined by a marble bridge.

Frank, Chuck and Denis, anticipating another shopping expedition, wisely left our group of can-can girls, hired a "tuk-tuk," a three-wheeled motorcycle taxi, and charged through the hay-ridden riverbanks across from the rear of the

Taj. They survived the daredevil ride through the rutted fields, goats and cattle, and had an exciting afternoon observing riverside cremations, collection of bones and ashes, and holy men preparing for meditation, then descending into a coma-like trance. They were subsequently known as the "Tuk-Tuk Cowboys," suitable counterparts for the fifteen "Can-Can Girls."

Agra Fort—yet another unbelievable fortress of towering 70-foot crenellated walls, inconceivable luxury within, white marble palaces inside the red sandstone walls, blue ceramics of delicate designs imbedded in the impregnable walls, court-yards and gardens and palaces within. We dodged vendors as we crossed the bridge above the sunken moat, once filled with foreboding crocodiles. Akbar's capital both before and after Fatehpur Sikri, Agra Fort in its splendor became the final prison of Shan Jahan as he sat confined in his elegant mosaic marble room, peering through the gracefully arched windows at his beloved Taj Mahal in the distance across the river.

"Now I take your attention, personally, on the back," advised our mala-propian guide. (In other words, "Look over here.") He pointed out the many overhanging "walconies" and the fountain which was "gifted to his wife as part of the love." These were some of the few comments we could decipher. The Indian love for the present continuous tense, excessive use of "the" ("Where is the Laila?"), reversal of v's and w's, clipped pronunciation (it took me two days to fig-ure out that all the beautiful "lockers" we saw in various cities were actually the "law courts"), and excessively formal expressions ("You are maintaining a diary?" inquired a shriveled pink-turbaned, white-bearded old gentleman at the Jodhpur fort) combine to create what I call "Indo-English" which probably becomes more Indo and less English with the passing of years after departure of the British Raj.

"You are maintaining a diary?" asked the pink-turbaned gentleman
in Jodphur

Well, having been suitably awed by the Agra Fort, we continued on with our indecipherable guide: "From vere is de vay of de hotel I vill take you for de shopping...."

NEW DELHI—Back to the Garden City of New Delhi with its wide open spaces, tree-lined boulevards, paucity of cars, huge "squares" and green, green, green for our final day of individual explorations, getting lost among the broad avenues, picking our way through the Tibetan bazaar, and returning to the magnificent Red Fort for an evening sound and light show, complete with horses' hoofs clomping, soldiers yelling, women giggling, elephants trumpeting amid horrendous colored lights illuminating the pure white marble buildings, not to mention the excitement of seeing (for a fee, of course) someone practice levitation.

We left India that night, but we didn't really leave, not till we landed in Bangkok, because our Air India flight embodied all the craziness of India within its fuselage walls decorated with temple nudes, its purple and gold and red cushions, and its unruly passengers walking the aisles and drinking throughout the "Fasten Your Seatbelt" stages. One particularly rowdy barefoot Sikh in front of us squatted lotus-like in his seat, whiskey bottle in one hand, glass of wine in the other, bright yellow airplane pillowcase pulled turban-like over the lifelong knot of hair atop his head, singing songs and assailing stewardesses. The can-can girls were in the next compartment, Frank was stretched out among the Sikhs in front of me, next to one in a beautifully speckled Jackson Pollack turban, and I contemplated our brief brush with India and bade farewell to Rajasthan, especially Udaipur. Its whitewashed doorways adorned with printed elephants and horses, its palaces and forts, lakes and winding village streets, its riverside laundries where saris and sheets intermingled in the sacred waters, its peacocks, baboons, camels and cows with brightly-painted horns, its brilliantly sari'd women and brightly-turbaned, earringed and moustachioed men beckon me to return.

In-Laws Are Out-Lawed!

We are fortunate to have shared our Egyptian and Thai adventures with friends (well, hardly anyone came!) and family members (well, it seems they ALL came—and stayed!). By "fortunate" I include good fortune as well as bad…

A few incidents that will not be soon forgotten:

Frank's mother's first visit to Cairo. How we had cleaned and cleaned in preparation for her visit! The maid, whoever it happened to be at the time, scrubbed and swept and dusted. I organized and re-arranged and assisted in the general spring-cleaning, whatever season it happened to be. Soon Frank's mother had crossed that invisible line in the Mediterranean, leaving her native Greece for the wilds of Africa—us. She came in, looked around and then began her microscopic inspection of every inch of every surface. The lower rungs of chairs. Underneath the carpets. The underside of each table. Inside the lampshades. She bent double to dust the previously dusted. She attacked unseen surfaces with gusto. She crawled, she peered, she swept, she rubbed. She spent most of her first day re-cleaning my laboriously cleaned apartment. Towards the end of the day, she sighed, sat down and announced, "Now I can sit. Finally, it is clean."

My cooking skills did not pass muster, either. Of course, we relished Frank's mom's home cooking—and she looked forward to cooking for her son, who kissed her goodbye early every morning, returned late each night to eat her home cooked food, and then retired to work some more. I, on the other hand, without car and without adequate language skills, tried to pass the lengthening days with limited chitchat and a feeble show of cleaning. The time that Frank's mom came for Greek Easter with Frank's brother, Frank instructed me to cook vegetables for the 40-day Lenten fast. So I did. Mounds and mounds and piles and piles of veggies of all sorts. When they arrived at last and sat down to eat from my proud table of tediously prepared Lenten fare, she took a bite, made a face and asked, "Does this have BUTTER?"

"Well, yes," I replied, oblivious to the fact that dairy products were taboo during this period. I glared at the culprit.

"Why didn't you tell me not to use butter?" I chided.

203

"Oh well, I forgot," Frank replied, as he passed around the bread—again. So his mother and brother were reduced to bread and water for their welcoming meal to Egypt that Easter. I'm sure this tale has become part of the family archives—in Greece.

Frank's mom, a very religious woman, spent many hours sitting and reading her prayer book. I strived to find activities to take her to, but since my life was limited to a British *mah jongg* group, a primarily southern ladies Bible study, and occasional forays into the medieval bazaar, these became her haunts as well. She brought her prayer book along, since no one spoke Greek and my translational skills were limited. The cakes and cookies served for refreshments at these activities were always a high point, except that she fasted on Wednesdays and Fridays—and the meetings were always on a Wednesday or Friday. Eventually, she made an exception to her self-imposed fasts and made a deal with God to trade Wednesdays and Fridays for other days of the week when there were no meetings with refreshments. She was a kindly presence at these various activities, always welcomed and smiling, sitting and reading her prayer book. (Lord knows we needed praying for in those days. Rabies, rats, bomb threats, broken bones—trouble in Paradise!)

When we lived in the little Villa Isis, Frank's mom, whom we called "Yiayia" (grandmother), came to visit again—and was a lifesaver when Leah and I stayed behind in the U.S. for my operation. She cooked her wonderful foods for Jared and Frank, and she saved the day by assembling Jared's Superman Halloween costume from some Superman pajamas I had sent over as well as making him a magic red cape. He looked like he was ready to take off and fly away! When Leah and I returned at last to Cairo, Jared used me as translator: "Tell Yiayia this…" "Ask Yiayia that…" One day I returned early from some errand and heard Yiayia asking in Greek, "Jared, where are your shoes?" I was struck dumb when I heard the prompt response in a little five-year-old voice in perfect GREEK: "Upstairs, Yiayia." When asked by another visiting Greek if her daughter-in-law understood Greek, Yiayia shrewdly replied, "When she wants to." I guess she wasn't too far off the mark.

Yiayia gradually learned that the Greek custom of politely refusing anything a minimum of three times did not mesh well with American manners. After "No, no, I can't" and "No, no, I don't want any," I would say "OK" and move on to something else, in my ignorance leaving a hungry grandmother at the table. (The first time I was introduced to this old-fashioned Greek custom was a few years before during her first visit to the U.S. when I tried to launder her sheets each week. She protested so vigorously each time that I relented and let her hand me only her pillowcases to wash. Before her departure, she drew me aside and said, "For me, never mind, but when anyone else visits, you be sure to wash their sheets!") In fact, later in Thailand when she and her sister came for an extended visit, we were all at the table, and her sister began refusing servings of foods. I saw Yiayia nudge her and whisper in Greek, "If you want to eat, you'd better take it now!"

Food—or lack of it—created a major brouhaha during a visit at our little Villa Isis. Yiayia complained of shortness of breath and chest discomfort. With her history of heart problems, this created a major alarm and we summoned the doctor right away. She finally admitted to the doctor that she had not taken her heart medication that day.

"Why not?" asked Frank, eyebrows raised, peering over his glasses.

"I cannot say," she said, looking down.

"Well, WHY can't you say?" bellowed Frank.

"Because I cannot."

"WHY DIDN'T YOU TAKE YOUR HEART MEDICINE???"

"Well...." she finally admitted, "it has to be taken with food."

"Well, why didn't you take it?"

"I cannot say."

"Why not?"

"I did not eat today...."

"W-H-A-T???" (You have to understand that this is the fatal blow for a Greek—eating is life, eating is love, and not feeding someone is tantamount to depriving them of life.) "I...did...not...eat...today."

"YOU DIDN'T EAT? WHY DIDN'T YOU EAT?"

Back to square one: "I cannot say."

Of course, all eyes turned to me and I became the focus of the inquisition.

"Didn't you give her lunch?"

"Yes, I offered her chicken left over from last night. She didn't want it."

"So?"

"I said I could make her a salad. She said no. I offered her something else and she didn't want it. What was I supposed to do?"

"YOU ARE SUPPOSED TO PUT THE FOOD IN FRONT OF HER ON THE TABLE, no matter what she says. Just put it out and she'll eat it. Don't you understand anything?"

At this point, Yiayia was given food, took her pill and the doctor left—hopefully not to return for another cultural misunderstanding emergency.

Yiayia was very attentive to the kids and the household and noticed much that passed me by. It was she who sensed that Jared's arm wasn't right after a fall—sure enough, he had broken his arm in two places. It was also Yiayia who informed me that my timid little maid, Layla (who would entertain Leah by clicking chicken feet in front of her face as she sat in her baby-seat at the kitchen table) was stealing. "No, I can't believe it! She would never do that," I protested. Well, Yiayia had been counting each piece of fruit each day and saw food disappearing. My electric knife soon was missing one of its two blades and rendered useless. My new silk dress was missing. Packages of nylons from the U.S. and other items, which I had earlier assumed I'd merely misplaced, now fell into the newly-established category of stolen goods. I just hated this. I really liked Layla and had worked hard to train her. By this point, I was helping newcomers interview prospective maids with my "kitchen Arabic" and felt that I was a good judge of character. Alas! Well, with the help of my friend Shahira to translate the finer points, I spoke to Layla, nearly doubling her salary and telling her how much we liked her and wanted to keep her. I put the money on the table, and then began removing it bill by bill ("This is for the knife...this is for the silk dress...this is for the nylons....") until she was left with her pre-raise amount. I told her that we really, really liked her and wanted her to stay, but if even one item were ever missing again, that would be the end. I don't think anything else was taken after that, but then again Yiayia had returned to Greece and without her eagle eyes, one can't say for sure!

Yiayia saw a different world indeed after we moved to Bangkok. She liked cosmopolitan Bangkok and thought its people were very religious, since there were so many temples around. She somehow didn't get the gist of the numerous clubs, billboards and evidence of prostitution all around us. We let her continue in her pleasant delusion. Yiayia stayed with the kids when Frank and I ventured to India and Burma. Imagine our shock when we returned and found her with carrot-orange hair. No, that is not a strong enough description. I had previously taken her for a shampoo to the hairdresser across the street. Yiayia later returned on her own to have her hair dyed. Well, fine western hair is not at all the same as thick dark Asian tresses, and what would have been merely a reddish highlight on an oriental head looked more like a fluorescent traffic cone on Yiayia! Frank and I were in shock and sent her back to the hairdresser for additional shampoos several times, all to no avail. It had to grow out.

Yiayia returned to Bangkok with her sister, Theia (Aunt) Tassia, for a record-setting series of shopping expeditions—with Yiayia's reluctant daughter-in-law as tour-guide and translator. You have to understand that I had established relationships with various merchants, seamstresses and shoemakers based on my distaste for bargaining. They all understood that and offered me their best price at the beginning, so all was well and I was relieved of that distasteful task. Until Yiayia and Theia Tassia arrived. "Tell her it's too much!" Theia Tassia would exclaim, vigorously gesturing, thumbs down, to lower the price when I fudged on the translation. This happened time and again, as each item ordered required numerous fittings, which became a trial indeed, as the elderly sisters kept changing their minds and making new demands with each visit. I did learn more Greek, though; for instance, Greeks call the "toe" of the shoe the *miti,* or "nose." Makes sense. Colors of shoes were changed mid-stream. Styles were altered after the leather had been cut. Straps and buckles were added and deleted with abandon. Prices were debated. And all this from Greek to English to Thai. Gems were purchased—and carefully and surreptitiously sewn into hems of dresses. Shopkeepers would look at me and say, "You are very good, Madam." Every detail changed a hundred times; half the items returned to be redone; questioning my arithmetic in charging for these thousands of items; insisting that the dressmaker's girls rummage through their trash bags to get every scrap of leftover fabric from every blouse, suit, skirt and dress ever made for them—probably thirty items—and then complaining about them instead of being happy. One night I dressed to go out and Theia asked, "Why are *your* pleats in the back only and mine in the front *and* the back?" Guess it adds excitement and meaning to life to recast every occurrence into a Greek tragedy of sorts. In one of our many shopping forays, I finally found some fabric that *I* wanted to use for a skirt; Theia Tassia grabbed it, bought it and said she'd give it to her maid back home, or perhaps to a neighbor she didn't like.

Oriental and Byzantine ways have more in common with each other than with the West, and so Yiayia and the Thai merchants and seamstress actually had a certain unspoken cultural understanding of each other, rendering language unnecessary. When Yiayia had me phone the seamstress for the hundredth time, it seemed, this time to tell her to change the black collar and lining of the brown, rust and black dress she was making for Yiayia, I asked her why she would want to have a WHITE collar and lining made for a brown and black dress.

"So the dirt won't show around the neck," she replied.

"But..." and this in my halting Greek as I strived to find the right words "...the dirt it show on the white color and the dirt it not show on the black color."

"No."

I had to request Frank's intervention to explain, again, that dirt shows on white, but not on black.

Yiayia remained adamant. The black lining had to go and be replaced with white. When I at last telephoned the seamstress and profusely apologized for this bizarre request, she understood perfectly and agreed to make the change. Frank had to explain to me that having black next to the skin would make Yiayia think of death. My cultural background had blinded me to superstitions easily understood by a Thai dressmaker and a Greek grandma. Yiayia returned to Greece with a lovely new dress with a lighter (but not white, thank God—the seamstress had some sense!) collar and lining.

Excerpt from 21 March 1896 letter to Frank's cousin:

Your article on stress arrived today—the day Frank was moved from intensive care into his private room. Don't be alarmed—he's doing fine. He's been under a lot of pressure lately at the office, has overseas visitors with different views, has been revising for several hectic weeks the speech he's supposed to give in two weeks in Singapore, developed severe tendonitis and could hardly walk; Jared broke his arm six days ago and is in a shoulder-high cast; I've recovered from an eight-day tropical fever that wiped me out, but nevertheless had to arise from my deathbed to help Theia Tassia buy two gems which she proceeded to hide in her bra—along with five fake watches—while she and Frank's mom went into hiding to sew all the Jim Thompson ties inside her skirt for her return to Greece after SIX weeks here...well, this begins to give you an inkling of our crazy lives here. I've spent all week taking Frank's mom to: internist, cardiologist, ophthalmologist, ear specialist, neurologist—to find out that, yes, the doctors in Greece were right and, yes, her medicine is OK. Four days dragging around getting ear and eye exams, X-rays, barium upper G-I series, zillions of blood, etc., tests—and, yes, even the treadmill cardiogram—and then *Frank* ends up in the emergency room with chest pains (second time in one day) and 220-140 blood pressure. Thank God a friend came to dinner and helped get a cab. Our street is wrecked for construction and so we have to park the car three blocks away for overnight. Oh, yes—tomorrow we have four houseguests coming form Singapore for eight days, and another houseguest arriving Sunday.

The good news is that it was NOT a heart attack—the heart muscle was not damaged. But it was a heart something, probably angina from reduced blood supply to the heart which requires more blood when under stress. Now dosed up on blood pressure medicine and lying down, his blood pressure is normal. Wires and patches and tubes can't keep Frank down, and he is dictating telexes and reviewing his speech and cracking jokes with the nurses. In the midst of all this, we have to get hamburgers and hotdogs and beer for the team baseball picnic tomorrow (simultaneous with arrival of houseguests at airport). We've been invited to lunch at the U.S. Ambassador's on Tuesday, too.

With poor Frank laid out on a stretcher-bed in the hospital hallway at 9-10 P.M., they insisted that I give them (1) an $800 deposit, which I don't exactly carry around in my purse (had just paid much more than that for all of Frank's mother's hospital tests, examinations and lab work), and (2) Frank's passport, which was locked up in his office downtown. Finally, 45 minutes later, he—from his hallway gurney—talked them into waiting till morning for the passport and cash. He was taken to a private room, and then the doctor came and put him in the intensive care unit for the night for observation. He came out fine, but the sight of him all hooked up to EKG wires and an IV was disturbing. This was the evening of the day I arrived at the very same hospital at 7:15 A.M. with his mom for additional tests and doctors till 2 P.M. Now I'm returning tomorrow for Jared's broken arm.

On the bright side, Leah is great—happy, healthy, new words every day and still asks where you are. Whenever she bumps into something, she wants to go to the hospital—after all, nearly every one else in the family goes there—nearly every day!

Please don't worry about Frank—he'll be fine. I think he needs to recover from the lethal combination of his mother and aunt in cahoots together—very demanding and critical of everything. He had just spent considerable time and over $100 in phone calls and telexes and sending checks to Singapore to order the video camera that Theia Tassia's son wanted—and then she called to say, "Never mind...we'll get one later." And so Frank had to race to the office to call Singapore again to cancel the order before his check was cashed. And today we received a letter from Theia to please buy a purse—color, size, etc.—for another lady who heard about the ones we've already bought. We were starved for houseguests in Egypt, but six weeks with two little old Greek ladies egging each other on is enough to do us for a long time—no wonder Frank landed in the hospital where he could recover.

Frank's mom will stay on another month if I can prove to immigration authorities that her son is in the hospital. My afternoon at the immigration office with her was futile because I didn't have a letter that nobody said I should have. They won't accept the hospital's letter, want Frank to appear, which he can't because he's hospitalized which is the reason we're here in the first place, and now they don't like Frank's mom's passport because someone in Albania changed the word "Greece" to "Albania" for her birthplace. Seems everyone's claiming that bit of land, but its repercussions leave us in hot water in Bangkok.

Oh yes, two days before all this, after I dropped Jared at school for only two hours because of his broken arm, the car broke down with Leah and Yiayia and me, I got them where they were going, it broke down again, I took a tuk-tuk in the blazing heat to be an hour and a half late to an embassy meeting, then got a lift to get Jared from school, but couldn't find him anywhere (someone had taken him home). The day after that he had such a four-hour tantrum ("You're the worst mother on earth!" after I had spent all morning making a baseball photo album to surprise him...) that I called the school psychologist and told the maid I was going back to India and would return in two years. Finally, when Frank limped in with his tendonitis, I ran off to the grocery store in search of solitude. And the next day, *Frank* ended up in the hospital. What irony.

Thanks for the stress article—good timing!

PS Jared's baseball team has a perfect record—no wins, all losses. Tomorrow is our last hope!

We Nearly Killed the Ambassador

March 1986

Medical emergencies in foreign countries are always quite frightening, compounded with language miscommunications and cultural differences. We had become good "customers" at our local Samitivej Hospital, having used its emergency services when Leah fell and split her skull on the only non-padded and non-rubberized surface in our ultra child-safe house. We've since returned with Jared's excruciating earaches, necessitating a small puncture in the eardrum to relieve the pressure—I in my housedress (most patients arrive jeweled and properly clothed) rocking the poor howling young boy as we waited for the hospital to "open" and for a doctor to arrive. We had also taken Frank's mother there for three days of extensive tests from head to toe, proving that she was in good health and that we were good children who showed our love for her by subjecting her to every imaginable diagnostic test, at considerable expense. With me translating the questions from English and the answers from Greek, it's amazing that she survived.

So we were quite familiar with our little hospital, with its private rooms complete with couches and chairs for visitors—and even room service...with alcoholic spirits to keep one's spirits up indeed. Never did we imagine that Frank would be hospitalized for a week for what we originally thought was a heart attack, but which turned out to be, most likely, an extreme reaction to medication for tendonitis. (One never knows where and how much of the medicine here is actually produced. It seems that his dosage was incorrect or the pills were mislabeled.) At any rate, it was with horror and fear that a friend and I rushed Frank to the emergency room, from which he was placed in an outdoor hallway for what seemed like hours awaiting transfer to the ICU. The young emergency room doctor, who looked to be about fourteen years old, came up with numerous possible diagnoses for Frank's extreme condition, but I couldn't understand his very halting English ("Maybe heart, maybe not..."), and his pale and pimply face didn't instill much confidence. When I was finally allowed to visit, after trying to sort through red tape and promising to pay for all treatment, I had to walk past bed after bed of patients in various stages of near-death, or so it appeared to me. Finally, I found Frank behind the curtains in the last bed, tied and tubed, gray and near-comatose.

Well, he did improve and was moved to a regular room from which he daily gave me instructions on what to tell the office, what reports to request, what messages to convey. We still didn't know the cause of his sudden illness, but later realized that he became successively more violently ill each time he took a dose of his new medicine. At the time, however, we thought it was his heart so we were very nervous indeed. He was scheduled for release a week later, just in time for a special luncheon which we felt most honored to be invited to at the residence of the American ambassador whose wife, Melpomene Brown, was a Greek-American from Boston! She had met Frank's mother at a previous gathering, where they abandoned traditional diplomatic protocol and conversed happily in Greek. I saw Mrs. Brown gesturing upward with her hands and overheard her saying to Frank's mom, in Greek: "We are EAGLES! We will rise like eagles!"

Thus we were on the guest list for an exclusive luncheon of Greeks living in Bangkok—there were fewer than twenty in all—in the ambassador's private quarters in celebration of Greek Independence Day on March 25. We had been awaiting this occasion for well over a month with great anticipation. In fact, Frank's mother had brought from Greece the *tarama* (fish roe) necessary to prepare the traditional *taramasalata*, which the ambassador's wife had requested. So we were especially pressed to retrieve Frank from the hospital expeditiously and head directly to the embassy residence. How organized I was! I had his best suit cleaned and shoes polished. I gathered necessary paperwork for checking out of the hospital. I arranged for the driver to arrive early to collect Frank's mom and the taramasalata, and me with all of Frank's clothes, and drive us to Samitivej, where we would pick up Frank and proceed directly to the ambassador's private residence.

I neglected to factor in a few variables, however:

• The king's son's girlfriend was moving into a large mansion at the end of our street. Thus, the blacktopped street was suddenly and without notice ripped up for the entire block, to be replaced with concrete, an extravagance indeed, but necessary to ensure a smooth ride for the prince during his comings and goings to visit his girlfriend.

• The masculinity of our small, very thin and wiry, rather sullen Muslim kickboxer driver, Musa (Moses), was compromised when I, rather than Frank, requested his services to drive us to the hospital. As a result, he did arrive, he did take the car—and then he disappeared with the car for the rest of the day, later saying that he "didn't understand" that we wanted him to drive us somewhere. (He assumed that we wanted him to come and take the car for a spin and enjoy himself for the rest of the day. He later said that he did not hear me say, "Come back at one o'clock to take us to the hospital" due to noise from the cement mixer just outside our driveway.)

• Frank's mother's desire to appear glamorous for the event combined with her insistence on making the taramasalata in a most unusual manner.

At any rate, Frank's mom prepared the salty, smelly roe in the blender, combining it with bread, mayonnaise and other ingredients. When I returned from assembling all of Frank's clothes to take to the hospital, I saw her putting the rubber spatula down in the lidless blender as it chopped away. "STOP!" I yelled. "No! No! The rubber is being cut up in the taramasalata!" In my slinky silk clothes, freshly bathed and cologned, I sat down to fish out camouflaged pieces of rubber from the various bowls holding the strong-smelling taramasalata. "These pieces are big enough to choke an ambassador," I thought. "I have to find them all. We can't kill the U.S. Ambassador to Thailand—especially on Greek Independence Day." I finally retrieved what I hoped was the last piece of rubber from the last dish, but my fingers smelled of fish eggs for the rest of the day.

Gathering all of Frank's clothes, still in their bags from the cleaners, I grabbed Frank's mom with a tray holding six bowls of taramasalata and headed outside. That's when I discovered that Musa was nowhere in sight and could not be reached by phone. In desperation, I decided to wave down a taxi at the corner. I had not counted on the cement mixer laying wet cement in front of our house just at that moment. I went back to change to rubber flip-flops to negotiate a narrow board laid over the wet concrete. Just as I was making progress, Frank's trousers slipped off the hanger inside the plastic bag—right into the wet cement. What next? I had to tiptoe backwards in my flip-flops to the house in search of different clothes—tried but couldn't remove the cement from the suit trousers. So I had to find a totally new outfit, neither as nice nor as well-matched. Grabbing Frank's mother, the clothes and the taramasalata once again, I traversed the wobbly board over the wet concrete till we arrived at the corner where we hailed a taxi which naturally was headed in the opposite direction from the hospital due to the one-way street system. Opening the windows to let the salty smell of the taramasalata dissipate, we were finally on our way to the hospital—where I asked the taxi to wait "a few minutes." I should have known better.

As soon at we entered the hospital, laden with our six odoriferous bowls, Frank's mother began looking despondent and complained about the color of her nail polish, how it didn't match her dress well enough, how it wasn't nice enough. "Why NOW?" I thought, but most opportunely spotted a beauty salon in the lobby of the hospital and shooed her inside for a manicure. At least that got rid of the taramasalata smell for a while, as it combined malodorously with the reeking odor of nail polish, creating a deadly duo which I feared would stifle anyone in the salon. But never mind them…on to Frank who, instead of being ready to be wheeled out, was still lounging in bed in his pajamas. "Why aren't you ready?" I panted. "I have the taxi waiting downstairs and your mom getting a manicure and your trousers fell into wet cement and the driver took the car and never came back—and we will probably kill the ambassador with a piece of rubber in the taramasalata!!"

"Calm down," he said. "They can't release me till they figure out the medicines I'm supposed to take, and no one's been in here for hours." Well, I started hustling around, calling nurses, then trying to check out downstairs, promising all our future earnings in payment on various legal documents. I don't really remember what I did or what I signed—just that it took a very long time, and of course the taxi had left by the time we were finally ready. Somehow, I got Frank into his mismatched clothes, retrieved his mom from the salon, leaving a trail of fish odor behind her, and found a new taxi to deliver us to the embassy residence, where we were enthusiastically greeted by the tall dignified ambassador and his energetic wife, who knew nothing of Frank's release from the hospital just minutes before.

"Now sit quietly and don't strain yourself," I said. "Watch what you eat." "Don't drink." "BE CAREFUL." Well, we were transported for the afternoon and evening to Greek soil, complete with fireworks outside the window. The taramasalata was a bit hit. We met every other Greek in Bangkok and commiserated that there were no Greek restaurants in the whole country. When dinner was over and it was time for lively and animated Greek dancing, you can just imagine who the ambassador's wife chose to lead the dance.

He did.

He didn't die.

And neither did the ambassador.

Nice Days, Naughty Nights

1985-1986

Jared's happily in first grade learning to read and awaits his Tuesday riding lessons at the Polo Club with great joy. He dresses all in white for his Monday and Thursday Tai-Kwan-Do lessons in Korean martial arts. Wednesday he takes gymnastics, and after the 8 A.M. Sunday school, he and Frank usually go to one of Bangkok's many department store arcades to ride the toys and endure the flashing lights and jarring music (I refuse on that one). So at last he has a full life after the paucity of activities in Egypt. He's developing allergies to the Bangkok pollution and dust, however, and may have to begin twice-weekly injections…poor guy.

Leah gets out three times a week—one play-group morning, one afternoon play-group, and Sunday morning church nursery. Her life is rather restricted, as I don't have a car here (they wanted $30,000 to bring my eight-year-old car into the country), and even if I did, I probably wouldn't risk Bangkok traffic. "The driver fled the scene" appears daily in the paper. Yesterday's variation was "The crane operator fled the scene" after he dropped an air conditioner eight storeys below onto a fish vendor—with predictable results.

Our rainy season will end soon, and the snakes will return to their holes, thank God. Jared came home from school one day with a story about the "cobra in the playground." Seemed rather outlandish to me, but I did ask his kindergarten teacher about it at the end-of-year party. "Well, I don't know anything about snakes," she said, "but it did move with its head sticking up," gesturing with her wrist and hand the perfect outline of a cobra! As it turns out, the school custodians were charged with inspecting the children's playground—next to a canal—before each recess. This was a young cobra, which escaped their attention. When Jared and his friends spotted the snake with its head reared up, they called the custodian—who dispatched the young cobra with practiced expertise.

This is the Bangkok we don't know. We collapse at 8 P.M. and are up at 5:30 A.M. (Enclosed with this letter is a page from *The Bangkok Post*, October 22, 1985, full of advertisements for numerous VD clinics such as "VD Polyclinic:

215

General Check-up, Dental, VD Specialist, Treatment for Herpes," some of which do house-calls; private clubs and "escort services," such as the "Happy Boy Cocktail Lounge—For men only"), "Joker Club—ONLY SWINGERS ALLOWED," "ATAMI—Experience a new kind of sensation in our new deluxe rooms," "CLEOPATRA—A Touch of Happiness! Massage Palour & Coffee Shop," "DARLING—At Darling, you'll get an experience so relaxing you'll never forget. Come try us…We'll make you really feel good.")

Other interesting "publications" are restaurant menus which graciously try to translate for the convenience of their foreign guests. Samples: Bansuan Flesh Perfume (or Duck Perfume, Hen Perfume or Goose Perfume). Try a refreshing salad such as Morning Gory Salad. Fried foods include Fry Plesh's Fish, Fry Parachute Jump, and Pontoon Broken. Main courses include Joke Fish Three Taste and Everything Curry. For dessert, try some canned fruits: Tin of Supper, Pineapple of Tin, Rambutan of Tin or Truffle of Tin. Beverage? Why, a bottle of Spite, of course! Our good friends, the Kuglers, took us to Thailand's largest restaurant, a huge outdoor structure seating several thousand at a time, designed in the shape of the map of Thailand and built on stilts over water, a kind of Siamese air conditioning *au naturel* with water-cooled breezes to cool the customers. The restaurant is SO large that waiters and waitresses whiz along on roller skates, precariously balancing huge trays, careening loftily as they speed up and down board walkways with curved bridges and ramps to reach their far-flung customers. After years of experience in hardship posts in South America and Indonesia, Bill Kugler proudly displayed his culinary expertise by insisting on ordering for the table: TOAD CURRY and tiny little roasted birds whose heads one was expected to crunch. Well, I went hungry that night.…

Other meals in Thailand were as memorable, but in a more delectable way. Frank joined the Bangkok branch of France's esteemed Chaîne des Rôtisseurs, a—shall we say—gentlemen's eating club, founded in 1248, whose monthly meetings are held in great style at Bangkok's best restaurants. I remember one at which wives were allowed—a progressive dinner at the various restaurants at the Royal Orchid Sheraton Hotel on the banks of the Chao Phya River in the center of Bangkok. We rode up in the elevator with not one, but *four* ambassadors—of Germany, Egypt, Poland and the U.S.. The first course, at the Zensai Japanese restaurant, was a variety of raw seafood in artistic designs on ice in a black lacquer box with a 10-inch-high Japanese *torii* spirit gate from which was hung a fish "net" made of tiny woven strips of some white vegetable—most impressive! We were a bit confused by our three-inch square birch boxes filled with what appeared to be water—finger bowls? Better watch the others and see what they do… Surprise—it was sake! Quite strong, but so smooth—and how easily it went down…like water, to the accompaniment of Japanese music in the background.

We needed the handrails on the stairway to reach the next destination—Giorgio's, the Italian restaurant where we were served a wonderfully rich *crema di zucca* in individual carved gourds, accompanied, of course, by a hearty red Italian wine, with the proper temperature announced to the group. Lyrical romantic Italian music lulled us. So full—and wobbly—that we could barely move, we were then directed to the terrace swimming pool where we were greeted by peasant-clad waitresses IN THE POOL wearing traditional Thai farmer straw hats, and walking through waist-high water to the raft which bore a one-ton ice sculpture covered in purple orchids and surmounted by the largest magnum of champagne I have ever seen! They scurried, if that is possible, through the water, ferrying us goblets of champagne sherbet to "cleanse the palate for the entrée." Although we wished to linger, we quickly moved along to the next course, watching the gigantic ice sculpture rapidly melt in the tropical evening heat.

As if that weren't enough, we were then escorted to the main dining room, where spectacular plates of roast prime rib of beef were accompanied by artistically braided bread which snaked its way down the center of the long table, and, of course, a rich and luscious bordeaux at the specified temperature…. As my father noticed, no wine glass was ever allowed to fall below the halfway mark…and his certainly never did!

On to the Pompadour Room, where we staggered in and thankfully dropped to our seats in the semi-circular amphitheater, and then were served yet another wine, a lighter one this time. After a few moments of silence, trumpets blared and suddenly a host of virile young waiters dressed in soccer uniforms burst into the room, jumping and yelling, bearing soccer balls made of white chocolate. As the handsome young men served each of us, they lifted the lids off the soccer balls revealing vanilla ice cream onto which they ladled cherries from a gigantic sculpted soccer ball on the stage. The intoxicating cherry sauce was quickly ignited—and Cherries Jubilee Flambée, according to my father, "became a spectacular reality. As we enjoyed the dessert we were entertained with lively Mexican mariachi music and dancers—obviously a salute to the upcoming World Cup soon to be held in Mexico City."

Enough? Not in Bangkok! On to The Club, the hotel's snazzy nightclub, for Irish coffee, petits fours and pralines, complete with a floor show with live music and the most luscious, sinuous, skimpily-clad and voluptuous young women singing and dancing provocatively. After all, this is Bangkok—what else could one expect? How many minutes did it take for our satiated and fuzzy minds to put two and two together and realize that these gorgeous young women, with their alluring dance movements and lovely throaty voices, were transvestite queens, imported from Pattya for the occasion?! (I learned the secret of uncovering the masculine nature of these alluring and ultra-feminine entertainers—look for narrow hips and broad shoulders...a dead give-away.) The next day, we had a hard time distinguishing reality from fantasy as we recalled this special evening. In fact, my father, after all his spirited indulgence, couldn't remember the nightclub portion, which he had so enjoyed, at all!

Other Chaîne des Rôtisseurs events were nearly as memorable, such as the dinner where we were served "essence of duck," each plate a miniature Toulouse Lautrec *Jane Avril* poster "painted" with a brown paste which how many poor ducks had sacrificed their lives for? Toulouse Lautrec, in full costume, painted on his easel to the accompaniment of can-can music as we ate—with of course the proper wine at the proper temperature, as announced. This was followed by English hunting lords racing into the room in full attire, as the hunting horns were blown, preceding our main course of red hart just flown in from the Alps. And on and on.... The favors were great, too—large brandy snifter with goldfish swimming round and round inside...a plate from the royal kilns, commemorating the attendance of the king's sister at the dinner...a chef's apron enumerating all the courses of the dinner. And so on.

Meanwhile, back at the ranch, we greedily ate our luscious pineapple and pomelo (a sort of overblown grapefruit, but not as tart). Pineapple will never again taste the same—it is SO sweet! Rambutans, the lovely white-fruited, fuzzy brown-covered crunchy fruits which tasted a bit like apples. Carambola, the magical star-fruit, a pedestrian-looking fruit until sliced, which is then magically transformed into a series of thin lemony-colored stars. The king of fruits I never tried—the durian, a large and extremely rancid smelly fruit which, due to it odoriferous nature, is forbidden to be served to the royal family. Once our maid put her durian in our refrigerator—and all the contents were contaminated. She had to wrap any future durians in layer after layer of paper and plastic to contain their strong fumes. We especially enjoyed the mild Thai curries, made with luscious coconut milk fresh from the shell. The Inverse Pastry Law, coined in Corfu many years ago, applies here as well. The more blah in appearance, the more luscious in taste! My favorite order in all of Thailand was the famed Oriental Hotel's cauliflower and potato curry—a white sauce with white chunks served over white rice on a white plate. Of course, the fuchsia orchid garnish helped. My second favorite food was discovered, unfortunately, toward the end of our time there—pumpkin flan made with coconut milk. The cholesterol count must have been in the thousands, as was the luscious and rich flavor. From the deprivations of Egypt we happily acclimated to Thailand's plethora of restaurants of every type—the best Scandinavian, Italian, French, seafood, etc., restaurants we had ever experienced. All this, and street food served on the sidewalk on banana leaves in lieu of plates or napkins. Leah soon addressed these street food vendors by name in Thai.

My father soon received a glimpse into the more seamy, not seemly, side of Thailand, as we decided to take him and another visitor to the famed porno nightclub street, Pat Pong, an area I had never yet visited. As we were suddenly and most regretfully scheduled to move back to the States in a month or so, I thought this would be my last chance to see what nearly every visitor to Bangkok experiences, a salacious Siamese sex show. (We prepared my father by taking him to our lovely bird-filled, open-sided international community church every Sunday morning for the previous month. His name appeared on the guest list with other distinguished visitors: Aracel Trinkinhov, Felix Cicero, Byong Su Chun, Myint Myint Than, Sranyoo Chanate—and Verna Volz!) After the initial shock of scantily and suggestively clad girls and women, bright lights, sleazy touts and crowds of people pressing upon us, the novelty wore off and it seemed old hat…or old G-string, or whatever. Each of us was approached by someone—and nervous we were! I clung to Frank while the garlanded girl spoke to me of her daughter back in the village. I saw her later that evening on stage suggestively wrapping her body around a pole. We were not prepared, however, for some of the more athletic displays, girls leaning back and forcefully emitting darts from their nether regions—each dart reached its mark with accuracy and burst a balloon high up on the other side of the stage. What muscle control! The highlight of the evening, for us, was not the grand finale—the twenty-minute live sex act consisting of sex in just about every position possible, choreographed to different styles of music ranging from ballet to rock—but rather the artistic portion of the evening in which a young artist, who held her brush/magic marker in a most unorthodox way, which I will leave to the imagination, squatted on the stage—and drew pictures. After a special request, she proceeded to get a new piece of paper from her sketchpad, squat over it and write, in quite legible and clear lettering with perfect spelling:

HELLO
NED
MY
DARLING

My father still has his sign.

Bridge Over the River Kwai

May 1986

Careening down the highway through the jungle on a large tour bus whose driver was watching TV as we prayed for a safe arrival, we were on our way to Kanchanaburi, a neighboring province across the river and site of the famed Bridge over the River Kwai (or Kwae, as it is known here). What a destination for our family outing with kids, my father, and another family from church. Remember my father's name in the church guestbook along with a Verna Volz? It all started there, as Verna Volz helps run the River Kwae Equestrian Camp, promising a taste of Thai country life and a respite from Bangkok's noise and pollution. Imagine two women of a certain ago running a sports camp in the jungle! Established in 1962 by Lee Rhodes, a long-time riding instructor from Germany, as a rural retreat from her 40-year-old riding school in Bangkok, the camp was carved out of dense jungle, but—not to worry—there hadn't been many cases of malaria for a while.

We pulled in, gratefully, from our rather perilous bus trip, although we had enjoyed the usual oriental amenities, including a bus hostess to serve soda, arrange pillows and assist passengers on and off the bus. From there, we climbed onto the back of a pick-up truck driven by the intrepid Lee and headed off to the camp. My father was invited to share the front of the truck with Lee, and thus began a three-way friendship, along with Verna Volz, reinforced by nightly postprandial discourse, well lubricated with Klosters beer. These wiry, gray-haired women were clever, interesting—and tough, in their overalls and baseball caps, with glasses suspended from their necks on cords. Driving trucks, managing people and livestock (forty horses!), feeding guests and crew and giving riding lessons filled their days. As if that's not enough, they also offer archery, air rifle target shooting, canoeing on the River Kwae, swimming, rafting, obstacle courses, biking, hiking trails, soccer, cave exploring and on and on. How can two older women manage all this? They do have local help, but basically they run everything themselves.

We stayed in one of the four guesthouse bedrooms (described by my father as "early U.S. motel quality") in a garden compound. Gardens are always appealing in Thailand, but one must never disregard what lurks beneath the lush tropical foliage. I was curious about the moat that surrounded our building—truly, a moat! Probably 18 inches deep and about a meter wide, the bricked-in moat extended from the exterior walls of the guesthouse around the entire perimeter, except for the door, of course. One can only wonder what creatures this moat is meant to discourage…. Reminds me of olden Thai libraries, where many of the books are made of lacquered palm leaf to prevent disintegration from the intense and incessant humidity. These traditional-style Thai libraries were always built in the middle of a lake or pond, elevated on stilts, in an effort to protect the books from southeast Asia's menagerie of hungry cockroaches and other creeping visitors. And so we slept, like books in an old Thai library, surrounded by water. We had beds, too, not hammocks or mats on the floor or the low wooden tables with colorful pads and triangular bolsters found in many traditional Thai homes. And little Leah had a little cot instead of a basket suspended from the rafters, like many Thai toddlers.

The next day was the first of several whose primary activity was mounting up and riding round and round and round the ring. How happy Jared was in his new cowboy boots and red camp tee-shirt. The children, including tiny two-and-a-half-year-old Leah, were all helmeted and assisted onto their mounts where they learned proper grip and posture. I'll never forget watching Leah, her head encased in large helmet, feet in shortened stirrups, gripping the reins with great concentration as she circled the ring on a large spotted pony. Well done for her first time in the saddle! Jared continued for the next session, posting with grace and ease, no longer requiring an attendant. Perhaps his previous experiences riding Arabian stallions around the pyramids made these lessons seem, literally, like kid stuff.

By the conclusion of the riding lessons, Frank, who suffered from jetlag following his flight from Greece yesterday, made an appearance and we all prepared for a treat—a four-hour cruise on a rice boat up (or down?) the River Kwae to the site of the famous bridge. As my father wrote: "All of us, with the kids, piled into the camp truck and were driven down to a sort of dock on the bank of the River Kwae and unloaded. We made our way down a steep path to the dock below (what dock? it was just a big step) and walked a plank out onto a nice large river boat for a scenic ride down the river past the bridge at some distance and then back up the river again. A most enjoyable excursion. It was a large and comfortable boat about forty feet long and wide of beam. The forward section was a framed bow structure covered with canvas. Aft it was covered by a wood deck over the galley and service areas, which included a head (toilet to you landlubbers). A broad serving area separated the galley from the passenger area. A crew of three men and two women were aboard. The men took care of the boat and engine and spare powered boat, and the women prepared a very nice meal of ham and egg stuffed pancakes, similar to the stuffed bread I had found in Egypt except much better. Fruit was available for the taking and the kids ate plenty of Thai rambutan, a small fruit about the size of an orange but covered with a prickly bunch of spines. When cut into, a delectable flesh was found that covered a big round seed about the size of a golf ball. Also soda and two Klosters for a granddad." The lulling lapping of the waves against the gently rocking rice boat soon found nearly all of us asleep on the floor of the boat. My father waxed poetic during the lazy languor of that long afternoon:

> Here we go down the River Kwae
> While the scenery slips quietly by
> There's the bridge o'er the River Kwae
> Up o'er the water so very high.
> We ate our lunch, a great repast
> Boats go zooming by so fast!
> We turn around and head upstream—
> I've seen this bridge before, it seems….
> We pass along the distant shores.
> What can that be? Do I hear snores?
> It surely is, it seems to me.
> The motor purrs so comfortably.
> We've seen the bridge, had our repast,
> Came back upstream, and docked at last.

My greatest memory of our River Kwae experience is not the famed River Kwae, not the equestrian activities or even the encroaching jungle—but rather, puppies and kittens! Buddhist in spirit, the camp respects all animal life…and it was certainly full of all kinds of farm animals in addition to the horses and ponies. But most especially I will always remember Jared and Leah lying or sitting on the floor, always with a warm little fuzzy puppy or silken kitten—sometimes several—cuddled into their laps. What euphoric expressions lit up their faces as they stroked, hour after hour, these lovely little creatures who ran up to snuggle in welcoming arms. In one picture, Jared has a tiny yellow kitty sleeping on one leg, a black one on the other leg, with a gray striped kitty leaning against his thigh, while Leah has a little white puppy crawling on her, with brown and black pups awaiting their turns. I think I've never seen Jared happier than in the photo in which he proudly sports his new cowboy boots, his riding camp tee-shirt and a riding helmet while his arms encircle a sleeping puppy wrapped in a towel. What bliss!

Next day we trekked through the thick brush to the site of a downed Japanese plane, of particular interest to my father, who had served in the Pacific during the war. Over forty years later, the plane's mangled remains created an odd modernistic sculpture, with bent propeller blades protruding from masses of warped and twisted metal. One could make out some Japanese characters painted on what must once have been the fuselage. I wish I could remember what Verna explained about the plane. Oh well...I remember the kittens and puppies. Life over death. Love over war.

Regretfully departing this enchanting camp, we headed to Kanchanaburi and to visit the bridge. As my father noted, "The scenery was beautiful on the road to Kanchanaburi and so was our driver," a young Thai woman! The bridge itself is a reconstruction of the original which, as we all know from the movie, was blown up in 1945. (Actually, the bridge was bombed by war planes rather than being blown up by a demolition team as portrayed the movie.) Allied prisoners, along with forced local labor, were forced to build two Kwai River bridges in 1942 to help transport Japanese supplies and troops from Bangkok to Rangoon. The actual bridge at Kanchanaburi took eight months to build—and under horrific conditions. It is not the towering graceful bamboo and wooden structure from the movie, but a rather unremarkable-looking concrete, iron and wood bridge. About a hundred thousand forced local laborers and 16,000 prisoners of war died working on the 258-mile "Death Railway," and 7,000 of them are buried in a nearby cemetery. I could not make myself go into the local museum, as its displays were too graphic and brutal.

The widely spaced horizontal railway trestles of the open bridge were topped with single lengths of board, placed one after the other, making a very narrow path to tread. Everyone from Pakistanis in white tunics to saffron-garbed monks trod, oh so carefully, along the narrow boards stretching down the middle of the bridge. And what a crowd it was. The problem was that once you started crossing—and it was a VERY long bridge, one hundred meters or so, spanning the wide river—you could not turn around. I had to focus straight ahead and try not to glance down into the depths of water far below through the spaces between the trestles. And of course, we were smack-dab in the center of the bridge, too far from either side to use the railings to steady our step. I felt like an acrobat in a tight-wire act. Somehow, I guess we managed to get across, wondering how on earth we'd ever get back, as traffic was one-way only on the narrow board. Eventually, the flow was halted, and we all returned in the other direction, peering down from the bridge upon the narrow canopied longboats below and floating houses with thatched roofs emulating the peaks of temple rooftops. At the entrance to the bridge was an unexploded 500-pound U.S. bomb that was (we hoped) a dud.

Into Kanchanaburi proper, where we felt we were stepping into the past as we rode along, two by two, in tricycle rickshaws, *samlors*, the precursor of our citified Bangkok "tuk-tuk," a sort of motorcycle rickshaw powered from a propane tank at the rear. (We always prayed we wouldn't be rear-ended in Bangkok's snarled traffic jams.) We stopped at a local restaurant with bamboo walls and a large white monkey, with black feet and face, tied to a tree out front. Little Leah's determination and tenacity in conquering a foot-long thin slippery noodle from her bowl of soup with chopsticks, the only utensil around, forewarned us of the persistence with which she would pursue her goals in the future. We flagged down four *samlors*, separated into pairs, and our four "drivers" gave us the ride of a lifetime as they turned the trip back to the bus station into a kind of oriental chariot race!

Indeed a weekend to remember.

Show and Tell
(and Shop, as Well!)

"Show and Tell" has always been an interesting assignment for our children. Bringing a chunk of pyramid or bone of mummy to their elementary school classrooms was somehow more exciting for the displayer than the other children in the classroom, as we all lived in such exotic locales that these items were considered old-hat, not nearly as exciting as bringing in a plastic action figure or Barbie doll from the U.S.. However, we persisted. My favorite show-and-tell contribution was a basketball-sized chunk of elephant poop—or *spoor,* shall we say, to be polite—carefully gathered and transported from the roadside of Khao Yai, Thailand's largest and most famous national park. Khao Yai (and you MU.S.T drop your voice when you say "Yai" or no one will know what you mean) is Thai for "big mountain" and consists of extremes of altitudes, climate, vegetation and habitats—and such inhabitants as elephants, gibbons, tigers, leopards, bears and over three hundred species of tropical birds. Known for cascading waterfalls and rushing streams in the thickly forested hillsides, Khao Yai is a popular destination for Thai tourists who get not only a change of scene, but a change of temperature as well!

And so we ventured with the children and our friends the Fothergills into the mountainous realm of Khao Yai. We had settled in to our spartan quarters for the night and were just beginning to relax when we heard a blood-curdling yell and much thrashing and pounding through the paper thin walls separating us from the Fothergills. Frank rushed over—and discovered that Bill Fothergill, in opening his bedside drawer, had disrupted a whole colony of some kind of tropical bugs. "BUGS! BUGS EVERYWHERE!" he yelled as he tried to beat them back. Defeated, he had to run to the office and demand an immediate change of quarters.

"Well, it serves him right," I smiled, recalling how Jared, just a few weeks ago, had sheepishly asked me not to look under my pillow when I went to bed. He wouldn't tell me why. Of course, the first thing I did once he left the room was to race to my pillow and check underneath, where I discovered two or three smelly dried fish! I'm sure I would have uncovered them soon enough from their unpleasant odor, but at least I was saved from making the discovery at that vulnerable moment of drifting off into sleep, slipping my arm under my head and my hand under the pillow. Upon questioning, as it turned out, Bill Fothergill had planned the prank, using Jared to do the deed. It would take me some time to slip some dried fish into Bill's shoes, but until then, I thought the revenge of the bugs would suffice as retribution.

Away from the infested rooms and into the park, we hiked along some marked trails, followed by a forest ranger. I kept hearing loud, slow "swishing" sounds, as of leaves and brush being swept from side to side. "Elephant?" I asked, for the park was known for its elephants. The ranger waved his stick and replied, "Big snake. Big, BIG snake." Well, that about did it for me. Never mind the waterfall we were walking towards. Just get me back to the road, I thought, as I raced along the footpath up to the paved road. From then on I thought we should do our touring by car instead of foot. So we drove along the roads, noticing frequent large clumps of straw-like balls along the roadside. When we learned that these were elephant droppings, I thought, "What more perfect 'show-and-tell' could one bring into class?" And so we spotted a large one, stopped and inspected it. Surprisingly light and odorless, it appeared to be just a large wad of straw held together by a hardened light-colored mud-like substance. I scooped it up, wrapped it, put it in the trunk—and thus it was that Jared's show-and-tell the next week was a very large clod of elephant dung...although a gaudy plastic action figure would have made a better hit with his classmates.

Thailand abounds in wonderful items for show-and-tell for adults, too. Hand-hammered bronze ware, blue-and-white Chinese-style porcelain and ceramics, brass statuary, carved teak furniture and statues, hand-woven silks, batiks, Indonesian *ikat* fabrics, embroidered and appliquéd hill tribe quilts and cloths, gilded dragons, reed and bamboo xylophones in the mournful and eerie eastern scale register (I still regret not having bought one) as well as other fanciful instruments, such as the nose flute which is played by exhaling through the nostrils. I had gradually acquired my various sources and outlets which I tried to visit every few weeks, never knowing what they might have in store for me. It must have taken ten visits to buy my set of dishes, as there were just a few that were "up to snuff" at each visit. You see, I didn't shop in the elegant large department stores. I prefer to snoop through stalls and alleyways—and have found a hoard of treasures that way...a little at a time.

Toward the end of our stay, when we knew we were leaving in a month, the shopping got serious. The items got bigger. Frank got involved, and suddenly we were shopping for a large teak roll-top desk, teak tables, chest-high brass candle-sticks from the Thieves Market to donate to our church when we returned.... "Shop Till You Drop" became our motto in those last desperate days when we had to order everything custom-made, push for deadlines, check for progress, cajole, plead and beg for completion and delivery by the time our things were packed up and shipped. Some made it, some didn't. I had ordered a lovely rattan chair and paid for it in advance (big mistake). When it wasn't ready in time, I was given a lamp in lieu of the chair. Didn't seem fair—but I DO like the lamp.

Fortunately, we had made our really major purchase earlier—an antique Chinese screen from the antique market, which we had delivered to the furniture maker to disassemble and use as doors for a china cabinet, designed to look like a screen, not a cabinet. This meant ordering special invisible hinges from California and having them shipped over. It was a much more involved project than we ever imagined, but the result is quite magnificent. I remember how we first started the "screening process"—only an aged and shriveled Chinese lady was squatting in the darkened shop. I spotted the lid of an old painted Chinese case which I was immediately drawn to. In a central medallion were tiny Chinese male figures with topknots on their silver-leaf heads walking among gilded banana trees on a black background. All four sides of the wide flat box were painted with similar figures. "Hmmmm, this would make a wonderful table if it were put on legs," I mused. I wanted both boxes right away, but we had to wait till her son, or whoever, returned. We returned later, and thank goodness the boxes, which were Chinese wardrobe cases, were still there. The deal was made, without my ever having seen the top of the second box. Imagine my delight when it was uncovered and turned out to a female wardrobe box, with elegantly coiffed and robed ladies of gold and silver-leaf lounging about. Thrilled with our success, we asked if they knew of any interesting old screens. So far we'd had our fill of rosewood and inlaid screens but couldn't seem to find anything else. "Come back next week," said the old woman's son.

We did—and we were astounded to see a large six-panel screen, painted in the same manner as the two wardrobe boxes we had purchased at our last visit. The paintings, with bits of Chinese calligraphy, related a traditional Chinese tale about a young woman and her woes. On the reverse side of each panel were six bats arranged in a circle, with their wings spread wide, painted in gold. Bats symbolize good fortune for the Chinese, so it seemed even more appropriate that this screen become a cabinet, placed next to our rosewood secretary with the Chinese symbol for long life ("Pantazopoulos" in Greek) carved on its lid.

Leah's *howdah*, lacquered carved teak elephant seat, bed/settee was another coup. Towards the end of our stay, we had dinner at a most exotic household whose embassy occupants had known our friends from Egypt when both families were stationed in Indonesia. It's a small world, this expatriate life, a mingling of embassy, commercial and missionary folks and they all seem to meet up again in some other country, on some other continent. After a while everyone knows everyone else, or at least knows of them. So that's how we ended up, with my friend Karen of the 40th birthday Knight of Knights, now living in the Philippines, at the home of our acquaintances and her former neighbors in Indonesia. At any rate, we sat upon the most beautiful carved elephant seat, a sort of enchanted sofa—and by the end of the evening I had directions to the carpenter's shop. We ordered a full-sized *howdah*, large enough to sleep a growing girl through the years—and we were fortunate to find wonderful hand-woven Jim Thompson fabric for the cushions.

Actually, Jim Thompson is another Thai tale of mystery. One of the first Americans to enter Bangkok after the second world war, as an embassy employee, he fell in love with the land and settled here after his discharge. He discovered some poor Thai Muslims along a canal, remnants of a dying silk cottage industry whose hand-dyed lustrous textured silks woven on crude bamboo looms were considered inferior to thin smooth machine-produced silk fabric. Thompson persuaded one of the former silk workers, now a plumber, to weave a sample which he then took to New York—and the rest is history. Thai silk, this handmade silk from the little canal in Bangkok, became a staple of the fashion industry, the canal became the center of a flourishing new industry, and the poor Muslim silk weavers now earned enough to become hajji's and make their pilgrimage to Mecca. Jim Thompson moved to the canal, assembled some old Thai houses from the north of Thailand into his elegant traditional-style Thai home, now a museum, and founded his Thai Silk Company in 1948. The name "Jim Thompson" is synonymous with silk. That would have been a very happy ending indeed had it not been for Jim Thompson's mysterious disappearance while on holiday in Malaysia's Cameron highlands in 1967. He walked out of his cottage—and never returned. Not a trace. Not even a tatter of silk to follow for a clue…. Kidnapped? Murdered? Dragged away by animals? Theories abound, and we shall probably never know. But his name has become an integral part of Thai history, thousands of Thai families have better lives because of him, and our furniture looks better, too.

And so do we, rustling about in our silken dresses, tie-ing our Thai ties, plumping our silk cushions. Thank you, Jim. It's not so easy, though, as most clothes are custom-made, not off-the-rack, and what may seem like a good idea on paper doesn't always turn out that well when in full size and full color. People select their favorite tailors and seamstresses who keep on hand complex measurements of each customer. I never realized there were SO many parts of the body to measure. The measurement process was akin to a thorough medical check-up, perhaps even more detailed. My favorite tailor sign appears a few blocks down on Sukhumvit Road where a large sign is posted in the window: "WE MAKE GIANT CLOTHES FOR AMERICANS AND AU.S.TRALIANS."

And we *must* seem like giants to them, for Thai's, like many Indians and other Asians from really hot locales, tend to have very small bones and are quite thin. Our driver Musa's thigh is about the size of Frank's arm—but I'm sure it packs quite a wallop, as he's a kick boxer when he's not driving for us. I remember from a visit to Key West that animals in torrid climes always have long thin legs and more body surface area, hence their long, lanky lean cats and the tiny Key deer, in order to cool off. The further north you go, the more chunky and compact the animals in order to maintain body heat, ending with, I suppose, seals, penguins and polar bears. (Does that suggest something about those of us from Boston?)

Carpetbaggers! Our expanse of bare floors was soon covered with carpets from a variety of traveling merchants, usually Pakistanis who tried every way they could think of to get their hands on the membership list of the American Women's Club. We never revealed this coveted source of potential clients, but the men managed to unearth most newly-established foreign residents to ply their wares. And what wares they had! It was always a thrill to see each "new" carpet unrolled with a flourish across one's floor. *Bokharas* were their mainstay, although they occasionally came up with a more unusual item. These rugs were not nearly as interesting as what we had acquired during our years in Egypt, such as our large "Jared broken tooth rug," spotted in an open shop doorway as we rushed Jared to the dentist in Cairo after his front teeth were knocked out at his nursery school. Subsequent dental visits took us by this enticing dark hole of a shop several times—and we eventually stopped in and bought two of our very favorite carpets from them, a large Persian Shiraz full of antelope and birds hidden among its intricate designs and a wonderful Caucasian whose zigzags and geometric patterns I prefer to the frou-frou flowery designs of more ornate carpets.

Mesmerized by these tribal carpets whose histories we can only surmise, we added yet another mission for our favorite destination in Cairo—the Khan el Khalili, the labyrinthine maze of canvas-covered walkways in the historic medieval *souq* covering many blocks next to the large El Hussein mosque. The Khan el Khalili was my favorite destination in all of Cairo. A few visits to the pyramids,

OK—but the Khan el Khalili *never* failed to promise mystery, adventure, hide-and-seek, hope, disappointment and, perhaps on a really good day, elation! My friend Karen spent so much time there in search of exotic wares that her little yellow Renault, whose air-conditioning consisted of a tiny fan on the dashboard, was christened "Karen's Khan Krawler."

The Khan el Khalili has many narrow little lanes, dead ending, turning, criss-crossing, and angling off in all directions. There is a street for perfumes, whose tiny shops entice you inside to sample alluring scents with enchanting names from tiny vials scattered on dusty shelves. A large turbaned man in long robes shuffles over to the shelf, retrieves a tiny vial of old colored glass, removes its tiny lid—and suddenly the shop is suffused with rich musky scent, or perhaps the lovely light wafting scent of orange blossoms, transporting you to the countryside on an early spring day. Or a darker heavier cloying floral scent which seems to seep into your pores till you need to excuse yourself and go outside for a breath of "fresh" air ("Eau de Cairo"?). Perhaps this is where our driver came when Frank sent him home on a hot day to take a shower after it became unbearable for us and our houseguests to continue closed up in the car with him. Well, he returned a few hours later still unwashed but absolutely *drenched* in heavy flowery cologne, which exacerbated rather than disguised his earlier earthy aroma.

Another Khan el Khalili street is lined with stalls for aromatic spices, seeds, powders and kernels piled high in their wide rolled-back canvas bags. Thousands, perhaps millions, of nuts piled high in barrels fill the sides of the narrow lanes, and the Egyptian sweet tooth is tempted by Turkish delight, nougat, and candies in all colors, shapes and wrappings. Dates, wonderful luscious dates, long and narrow or short and plump, pale and shiny or rich and dark, all surrounded by hordes of hungry flies—one reason for the continued use from pharaonic times till now of *kohl*, black eyeliner powder sold nearby in fanciful little vials, to be painted in a thick line on upper and lower eyelids to repel flies, which transmit trachoma, a widespread eye disease leading to blindness. When you next look at Nefertiti's elegant face with dramatic eyeliner, just remember that it's not for vanity, but for good health!

Displayed next to the dates are barrels of *zeebeep*, raisins. (That's my favorite word in Arabic and absolved me from having my bags inspected at the Hilton; when the guard inquired what was inside, I exclaimed, "*Zeebeep!*" I got a smile and was waved through without further ado.) Pajamas, pots and pans, plastics—anything you want, and much that you don't, is found somewhere in these crowded lanes. Wedged in between shops is a tiny stall smaller than a bedroom closet with steaming vats of chemicals. Dippety-do! Dip in a dull tarnished candlestick, ring or bracelet, and in a few seconds you have a bright shiny silver-plated object, ready for new life. For the extra money, go all the way and select one of the three colors of gold plate: white, yellow or the one most favored by Egyptians, rose-tinted gold. Even the poorest-looking of women and young girls seem to wear some gold.

One whole section of the Khan el Khalili is full of tailors sewing long flowing *galabeyas* trimmed in lustrous silky cording, stitched on by hand in entwining arabesque designs. Oh, how many of these irresistible robes hang in our closets, resurrected for Halloweens and masquerades? Elegant little silk buttons are made by tightly wrapping thick threads of silk around little "spitballs" of squashed and rolled up pieces of cardboard, teaching one that there is often more than meets the eye in elegant attire. Also in that *quartier* are the *tarboosh*, or fez-makers, purveyors of that once common symbol of respectability. You didn't have to be a Shriner to wear a fez here in the old days. Suspended from overhead awnings were scarves and shawls of gauzy fabrics, jingling with coins and beads sewn around the edges, headdresses with little jewels forming beaded bangs on the forehead, embroidered Bedouin dresses and robes, long narrow women's face masks adorned with silver or gold coins, sequined and beaded belly dance costumes in every color imaginable. (How I secretly coveted one of these, but never had the nerve to get one....)

And my personal favorite—the coppersmiths. How many little curved glasses of super-sugary tea have I consumed during visits here? One would never point, pay and purchase. The etiquette of shopping requires sitting down and taking tea, ordered from somewhere down the alley and brought in on a swinging tray suspended from three chains, and then politely conversing until the business is transacted. But such copper was well worth the wait. Giant *fool* (fava bean) pots, thick, heavy, hand-hammered, and blackened on the bottom from years over a charcoal fire... Saudi-style brass coffee pots with their hourglass figures and elongated narrow curved spouts, like the beak of an ibis... Trays! Trays! Trays! Old trays, new trays, trays for table tops, trays full of Arabic calligraphy, trays with birds or antelopes stamped around their edges.... I think I never once left the coppersmith *quartier* without a tray of some type. (I remember proudly giving an old copper tray, delicately adorned with birds and flowers, to Frank's mom as a house gift. She took one look, put it aside and said she'd had things like that in her kitchen as a child. In retrospect, I should have bought her a cheap shiny souvenir trinket—it would have pleased her more.) There were more unusual objects, too, such as the old Ramadan water pot now sitting on our floor, old pitchers, miniature fool pots (great for flower arrangements—if they don't leak), copper "mugs" with curved brass handles, copper plates with crimped edges, copper bowls with scalloped borders, large ornate casseroles whose interior has been tinned for cooking (something about lead poisoning…so I hang them on the wall or set them on a shelf instead of cooking in them). Magical extraordinary things, all of copper, all handmade—and all just waiting for me!

Frank preferred more high-class haunts, such as Nassar Brother jewelers whose gold is all designed and handcrafted by the world famous Nassar brothers, always thick, always heavy, always expensive. Their tiny little storefront belies their fame and their illustrious clientele—including us! They also specialized in antiquities, some of which they were allowed to sell for export. Why, oh why didn't I throw caution to the winds and buy the tiny elongated pharaonic cat perched on a golden swing? Someone had worn this proud little feline four or five thousand years ago, and surely someone somewhere in the world is admiring him now. Nearly every expatriate in Cairo has a gold cartouche with his name in hieroglyphics. The only letter I remember is the "N"—a horizontal zigzag resembling geometric waves in water—"N" is for "Nile." For Frank's birthday one year I bought him a heavy gold key ring at Nassar Brothers (prodded by another ex-pat who said her husband and father loved theirs; unfortunately, it was not such a hit with Frank and languishes somewhere in a dark drawer), but the pièce de résistance was an old key I found, with three pyramids stamped into it, which I then had gold-plated and placed on the key ring. I thought it was pretty cool myself!

My favorite source of jewelry was not the endless gold stalls favored by locals, or even the inventive and prestigious Nassar Brothers preferred by Frank, but rather a dusty little shop tucked into a cul de sac. At first its touristy merchandise nearly made me give a quick glance, turn around and walk out. But I soon learned that this shop purchased old silver Bedouin jewelry—from its owners? from some desert peddler middleman? Whatever, the trays underneath the counter evoked Saharan sands, caravansaries, camels and goatskin tents, with a hint of Lawrence of Arabia thrown in for good measure. What wonders lay hidden under that counter! Bringing them out one at a time, shrewdly sparking my curiosity and impatience, he produced silver bangles, heavy silver rope bracelets, and necklaces of agate surrounded by crude, tarnished silver with "God Is Great" in Arabic, pendants in the shape of the Hand of Fatima and others with an open cutwork design from one desert oasis. I went back week after week, adding to my collection of heavy ethnic Bedouin silver bracelets. Each week offered some new treasure—a Brunhilda-style bracelet with spikes all around, as effective for self-defense as for adornment, or perhaps a three-inch wide hand-hammered bracelet whose designs were nearly worn off, or? Who wore them last? Where had they been? What rubbed the silver so thin? And who created them in the first place, and wouldn't he be surprised to see his handiwork end up in Bangkok and then Boston?

Of course no bazaar would be complete without the carpet dealers, and we did eventually buy three carpets (not bad, considering we were there for nearly five years) in a huge cavernous store full of antiques, French art nouveau glass, old English furniture—just about anything you could imagine, including ivory-handled horsehair fly whisks and mummy coffins, all shrouded in a thick coating of silty dust. The rather creepy setting looked like something straight out of an Amelia Peabody mystery, and I wouldn't have been at all surprised to see Ramses Emerson emerge from the shadowy depths of the gloomy shop. Aside from the pearl inlay *mashrabeya* chairs purchased during Jared's one and only visit there, when he disappeared for fifteen minutes following a stray cat, and the shopkeeper was "surprised" that we got him back!—Frank's only obsession was antique clocks. And so we now have old clocks, as my grandfather would say, "to who laid the chunk." They've all been refurbished and refinished, and did work when we originally purchased them, one each year, or perhaps more…with brass pendulums, one with beautiful flowers carved into the pendulum, another with delicate hands, and one with a porcelain face painted in Arabic numerals. Now that's the tick-it, as they say in New England.

The Khan el Khalili also offers the usual tourist stuff—small alabaster pyramids, in sets of three of course, little leather camel dolls with colorful woven saddles, quite lovely boxes intricately inlaid with miniscule pieces of pearl and ebony, whose varnish will turn orange once the box leaves Egypt, paintings on papyrus, scarabs, drums and gongs, backgammon sets, brass this and brass that, hanging lanterns with arabesque cut-outs, pharaonic statues, *narghilas* (hookahs, the water pipes with long rope-y tubes of gaudy fabric found in coffeehouses and on sidewalks) and anything else local merchants think *farangs* might fall for. Frank was not interested, and preferred to have elegant leather briefcases crafted by a particularly skilled fellow in the leather *quartier*. Of course, it was hard to resist the belts and lizard and snakeskin bags one had to pass on the way to the briefcases. Much easier to pass up were the stuffed cobras and lizards.

Another favorite destination was a tiny stall with an antiquities dealer who was permitted to sell only certain objects. I favored him because I could actually afford something he sold—mummy beads. These fragile narrow glass tubes, each perhaps half an inch long, originally used to adorn mummies, were arranged over the woven linen strips of fabric in which the mummy was wrapped. The mummy beads, usually turquoise, beige or rust-colored with a matte finish, were sewn on in a crisscross diagonal, forming a pattern of diamond shapes, so the mummy ended up looking rather like a harlequin in costume. Anyway, the antiquities dealer would string a few of the ancient mummy beads on a string or wire to be worn as a choker necklace. I bought quite a few for gifts—can you imagine giving someone 4,000-5000-year-old beads to wear? Well, never mind, as they were all crushed in our shipment and just added a bit of pharaonic débris to our belongings.

Speaking of antiquities, selling our VCR led to Frank's visit to the home of a member of Egypt's infamous family of tomb robbers, the Abd el Rasuls of Qurnah, I believe. Either that, or he visited a master forger. We had advertised our VCR for sale prior to departure, and a most imposing figure in robes and turban swooped in, handed us a fistful of cash and walked out with the VCR. We were happy to cross one more item off our "to-do" list. The next day the mysterious figure returned, saying he couldn't get the VCR to work with his television and asked if we would take it back. He must have been in a state of shock when Frank returned his money without protest (either that or he thought he'd found a real sucker), for he invited Frank to his home to select—for a price, a very good price, just a token really—any antiquity of his choice (straight from the tomb?). Had I been there, I would have chosen a carved stone statue, but we had the weight of our impending shipment to consider, and so Frank selected a painted wooden statue, just over a foot tall, wedged into a wooden base on top of what to my practiced eye did indeed appear to be authentic woven linen mummy wrappings. The *ushebti, a* mummy-shaped statue made of stone, wood or faience for a regular person, but of alabaster or gold for a pharaoh, would have been placed alongside the mummy in the tomb in order to serve its master when he awakened. In later dynasties there were one or more *ushebtis* for each day of the year, some inscribed with a warning that no other deceased person could be served by this *ushebti.* I guess "you can't take it with you" didn't apply in ancient Egypt.

And in that ancient Egyptian tradition, we *did* take it with us. All of it—carpets, tables, copper, a tall earthen water jar that cost three dollars to buy and a bundle to ship, our purloined *ushebti*, crushed mummy beads, Frank's clocks, Halina's paintings, chips off the old block (pyramid, that is), a rocking-horse made out of a camel saddle. When we wake up on the other side, we'll be well-provisioned, just like our ancient Egyptian forebears whose home we have been privileged to occupy for a few years.

Farewell to the Orient

May 27, 1986

Farewell to the Orient—Our departure is imminent, my shock just fading as I begin the massive reorganization of our household and lives. We are repatriating in one month—a month of sifting through our possessions and affairs, of bemoaning all those places we didn't see, all those things we didn't do. We have two long-term houseguests and one on the way—a way of life lately. Jared's school ends in three days, so the household will be even more lively. (I often wonder if I am the cause of our uprooting. When I first visited Frank's office upon our arrival, I unthinkingly reached up to wipe off the chalk smudges over the office entrance doorway. "Stop!" yelled Frank. "That's the blessing of the monks from the ceremony to open the office!" Well, I hadn't entirely obliterated the curlicue squiggles in chalk, but I now wonder if we would still be here if I hadn't impulsively reached up to "clean" the lintel....)

We sadly bid farewell to good friends, hosted their goodbye party which they couldn't attend due to the massive flooding, and now we will arrive in the States before them! We're joining all those departing people whom I pitied just last week! Our departure is not a total surprise, but the temporary limbo in which many overseas workers live had become permanent to me—thus my shock at our uprooting. For this is home now. Jared's second-grade teacher next year had been chosen. Leah was slated to enter pre-school after a year and a half on the waiting list, and I was about to embark on some morning activities at last. And it's sad to sever friendships which developed in the rich and fertile tropical climes.

Every time I bite into a luscious tropical fruit I wonder, "Is this the last time?" I savor each taste of sweet gooey "sticky rice," suffused with rich coconut milk, a favored conclusion to a Thai meal. But nothing is forever. Soon the palms will turn to pines, the tropical greens to New England's autumn golds, and our bodies will plunge from sauna to freezer. But there will be compensations—old friendships renewed, mobility (a car!), and surely pleasant surprises in store.

"We've been away too long," says Frank.

"My dog! My golden retriever!" dreams Jared.

235

"My maids," I sigh.

Perhaps the most wonderful part of living in Egypt and Thailand for six years has been the exciting interesting people we have met—from various nationalities, engaged in various activities, from professors to fish farmers to round-the-world cyclists. I think I fear returning to my New England niche, cozy and comfortable though it was, and never again experiencing the bit of wildness and craziness and exotic adventure and close friendships of expatriate living.

Anyway, we are returning, leaving early July and arriving in the U.S. perhaps late July, dragging various pieces of Thai blue and white pottery, Korean baseball gloves, Chinese paintings, Indian miniatures and bizarre Asian musical instruments to remind us that we were really there, and thankful for the opportunity, brief though it seems. We left with a baby boy not yet even two years old, and are returning with a nearly three-year-old girl and our second-grade boy!

See you soon....

Bangkok to Boston

New Year 1987
Return to the Americas…

As we snuggle deeper into our parkas, raise the thermostat another notch and suppress an involuntary shiver, we begin to realize that we really are back in New England after six adventurous years in the Middle East and Asia. Home again! Home? We're a bit like the Pilgrims encountering a new world. Jared has shed his beloved Masters of the Universe (the current rage of Bangkok) for a whole new series of characters popular with local second-graders. Leah has discovered little plastic ponies and has amended her grammar accordingly: "…wonderful-my-little-pony this and wonderful-my-little-pony that." I've discovered the joys of automatic teller machines, the astonishing rapidity of depletion of a bank account, the wondrous children's books available, and the frustration of life without child-care. I still cringe when I realize that the peanut butter and plastic nothings in my bag cost the same as some exotic objet d'art in Bangkok.

…and then Happy New Year 1988

Our roots are stretching deeper into New England's rocky soil, as six years of excitement and adventure overseas begin to fade into distant memories. Last year we went through the motions of living here, but my mind and soul were somewhere beyond the international dateline with occasional mental journeys from the Far East to Egypt's welcoming climate and Ma'adi's flower-laden avenues.

And now we're slowly relinquishing our hold on those days of sun and flowers as the children create new worlds of dance, school and friendships here, amidst the chill and frosts and snowdrifts. Ballerina Leah is a graceful and spirited four-year-old whose beauty, inventiveness and good cheer fill our lives with constant amusement and amazement and occasional consternation.

Cowboy Jared, our tall handsome nine-year-old sportsman, who is equally at home in the saddle or straddling home plate, has developed a wonderful circle of friends, all charter members of his newly-established Sleep-Over Club. He fondly remembers his two weeks out West with Frank—six hours in the saddle every day at their Wyoming dude ranch—and is awaiting a repeat performance this summer. Jared will not move down the street, let alone to another overseas adventure, so it seems we are here to stay.

To further cement us to our present location is the addition of various new family members—Coco, our large brown standard poodle, whose good manners and gentle nature have endeared her to all, and Kitty, our gold and white feline foundling who immediately assumed her regal role of household management…and has been discovered in every enclosure from refrigerator to clothes drier.

I am immersed in mundane daily activities from my futile attempts to make Christmas cookies faster than they're consumed to picking up rapidly multiplying pieces of toys which propagate in the dark. My New Year's resolution is to write the account of our one and a half year old summer's journey home through the South Pacific:

- Jared's introduction to nude bathing in Bali ("Oh, Dad, I saw her *yesterday*" with a yawn)

- and on horseback wherever we stopped—on the beach in Tahiti, at an ermine farm in New Zealand

- bringing SNOW to Sydney one shocking afternoon—and scouring department stores in search of wool sweaters to endure the unusual Australian winter chill after sweating through sultry years in Bangkok

- the sulfury smells of Rotorua, New Zealand, with its Valley of the ~~Dolls~~ Moths and Cave of Glow Worms

- sending an airport cab back to rescue a forgotten koala bear at the resort in Fiji

- our discovery that we had given birth to a party girl, as two-year-old Leah, covered in confetti and ribbons, danced the night away on stage at a Club Med nightclub in Moorea, Tahiti

- our brief stopover in the island kingdom of Raratonga, dragging baskets and carvings accumulated along the way—all safely transported from island to island, country to country, until they were lost on our LA-San Francisco flight

- and then the long unwinding as we slowly seeped back into "the American way," trying in vain to cope with culture shock after six years in desert, jungle, and magical kingdoms of the mind.

Epilogue

Twentysome years later—the house still looks like we just returned. Egyptian village scenes fill the walls, along with Tibetan thankas, Chinese fabrics, Thai leather cuttings, old maps of Arabia and Asia. Pencils are held in copper cups from Cairo's medieval bazaar, Tibetan masks glower over us, giant Thai klong pots hold umbrellas along with an assortment of canes from Cairo's Imbaba camel market and Rangoon's back streets. We walk on carpets, each with a special memory: That's the "broken tooth carpet"—an old Kazak carpet which we espied in an open-fronted shop as we rushed Jared to the dentist clutching only one of his two missing front teeth knocked out in Teacher Judy's pre-school garden. We returned the next day, still minus the missing tooth, but with a "new" carpet. One wall holds exotic musical instruments from Bali to Aswan to wherever. Somehow, they all seem so similar, regardless of their origin—one or two strings over a wooden or gourd bowl and a long carved neck, along with carved flutes and fifes and fluttery wind instruments and a multitude of drums. (After all these years, I *still* regret not buying that unwieldy dragon-headed Thai xylophone, covered in tesserae of gold glass, with its bamboo pipes and haunting Asian tones.) And then, broken ostrich eggs from Australia that I can't quite throw away—the shards are rather artistic, aren't they? Chinese stele rubbings, Rajastani miniatures (details painted with a squirrel's eyelash?), brass mirrors, Burmese silver cheroot holders, pots, bronze bowls, carvings, camel saddlebags, Indonesian rod puppets, the wooden Balinese monkey mask Leah used to chatter in when she was three, upside-down spittoons, old Chinese wardrobe boxes made into tables, an antique screen magically converted into a hidden china cabinet by Thai craftsmen who couldn't understand why we didn't want their workmanship to show, old clocks, samovars, tools, tongs, tables, tablets....

We may be living here, but in a way we're still living there...in all those magical places of so long ago. Could that be why our kids are scattered like dandelion globes to all corners of the globe?

"Why don't you ever take us anywhere?" they asked.

"But you've been around the world!"

"Well, we don't remember—we just want to go to Disney World like everyone else."

Jared escaped his cubicle at Fidelity and began a series of adventures, until and after his savings ran out, taking him through central Europe, and then Down Under for a year where he picked grapes as a migrant worker, was a door-to-door salesman, broke up concrete on a construction crew, cleaned youth hostels for a free night's lodging, and sampled all the Aussie beer he could find. He crewed on a 3-man catamaran, diving into the South Pacific at the deepest spot between Fiji and Vanuatu—10,000 feet! He caught and cooked his dinner from the sea's bounty, and returned as an accomplished chef. After a brief stint as a daytime governor (*vs* governess) and family cook with simultaneous all-night shifts as a waiter (well, he did get to serve the Red Sox starters and their wives at 3 A.M. one night!), he headed for his ancestral homeland—well, one of them, lived in Athens for a year and mastered Greek at the university, also playing on the Greek Milon baseball team. And now? He's at the University of Utrecht in the Netherlands getting his master's in international economics, and playing on the Amsterdam Lions lacrosse team. How much more international can you get?

Little Miss Leah headed for Europe whenever she could in high school and university, visiting and studying in France, Italy and the Netherlands, and then expanding to seven months in Egypt where she mastered not only the local Arabic dialect, but the hand gestures and expressions of her many new acquaintances there. Oh yes, she changed her name, too, as "Leah" sounds too much like the Arabic word for the backside of a sheep. She is now, in Egypt at least, Leila—or Lila or Lola or Lulu, depending on who's talking to her. And as if that isn't enough, when she returned she took up Portuguese, befriended Brazilians—and is now heading off to India to work after her university graduation.

Guess they carry the allure of those long-ago expatriate years within them—and are now creating exotic experiences and encounters of their own. What was it I said after my first honeymoon/business trip to Egypt? "Well, I've seen the pyramids—and never again as long as I live will I ever set foot in this country again!" Three years later I was living there, and I wouldn't change that experience for anything in the world. I am transformed, and my children have escaped their cozy American cocoon. *Al-hamdulellah*!!

A final note: At long last I have returned to Cairo. We raced to Egypt a few months ago to see Leah in her milieu before she returned to the U.S. for her final semester at the university. Jared flew in from Amsterdam, so the family was reunited at the site of those challenging and enchanting early days. Only this time, *Leah* was leading *us* around, maneuvering and translating as we traipsed and twisted through her favorite haunts and alleyways. Jared revisited the track he used to run around in kindergarten, and we found our little villa, newly faced in white stone but unoccupied for two years, and our wonderful apartment, our very first home overseas, now converted into a kitchen cabinet showroom for the son of the "hajja." Jimmy, the world-renowned hairdresser who won first prize at Cannes, has turned fundamentalist and his dazzling hair creations are lost to the past, as he is now just a barber, unwilling to touch other men's women's hair. Ma'adi's tree-lined streets still beckon, but the vista of villas is replaced by ornate and sometimes garish high-rise apartment buildings. There is an occasional charming corner, with an old villa tucked into a rambling garden, but one must hunt for it, and so a stroll through the streets has lost its enchantment. We found the site of our Knight of Knights and were thrilled to see the magnificent flame tree still towering over the yard. How many people have lived there during the intervening years? Oh, if only the walls could talk....

For every step forward, there's a step back. There is indeed a subway now—complete with a separate women's car at the rear of each train for its veiled occupants. The most striking change, on the surface at least, of our twenty-year absence from Egypt is the proliferation of the veil. Now middle and upper class women and even students have taken up the veil, and so the entire country seems aflutter with fabric, so much so that I couldn't resist tapping into Edgar Allan Poe's "The Bells":

THE VEILS
With apologies to Edgar Allen Poe

I

See the women in their veils—
Flowing veils!
What a world of mystery their varied folds foretell!
How they swish and swash and sway
In the tepid air of day!
While the sun that beats down harshly
On their faces, only partially
Reveals within the margins of each scarf,
Tediously pinned and tied to hide
Any tress of hair which dares to peek outside
The confines of the veils
Of the veils, veils, veils, veils,

Veils, veils, veils—
From the swishing and the swashing of the veils.

II

See the young girls in their veils—
Brilliant veils!
Topping denim skirts and running shoes,
Shirts of stylish patterns and stunning hues.
In the street or marooned at desktop
Doing homework or tuned to hiphop,
The veils are always there
Harnassing tresses of teenage hair—
Oh, those veils, veils, veils, veils,
Veils, veils, veils—
Those denim-topping hair-imprisoning veils!

III

See old women in black veils—
Blackest veils!
What long lives of drudgery and toil
Lie hidden in forbidden curl and coil?
What dearth and deprivation lie inside
Those weathered faces of brown and leathery hide?
Best to let them lie protected
By their veils, veils, veils, veils,
Veils, veils, veils—
The blackest and the bleakest of the veils.

IV

See the businesswomen in veils—
Designer veils!
Gucci or Armani, Dolce Gabbana, perforce?
Armed with laptops and leather briefcases, of course,
These elegant upscale women make a splash
In streets of Cairo. With rouged cheek and mascara'd eyelash
They elegantly dash from meeting to meeting,
Garbed in latest fashion, greeting
Clients and colleagues in their chic designer veils,
In their veils, veils, veils, veils,
Veils, veils, veils—
Their stylish, upscale-lifeish designer veils.

V

See virtuous, voluptuous, voluminous veils–
Varied veils!
Swirling veils, curling veils, whirling and unfurling veils.
Young and old, thick and thin—
All wear veils to keep hair in.
Though desert winds are blowing
And relentless sun is glowing,
Not a strand of hair is showing
Behind veils so long and flowing.
What's the point, I ask myself,
To hide one's hair, and then in stealth
Paint the eyes and rouge the cheek?
A bird in the bush tempts more than one in hand.
Isn't this true in every land?
If every woman walked unveiled,
Many would find themselves unhailed.
Once you've eliminated all the mystery,

Many a woman's appeal is history
Without those veils, veils, veils, veils,
Veils, veils, veils—
Without mystery, it's now history for the veils!

Unveiled we were, though well covered, Leah drawing an occasional feminine hiss at her curly locks streaming with abandon. Through endless alleys in medieval Cairo, with occasional *shisha*, or hookah, breaks and many glass cups of mint tea, we passed late nights and late mornings, happily tracked down some of our favorite former merchants in the medieval bazaar, never darkened the door of the Cairo Museum or approached or even glimpsed the pyramids or the Sphinx, and left Frank to remove the handkerchief covering his mouth ("I have to breathe, don't I?"), drink tea or visit his merchant friends while we immersed ourselves in Leah's Egypt. We crawled over a crumbling crenellated rooftop six storeys above a mausoleum's marble courtyard (no railing—I now understand Hitchcock's *Vertigo*) and clambered and climbed up through a pitch-black 1,000-year old minaret, with Jared lighting the way for his stumbling mom with the pale greenish light of his cellphone screen. Emerging onto the first landing of the ornately carved minaret into the dusky blue, we gazed down over the labyrinthine streets of Old Cairo and down upon the top of the massive bulbous white dome we had just looked up to from the street. As we climbed up, we climbed back—in time. I remained on this first landing while my daring children ventured to the top. Could I have foreseen this moment twentysome years ago? That we'd be here again, together, and in a soaring medieval minaret in the magic of night, with a flock of white birds swirling, dipping and disappearing in a graceful swoop, much as their forebears must have done when this towering minaret was newly built and the muezzin climbed its steep stone steps to call the faithful to prayer....

The days passed quickly and soon we were back home, leaving Leah's apartment with its lethal crisscross of wires on the floor, its creative plumbing, its banana trees and gardener who watered our laundry drying on the clothesline outside the window along with the plants, and her own magic Cairo, eternal city transforming itself for each of us, creating its own corner in each of our hearts.

No longer the reluctant expatriate, I am now a vicarious adventurer via emails and middle-of-the-night panicked phone calls from foreign lands. But then...that's another story.

978-0-595-40156-7
0-595-40156-2